THE NOTIONS
THE 'CAVERN'S CHOICE' FOR 1964

Their story as documented by their manager Frank Delaney

"IT'S MY OPINION THAT THE 'NOTIONS' WERE ONE OF THE UNLUCKIEST GROUPS OF THE ERA. CERTAINLY, THEY WERE ONE OF THE BETTER 60'S LIVERPOOL GROUPS BUT IT ALWAYS SEEMED THAT EVERY OPPORTUNITY TO MAKE IT 'BIG' JUST SLIPPED THROUGH THEIR FINGERS - THROUGH NO FAULT OF THEIR OWN!"

DAVE McCLURE - RHYTHM GUITAR - THE 'ABSTRACTS'

DEDICATION - by Dave McClure (Publisher)

Unfortunately, my life-long friend and one of the founding members of the 'Notions', Keith Balcomb, never got to see the finished version of this book. However, while it's only a minor consolation, I can take some comfort in the fact that he did at least get to see the almost completed final draft.

As Keith is no longer with us, I feel it is important that I dedicate this book to his memory and also to Cathy, his wife, Mandy, his daughter, Jean, his sister, Andy, his brother, and Steve Faulkner who played a role in keeping Keith motivated musically and assisted him with the task of re-connecting with the other 'Notions' members.

Unquestionably, my thanks also go out to Dave Delaney for his effort in providing Frank Delaney's documentation and to each of the individual members of the 'Notions' that contributed to this project.

Dave McClure

© 2017 Veloce Enterprises Inc.,
San Antonio, Texas, USA

All rights reserved. This work may not be reproduced or transmitted in any form without the express written consent of the publisher.

CONTENTS

Dedication	previous page
Foreword & Publishers Commentary	1
Meet the 'Notions'	5
Dave Armstrong	8
Keith Balcomb	9
Joe Short	10
Dave McCarthy	11
The 'Notions' Story – as told by:	
Dave Delaney	13
Local and National newspapers	37
The 'Notions'	
Their 'Gig' list	57
Other Groups that were on the same bill	109
The venues they played at	115
The 'Phantoms' & the 'Notions'	
A photo album	119
Posters & Handbills	153
Epilogue 'What happened after the Notions?'	
Keith Balcomb	176
Dave Armstrong	179
Joe Short	179
Kevin Short	180
Dave Delaney	180
Dave McCarthy	183

FOREWORD
&
PUBLISHERS COMMENTARY

FOREWORD - by Dave McClure

Rhythm Guitarist for the 'Abstracts' (A 1960's Liverpool group)

It may seem strange that a member of another group would not only be writing this foreword but would also be the person responsible for coordinating, producing and publishing a book about a 'rival' group. However, for a number of reasons both the 'Abstracts' as a group, and myself as an individual, are associated with the 'Notions' either by coincidence or sheer chance.

THE ASSOCIATION BETWEEN THE 'ABSTRACTS' & THE 'NOTIONS'

Obviously, back in the 60's it was not uncommon for the 'Abstracts' and the 'Notions' to appear together on the same bill and certainly, like many other Liverpool groups of that era our paths would have crossed on numerous occasions but never with enough time or opportunity to form any sort of relationship between the members.

However, the 'Abstracts', who had been performing together since 1962, had by the onset of 1964 slowly morphed from a Skiffle group into a R&B and Rock group and that change had necessitated both modifying and expanding our line up. Among a number of hopeful individuals that came to some of our early 1964 practice sessions was a 16 year old local lad that had a great singing voice and an uncanny ability to harmonize. However, as our primary musical direction was Blues and Rock, vocal harmony was not something that we considered to be an absolute requirement, so our search for additional members continued. A few weeks later we discovered that the local lad with the great singing voice had joined the 'Notions', his name was Dave McCarthy.

THE ASSOCIATION BETWEEN THE 'ABSTRACTS', THE 'NOTIONS', DAVE McCARTHY & DAVE McCLURE

A number of years after both the 'Notions' and the 'Abstracts' had disbanded my (then) wife, was working at a store in Ormskirk where she became close friends with a young lady customer who lived nearby. So much so, that we were ultimately invited to their home for an evening meal. During our dinner conversation it turned out that her husband was an ex-member of the 'Notions', his name was Keith Balcomb. Over the years following that first meeting with Keith and Cathy Balcomb our friendship has continued to grow and we have become life-long friends, a friendship that still exists to this day.

I am sure that if you have read this far you may be wondering what any of this has to do with Dave McCarthy! Well as the saying goes, here's the rest of the story. In 2010 the 'Abstracts' held their 45 year reunion and as part of that reunion I volunteered to produce a 'historical booklet' for the group members. Ultimately, by sheer accident, that booklet ended up becoming a 'real' book*. However, while researching information for the 'Abstracts' book, I happened to unearth yet another uncanny association between the 'Abstracts' the 'Notions' and myself. I discovered that my lifelong friend Keith Balcomb, was the person whom Dave McCarthy had replaced in the 'Notions' back in 1964. In fact, as I dug deeper it turned out that Dave McCarthy went directly from those practice sessions with the 'Abstracts' to the 'Notions' and that I had been oblivious to that turn of events for more than 45 years!

THE ASSOCIATION BETWEEN THE 'NOTIONS', KEITH BALCOMB, DAVE McCLURE & THIS BOOK

In the years after the 'Notions' disbanded, Keith eventually lost touch with all of the other members. However, in 2010 he had a chance meeting with ex 'Notions' drummer Dave Armstrong. As a result of that meeting, the original 1963 'Notions' line up got together for a social evening once again in October 2011. At that meeting ex 'Notions' lead guitarist Dave Delaney offered to provide all of the members with copies of the documentation that his father Frank had collected during the years as their manager. During one of his visits to the USA, Keith brought his copy along with him and I was amazed at the depth of information. More than 300 pages of notes, cuttings, gigs, fan mail, photos, etc., all neatly documented. This was not just a scrapbook but a historical document that would be of interest to many of the other groups who played on the same bill or venue as the 'Notions' because Frank had taken the time to include information about those 'other' groups.

Even though I realized that it would be quite a task to turn Frank Delaney's documentation into a book, I decided to accept the challenge. Most books about the 60's Liverpool groups tend to focus on the individual members however, I decided that, while this book would obviously be the 'Notions' story, it would also include details and information that Frank Delaney had accumulated that was not totally exclusive to the 'Notions'.

So here it is! A tribute to Frank Delaney's detailed record keeping. I hope you enjoy it as much as I enjoyed putting it together.

Dave McClure

NOTE

* 'The Abstracts – A 1960's Liverpool Group That Time Almost Forgot!' a book written by the individual group members and the 'roadies' ISBN 9781588501462 (Color) available from Amazon and most retail book stores.

WARNING!

As this book was written by individuals located on both sides of the 'pond', the reader should be aware that it will contain American and English grammar and spelling depending upon who (or whom) is writing a particular segment and, in many cases, it will contain a mix of both. Therefore we encourage the reader to be conservative in their criticism of the vernacular variances and just enjoy the story. However, where there would be total misunderstanding, we have attempted to include an explanation.

Finally, please remember that these stories were written by a bunch of musicians, not professional writers or 'English majors' and they will contain spelling mistakes and punctuation errors. We humbly request that you overlook any lack of grammatical expertise and just enjoy the tale.

MEET THE 'NOTIONS'
(In no particular order)

Dave Delaney – Lead Guitar & Vocals

October 7, 1962 – July 21, 1967 – 986 gigs

Dave Armstrong – Drums & Vocals

October 7, 1962 – July 21, 1967 – 986 gigs

Pete Little – Bass Guitar

October 7, 1962 – March 28, 1963 – 34 gigs

Dave Powell – Rhythm Guitar

October 7, 1962 – April 18, 1963 – 36 gigs

Keith Balcomb – Rhythm Guitar & Vocals

April 19, 1963 – April 19, 1964 – 211 gigs

Joe Short – Bass Guitar & Vocals

September 25, 1963 – Sept 5, 1965 – 505 gigs

Dave McCarthy – Rhythm Guitar & Vocals

April 20, 1964 – May 26, 1966 – 525 gigs

Kevin Short – Bass Guitar & Vocals

September 8, 1965 – July 21, 1967 – 391 gigs

PUBLISHER'S NOTE

An important fact that is often overlooked is that the predominance of all of the early 1960's Liverpool groups consisted of amateur musicians. However, it goes without saying, that many of those amateurs honed their skills during that decade and went on to successful professional careers. Liverpool group members such as Terry Sylvester, who went from the 'Escorts' to the 'Hollies' and Tom Evans who went from 'Them Calderstones' to 'Badfinger' are just two examples.

Unfortunately, many of the Liverpool amateur musicians were either full time school students or working a full time job and the demands of either took priority over music. Consequently, most of the Liverpool groups were faced with members 'coming and going' due to school, parental pressure or the demands of their employment. The 'Notions' were no strangers to that situation with Pete Little leaving to join the British Army and shortly thereafter the departure of Dave Powell, who's father insisted it was his affecting his studies at school.

However, for the sake of completeness, both of their photographs and playing 'stats' are included but, unfortunately, time has eroded their association with the other group members so it was not possible to include their personal 'Notions' recollections.

Should any reader know the whereabouts of either of these two individuals, please contact us through our website at www.VelocePress.com.

DAVE ARMSTRONG (Drums & Vocals)

I was born in Waterloo on 12th July 1946 and my early teen years were spent as a pupil at a boarding school in Hertfordshire; however, during the school holidays I always returned home to Waterloo.

I was at home one day when I heard someone nearby playing a guitar and I discovered that it was coming from Ferndale Road, the street next to mine. I found the house and introduced myself to the guitar player (who turned out to be Dave Delaney). We discovered that we were both interested in forming a group and he mentioned that he knew another guitarist, a schoolfriend by the name of Dave Powell, who would probably join up with us. We started off as a trio playing instrumental numbers and decided to call ourselves 'The Phantoms', since we played mostly Shadows' material, as did many of the local groups at that time.

Dave Delaney's father, Frank Delaney, took on the task of managing us and began seeking initial bookings. At this stage we didn't have a bass player but a friend of Dave Delaney's, Pete Little, offered to play bass for us. He didn't have an instrument or any equipment at the time, so he bought a bass guitar and a second-hand amp. As a result, we became a four-piece outfit and Pete started learning to play the bass lines. Our first real gig was at St Faith's Youth Club in Crosby on 7th October 1962.

After few more gigs, Dave Delaney, who played lead guitar, started to do some vocal numbers to broaden our repertoire. Unfortunately, a short while later, Pete Little decided to leave to join the British Army and so we were back to a trio again.

Not long after Pete's departure, Dave Powell had to quit the group as his father felt that his involvement was affecting his schoolwork. That left just Dave Delaney and me, so we recruited another friend of Dave's, Keith Balcomb, who played his first gig as the rhythm guitarist with the Phantoms in April 1963. Under Frank's management we were soon playing three or four bookings every week, but still as a trio without a bass player. Then, in September 1963, we added Joe Short on bass guitar and changed our name to 'The Notions'.

With this line up we became quite a popular group on the Liverpool scene and eventually caught the attention of Bob Wooler, the compère at the Cavern Club. We then started playing at the Cavern on a regular basis. In April 1964, Keith Balcomb, who had been with the Phantoms and then the Notions for a full year, was replaced by Dave McCarthy. From that point onwards the group started to develop close harmony singing and increasingly performed songs recorded by artistes such as the Everly Brothers. Bob Wooler named us as the 'Cavern's Choice for 1964' and over the next few years we played more than a hundred gigs at the Cavern, appearing with most of the top local groups of the time, such as the Merseybeats, the Escorts, the Big Three and many others. We also played at all of the popular Liverpool venues, including the Iron Door, Jacaranda, Blue Angel, Mardi Gras, Peppermint Lounge, C.I. Club, Downbeat and many more.

One of our favourite venues outside Liverpool was the Memorial Hall in Northwich, where we supported many of the top national artistes and groups of the day including the Hollies, the Kinks, Manfred Mann, P.J.Proby, the Walker Brothers, the Animals, Johnny Kidd and the Pirates, and many others. However, by 1967 the Liverpool music scene was starting to change and we decided to call it a day. Our final gig was in July 1967 and after that we all went our separate ways.

KEITH BALCOMB (Rhythm Guitar & Vocals)

Born in Seaforth, Liverpool, to Barbara & Eric Balcomb on the 10th August 1946, I was the oldest of three children, followed by my sister Jean and a younger brother Andy.

When Dave McCarthy took over from me on April 20, 1964 I had performed with the 'Phantoms' and then the 'Notions' for exactly a year and during that time we had played a total of 211 gigs. Even though I received offers to join other groups I decided to hang up my guitar. However, I did keep in touch with all of the 'Notions' for a while and even went to see them perform at various gigs for sometime thereafter. Unfortunately, as time passed I ultimately lost touch with the other group members and we slowly drifted apart and I eventually sold my guitar to a co-worker.

One of the highlights of my time with the Notions was at a Cavern gig when I met a young lady by the name of Cathy. It was somewhat of a chance encounter as she had actually gone to see the Escorts, who were playing on the same bill. I was on stage getting ready for our session when we struck up a conversation. That meeting ultimately cumulated in our marriage and in 1967, Cathy gave birth to our beautiful daughter Mandy.

Jean Balcomb and the Notions Scrapbook - by Dave McClure (Editor)

During the year that Keith performed with the 'Notions', his sister Jean kept a scrapbook documenting the group's activities. Obviously, the predominance of the items in that scrapbook were also duplicated in Frank Delaney's documentation. However, there were some notable exceptions that relate, on a more personal level, to Keith's time with the 'Notions' that I felt should be shared.

Keith with his sister Jean - circa 1963

During the formative period of the 'Notions' both Keith and Dave Delaney played Hofner guitars that they had re-bodied to look like Fender Stratocasters. Consequently, I was surprised to see Jeans scrapbook photo of Keith posing with what is obviously a genuine 'Strat'. When I quizzed Keith about it he told me that it was left behind at the Savoy Hall dance club on July 12, 1963 by another group that was on the same bill with them. As the 'Notions' did not want to risk leaving it behind in the unsecured 'bandroom' they made sure that the guitar was safely returned but Keith

'A Real Fender Stratocaster'
Keith did not own this guitar, but it's
certainly a significant part of both the
'Liverpool Sound' and the 'Hollies' stories.

could not resist the opportunity to pose for this photo. The guitar in question was left behind by Terry Sylvester who at that time was with the 'Escorts', later with the 'Swinging Blue Jeans' (1966-1969) and ultimately he replaced Graham Nash for a 12-year stint in the 'Hollies'. While we will never know if Terry used this same guitar throughout his career, this photo makes for an interesting piece of musical trivia, particularly as Dave McCarthy was approached by the 'Escorts' as a potential replacement when Terry Sylvester left the group and Dave Delaney traded his Gibson ES335 to Graham Nash of the Hollies shortly thereafter – coincidences are sometimes truly amazing!

JOE SHORT (Bass Guitar & Vocals)

Born on April 30th 1947, I was only fourteen years of age when my older brother, Kevin, began playing in a group. I really wanted to join in along with him but unfortunately, at that time, I could only strum a few chords on the guitar. Before I realised it, I was sixteen and I had still not been able to find a group to join. Fortunately, by a stroke of luck, I discovered that a guy who lived in the next road, Peter Little, was leaving the group he played in to join the British Army. I met up with the other group members only to find out that Pete was their bass guitarist. Unfortunately, as I couldn't play bass and didn't even own a bass guitar, I felt like this was not going to be an opportunity for me. However, Pete generously offered to loan me his bass and, with the help of a few lessons, I was soon able to start practising with the group at the lead guitarist's house in Waterloo.

I joined the group in 1963 and at that time they were still called 'The Phantoms'. Dave Delaney was the lead guitarist and his father, Frank Delaney, was their manager. Dave Armstrong was the drummer and Keith Balcomb was their rhythm guitarist. My first public appearance with the group was on September 25th 1963 at the NALGO Club in West Derby. At the same time we changed our name to 'The Notions'.

I well remember that the bass guitar that I had borrowed from Pete Little was difficult to play, as the strings were too far away from the frets. However, as the Notions progressed, I owned a variety of bass guitars including a Hofner 185, a Fender Precision and a Gibson EB-0. I think the Fender sounded the best but it was quite heavy and as we often played anything up to four hours a night I preferred to use the lighter Gibson.

Frank Delaney was a good manager, although at times I felt he was too successful, as we sometimes had two bookings on the same night. Also, whenever we played the late spot at the Cavern, finishing at around one o'clock in the morning, it meant getting home around two or three o'clock. Not too good when you also had a full time job to go to later the same morning!

Over the years we played on the same bill with many famous groups and performers of the era, such as the Kinks, the Who, Herman's Hermits, the Hollies, the Walker Brothers, Lulu and her Luvvers and many others. When Lulu appeared at the Memorial Hall in Northwich in April 1965, I remember thinking that for a 16-year-old she was a bit overbearing. Before the show she was giving her group a good telling-off about something in a very thick Scottish accent and, although they were much older than she was, they were taking the 'dressing down' in silence from this tiny girl in curlers. However, she was fantastic on stage with an almost magical presence. The audience was totally captivated by her performance and raw energy.

I remember playing at the Cavern in late 1964 and the Notions were on the same bill as Herman's Hermits just a week before their record went to number one in the UK. Coincidently, both groups were also booked to play the Plaza in St. Helens a few days later. As the Plaza booking was mid-week it would normally have been a very quiet night; however, when we arrived the place was completely swarming with screaming girls. What a contrast to the previous week at the Cavern, when Peter Noone was on the midnight to 1am slot with an audience of twenty to thirty people! They had gone from obscurity to national fame in the space of a few weeks.

Another recollection was playing on the same bill as the Who at Parr Hall in Warrington and they certainly lived up to their reputation of wrecking their equipment. Also, it appeared that I upset Roger Daltrey by taking an interest in a girl he had his eye on, as he took it personally and threatened to give me a thumping.

I played bass guitar with the Notions for almost two years and it was an experience that I value. It was rewarding to see people enjoying themselves and appreciating our performances. However, for personal reasons I made the decision to leave the group and handed over the position of bass guitarist to my brother Kevin who had originally started me on my musical path.

DAVE McCARTHY (Rhythm Guitar & Vocals)

I was born on 16th March 1947 and lived in Curzon Road, Waterloo. From an early age I was keen on music and, as a young teenager, I attempted to join a local group called 'The Abstracts', but was unsuccessful. At the time I was a pupil at a school in Crosby and one of my schoolmates was Joe Short. When I discovered that Joe played bass for another local group called 'The Notions', I went to see him play at a few of their gigs, a couple of which were at the Cavern Club. Joe introduced me to the other guys in the group and a short while later I sat in on one of their practice sessions at Dave Delaney's house, which was less than half a mile from my own. As I could already play the guitar, I jammed with them and sang high harmony with Dave Delaney and Joe on a few numbers. The group liked what they heard and thought that my voice fitted in well with theirs. Subsequently, their manager, Frank Delaney, asked me if I would like to join the group. Of course I jumped at the chance and so I then became a 'Notion'! After only a few rehearsals I played my first gig with the group on 20th April 1964 at the Jacaranda Club in Liverpool.

Whilst I could wax lyrically about my time with the Notions, I felt that much of the 'flavour' of the era could be summed up in a short story about the Notions topping the bill over the Who at Parr Hall in Warrington. What follows is a preamble leading up to that story.

It's funny how we tend to remember life in brief moments rather than complete segments, such as days, weeks and months. Personally, I remember very few, if any, complete days, but there is still one particular afternoon I won't soon forget.

The climatic zone between Liverpool and Warrington is not exactly Mediterranean in character but the warm breeze, which coursed through the open windows of the Notions' old Bedford van as we chugged steadily towards the town of Warrington en-route to our mid-week engagement at Parr Hall, created the impression, if you closed your eyes, that you could have been driving in Southern California between Venice and Santa Monica.

That early summer of 1965 was notable, not only for the weather, but for a radical development in British popular music. Up to that time the only really good popular music station featuring the latest American hits was 'Radio Luxembourg'. Kids would illicitly listen to Radio Luxembourg broadcasts from the small country of Luxembourg, behind their bedroom doors late on school nights, and invariably get busted by their parents. I don't think we had access to personal headphones in those days.

This was the summer of the independent, so-called 'Pirate' radio stations. These alternative radio stations, which furnished a welcome alternative to the stodgy old B.B.C. (whose coolest offering at the time was 'The Billy Cotton band Show'), were based aboard small, sea-going vessels operating in international waters just off the British coast, beyond the reach of British government regulations. One such facility, whose name I forget, was situated in the North Sea, just off the Essex coast, to serve the South of England. 'Radio Caroline', the station being named after the ship itself, out in the Irish Sea just off the Isle of Man, was the facility we picked up loud and clear in Liverpool.

In addition to the established American and British chart-toppers, these independent stations were responsible for opening the door to a variety of new record labels, artistes and songs, escaping the absolute monopoly of the air waves hitherto maintained exclusively by government radio stations such as the B.B.C. One of the more notable beneficiaries of this artistic breakthrough was a Beach Boys cover band from Shepherds Bush in West London, formerly known as 'The High Numbers' who, with their new national independent radio hit 'I Can't Explain', now rejoiced in their newly adopted name - 'The Who'. We were slated that particular evening to support the Who, currently touring the UK behind their new record, at Warrington's Parr Hall.

Now that I have your attention and have piqued your curiosity, you will have to pick up the rest of this story in Dave Delaney's missive!

THE STORY OF THE 'NOTIONS' AS TOLD BY DAVE DELANEY (Lead Guitar & Vocals)

DAVE DELANEY (Lead Guitar & Vocals)

It has taken several decades for me to get around to writing down my recollection of my years as a member of a Liverpool rock group during the 1960's. It has always been something that I felt I ought to do but somehow I never managed to find the time or the inclination to even start. Finally, I have put finger to keyboard, trawled through my failing brain cells and begun the telling of my own story - alongside those of the other members of our group.

I have to confess that what you may read in the ensuing pages did not come straight out of my own head. The credit for making the recounting of this story possible at all lies with my late father, Frank Delaney, who, unknown to me at the time, kept full and concise records of everything related to the group's activities. After his passing in 1994, I came across several large files of photographs, press cuttings, posters, gig lists and all sorts of other information that he had collected and assembled in chronological order during the years 1962 to 1967. By simply scanning through this wealth of material, I was able virtually to re-live the years of my youth that I spent playing guitar, singing and performing in public, in the company of a bunch of like-minded friends. His efforts have made feasible what would otherwise have been an impossible task and I dearly wish that he were still around to tell him what a fantastic job he did.

I also have to admit that, despite the massive advantage of a fully documented record, I probably would still not have taken on the task of converting this large quantity of factual information into a form that would convey the story of the events that the group and I experienced so many years ago. The necessary impetus came from my old friend and band-mate, Keith Balcomb, now sadly passed on, and his friend Dave McClure who, on seeing the fruits of my father's labours, insisted that it should be published - if for no other reason than to serve as reference material for all those with an historical interest in Liverpool's 'Mersey Beat' era. As a consequence, contact was made with all the surviving members of the Notions and each agreed to write about his personal memories of his time in the group in order to provide a human perspective to complement the factual information. What follows is my own account, with contributions from the other members included where appropriate.

My story begins on 9th December 1946 when I emerged into this world as the second and final entrant to quite a musical family in Waterloo, on the north side of Liverpool. My mother, Norah, and my father were both accomplished pianists and my Uncle Jim played a pretty mean violin. I can clearly remember the gatherings that took place at home every Christmas during the 1950's, when the three of them would play the popular melodies of the day, with the rest of the family and relatives singing along with them. Looking back, it is surprising that my parents hadn't thought of providing either myself or my sister, Irene, with music lessons. I can only think that they probably did consider the idea but that the cost deterred them, as money was always tight in those days.

Perhaps to remedy the situation in her mind, sometime in 1960 my mother purchased a guitar that she had spotted in a local second-hand shop and presented it to me with the words "See if you can work out how to play it"! The guitar was a Spanish-style acoustic, which, although it had quite a nice tone, was not the easiest instrument for a beginner to start out on. The strings were slightly rusty and the action was painfully high, but it was a guitar nonetheless! Unfortunately I didn't have a clue how to play it or even how to tune it, so after an initial flurry of enthusiasm, it was parked in the corner of my bedroom for several months, until my growing interest caused me to give it another try.

The main encouragement for my guitar playing came from, of all places, school. A few of my classmates were interested in building electric guitars, particularly ones like those used by the Shadows. The sound and shape of the Fender Stratocaster, when it first appeared in the hands of Hank Marvin, was a joy to behold. A schoolfriend, Dave Powell, made a very good copy of a Stratocaster completely from scratch, even down to the pickups themselves. It was a fantastic achievement at a time when it was not possible to buy even the most basic guitar parts from music shops. I decided to do the same but with a different approach. I felt it would be easier and better for me to acquire the relevant hardware from a donor guitar and bolt it onto a Fender-style body. In that way I could achieve the result I was looking for in a shorter time. The problem was that I didn't have a suitable guitar to cannibalise, so for the next few months, it was back to struggling with the Spanish acoustic.

In common with many of my contemporaries, I began the development of my playing skills by copying the instrumental records of the Shadows. It was a matter of pride to be able to work out, down to the last note, not only the melodies but also every special riff and nuance for which Hank's guitar playing became justly famous. Fortunately, as my own playing progressed, my father began to realise that my old Spanish guitar was not going to suffice and decided to help me out by funding the purchase of a Hofner Colorama solid-body electric guitar. Although this was one of the cheapest guitars in the Hofner range, it was quite a reasonable instrument to play and, most importantly, had the essential components that would eventually enable me to create my own Stratocaster look-a-like, i.e. pick-ups, controls, a tremolo, and a Fender-like neck. All it needed was the right body!

Having developed sufficient expertise to play a range of instrumental numbers, the idea of forming a group came to mind and Dave Powell, who could play to a similar standard as myself, was keen to be part of it. However, to progress the idea further we needed to find a drummer and a bass player - not a simple task at the best of times. As luck would have it, we didn't have to search at all for the drummer – he found us! Dave Armstrong, who lived virtually back-to-back to me in the next road, knocked on my door one day and said that he had heard us playing and was interested in being in a group. What a fortunate coincidence - and half of the problem solved at a stroke!

Dave Armstrong was about six months older than I was and lived with his mum and sister, Marilyn, as his father had died a few years previously. During his secondary school years he was a pupil at a boarding school in Hertfordshire where one of the teachers, who was also a drummer in a London orchestra, had become aware of his interest in playing drums and began coaching him. Being a boarder he was away for long periods each year, which is probably why we had not run into each other before then, but during the school holidays he would return home to Waterloo. On one such visit his mother bought him a drum kit to practise on at home to help him improve his technique.

We decided we would call our group 'The Phantoms', mainly because it had a Shadows-like ring to it. Given our ages and the fact that we were all still at school, my father stated that if we were intent on taking this step, someone would need to take responsibility for us and declared that he would act as our manager. He would look after getting some bookings for us and, as we had no suitable amplification equipment or the money to buy any, he funded a visit to that well-known Liverpool music emporium, Rushworth and Draper, to purchase an amplifier - a superb Vox AC30, in the standard 'tweedy' colours - which I promptly dyed black. That amp would have been worth a small fortune now, if I still owned it, especially in its original colour scheme!

Finding a bass player, however, was not quite so easy but, after a little persuasion, a cycling buddy, Peter Little, became the fourth member of the group. Unfortunately, at that stage, he had no idea how to play bass nor did he own a guitar! The latter issue was quickly resolved by a trip to Frank Hessy's music shop in Liverpool where Pete bought a Framus solid-body bass guitar. A second-hand bass amp was subsequently purchased, again by my father digging deep into his pockets. After a few practice sessions, Pete had picked up enough knowledge to play several instrumental numbers and so we decided that we were now ready to play our first live gig. Looking back, it is hard to believe that we actually thought at that stage that we were ready for a public performance - such is the arrogance of youth!

Of course, getting to a gig with equipment, little though there was at that stage, presented us with a new problem – we had no means of transport. We were all too young to drive and my father didn't have a car or even a licence, so we decided to put an advert in a local shop window for a van and driver. Luckily, we had a response almost straightaway, from a guy called Brian Tickle who owned a

Bedford van. That solved the problem for the first gig and, as things turned out, Brian remained our driver for every gig we played during the next three years.

After a few more practice sessions we played our first gig on 7th October 1962, supporting a popular Liverpool group, the Flintstones, at a youth club dance in St Faith's Church hall in Crosby. Despite feeling acutely nervous beforehand, everything went quite smoothly on the night, and the audience was very receptive towards this bunch of very young lads playing together on a stage for the first time. Little did we know then that this gig was the start of a musical adventure that would continue for almost five years during the period in which my home-town would become famous world-wide as the centre of 'Mersey Beat' music.

Following on from this successful first outing, the group went on to perform at several of the youth clubs and dance venues in the local area during the next few months, sometimes on the same bill as well-established Liverpool groups such as the Black Velvets, the Undertakers and the Fourmost. As we became busier with gigs and practice sessions, our equipment began to suffer from the frequent setting up, disassembly, loading and unloading it was being subjected to. This was particularly true of the bass amp, which was not a high quality unit like the Vox and looked like it had been well-used even before we acquired it.

On one gig the bass amp packed up completely for no obvious reason, which left us scratching our heads as at that stage we had very little experience of dealing with electrical problems in sound equipment. We realised that we had a real issue on our hands and so we requested assistance from anyone who might have the necessary skills. A minute or two later a guy came to the front of the stage and offered to help out. To our great relief he sorted out the problem very quickly and we were soon up and running again to continue playing. After the gig finished we began breaking down the equipment as usual when our helper re-appeared and introduced himself as Ian Wright. We had a quick chat with him, thanked him for his help and then gave him my father's 'phone number as he wanted to keep in touch with us.

A few weeks later Ian called to ask if he could be of any help to us on a regular basis. As we already had a good, reliable van driver, we suggested to Ian that he could be our 'Roadie' to help with setting up and maintaining the equipment. As he also lived in Waterloo, it would be an easy matter for him to assist with loading-up the van before we all set off for a gig. He was a very tall, well-built guy, so we called him 'Big Ian'. Thereafter Ian became the Notions' roadie and, with his good knowledge of electronics, kept our gear in great shape. We never again had to suffer an embarrassing equipment failure in the middle of a performance.

Ian stayed with the Notions for the next few years as a part-roadie, part-electrician and friend, until just after his 21st birthday when he got a 'proper' job working at Fiddler's Ferry power station, a few miles outside Liverpool. However, from there he moved on to other power stations around the country and so it was no longer possible for him to be associated with the group. Eventually we lost touch with him completely.

By this time I had been using my Hofner Colorama guitar in its original form for several months and I decided that now was the moment to modify it. I bought a piece of mahogany from a timber merchant near the Liverpool docks and set about the task of turning the Colorama into a passable Stratocaster look-a-like. To achieve this, the first and most important step was to get the shape and size right. A further trip to Rushworth and Draper sorted out that problem quite neatly. Jack Hobbs, the guitar salesman who briefly experienced fame by presenting the Beatles with their Gibson J160E acoustic guitars, kindly allowed me to draw around a real Fender Stratocaster with a pencil onto a large piece of cardboard. A few days later, using my new template and a few basic woodworking tools, I had turned the lump of mahogany into an accurate copy of a Strat's body. After a little more work and a coat of Woolworth's pinky-red household paint, I transferred the neck and hardware of the Colorama onto the new body and – hey presto – the 'Stratorama' was born! The original Colorama guitar and the modified version appear in some of the photos of the Phantoms.

As well as being a great fan of Shadows music, without which I would never have taken up the guitar, in the late 1950's I had also become attuned to the music of the popular American artistes, particularly Elvis, Eddie Cochran, Jerry Lee Lewis and others, especially the Everly Brothers. I had always been fond of singing but other than in the local church choir, I had never sung in public. However, from the night of the Phantoms' very first gig I realised that someone in the group would soon have to start performing vocals and move us on from being a purely instrumental outfit. As it transpired, that someone was me, and by the end of 1962 we had started to incorporate vocal numbers into our repertoire. Subsequently, as we became more influenced by the general 'Mersey Beat' scene, the group gradually replaced all the instrumental numbers with vocal material.

1963

Within the first few months of 1963, this fledgling group suffered two major setbacks, the first being the decision by Pete Little to leave the group in order to join the Army. This meant that, even though we no longer had a bass player, we had to fulfil several previously booked engagements as a trio. Then, in April, within a month of Pete's departure, the second blow came. Dave Powell's father insisted that he finish playing in the group to prevent it from interfering with his studies at school, given that there were only a couple of months left until the start of our GCE 'O' Level exams.

Although I was in the same class at school as Dave and was faced with the same set of exams, my father didn't seem unduly concerned about the number of gigs I was playing. In fact, his ability to obtain bookings was increasing remarkably which, as the group itself gradually developed, gave me the tricky problem of trying to fit in everything that I was required to do school-wise with the enjoyment of playing live gigs ever more frequently. I had to attend school six days a week and had a heavy homework load every night, some of it having to be done in the back of the van on the way to a gig or in the dressing room, if there was one, at the venue itself. It was quite a juggling act, but somehow, when the time came, I managed to get through my 'O' levels unscathed. Unfortunately, having lost two members and with only Dave Armstrong and myself remaining in the group, there was now the added pressure of trying to repair the damage.

We needed to assemble a workable group quickly in order to fulfil our commitments and our first thoughts were to try to recruit Keith Balcomb, a long-time friend, even though he had been playing guitar for only a short time. Keith originally came from Seaforth but was now living less than a mile away in Waterloo with his mum, dad, brother and younger sister, Jean. His birthday was in August 1946 so we were all of a similar age. Keith had been interested in guitars for a while and he had already picked up some basic chords.

Keith was keen to join the group as the rhythm guitarist and he persuaded his father to fork out for a new Hofner Colorama guitar, like mine had once been. As he preferred the shape of my Stratorama, we converted his Hofner in the same manner and so ended up with matching guitars. At around the same time we also acquired a second Vox AC30 amp which, together with the guitars, gave a good sound and a neat look to the group's equipment. Despite the fact that we had not yet found a new bass player, we decided that we would carry on as a trio until we could identify a suitable replacement for Pete.

Although he was faced with having to learn a lot of material in a very short time, Keith rose to the challenge and after we had practised intensively, using every spare moment during the next few weeks, he felt he was ready to embark on his first gig. This was a French-themed dance at St Nicholas's Church Youth Club in Crosby on 19th April 1963, where we each got dressed up in a trilby hat and trench coat to look like 'Inspector Maigret', the famous French detective who was very popular on TV at that time. I remember that our performance that evening went down really well and Keith had made a successful debut with the group in its new line-up.

Not long after Keith's first appearance, my father proposed that we should enter a Beat Group competition to be held at the Liverpool Philharmonic Hall. Even at the time we thought it was a crazy idea to put ourselves into the limelight without a bass player, but we did it anyway, mainly for the experience. Each group had to perform just two numbers, so we chose to do a vocal and an instrumental. The instrumental number was loosely based on the Shadows track 'Little B', chosen especially because it included a lengthy drum solo. Dave made a great job of this and received a big round of applause at the end. Needless to say, we didn't win the competition. A very polished group, the Escorts, emerged as the winners and the members were due to receive a recording contract as their prize, although apparently this never actually materialised.

However, with our line-up still consisting only of Dave, Keith and myself, the group continued to play gigs quite successfully for another six months, even managing to reach the finals of the Frankie Vaughan Talent Contest at the Crane Theatre in July of 1963. During this period the type of music we played shifted entirely to vocal numbers, with an increasing emphasis on so-called 'R&B' as opposed to everyday pop material. Our growing repertoire now included songs recorded by predominantly American artists, such as Chuck Berry, Arthur Alexander, John Lee Hooker and many others.

By this time, having played at quite a few venues and experienced the music of other Liverpool groups, we realised that an improvement in our equipment was badly needed, particularly the drums. Dave was still playing with his original Broadway basic kit, which didn't have much depth or tone no matter how hard he hit it. After trawling around the music shops in Liverpool several times, he decided that a Premier kit would be up to the job and was more affordable than the expensive American makes such as Ludwig, Slingerland and Gretsch. He ordered a set with twin small tom toms, in a swirly patterned bronzy-brown finish, and waited eagerly for their arrival at the end of August. When he first started to play with his new kit, the sound and appearance of the group was noticeably enhanced.

Of the numerous gigs we played during this time, certainly the most memorable was a dance held on 3rd September at Southport's Floral Hall where we were supporting the Searchers. By sheer coincidence, the Searcher's first recording, 'Sweets For My Sweet', hit the number one spot in the national music charts on the same day as the gig. They were totally ecstatic when they heard the news, no doubt buoyed up even further by the knowledge that they would now receive free a full complement of Vox sound equipment. This was the result of the approach to advertising that Vox took in the 1960's, whereby any artist topping the national charts would be supplied with brand new Vox gear. Not surprisingly the Searchers played a great set that night and, as Keith recalls: 'To our delight their bass player, Tony Jackson, jammed with us during the interval'. This, of course, only served to reinforce even more our view that we had to get a bass player into our line-up if we wanted to develop any further as a group.

As 1963 progressed we gradually became more involved with the increasingly vibrant Liverpool music scene and we desperately wanted to play at the top venues, particularly the Cavern Club, which was the 'Mecca' of all venues for a group to perform at in Liverpool. It was the home of the Beatles and the launching point of many of the better-known Liverpool artistes who were making an impact nationally, such as Gerry and The Pacemakers, Billy J Kramer and Cilla Black. However, we knew that it would be pointless playing there without the deep, thudding sound of a bass guitar. We were still a trio and although there were other three-piece groups active on the Liverpool scene, such as the Big Three, they all included a bass player in their line-up. So the search was on in earnest for a bass player to complete our own line-up and to help us to move forward musically. At this point, enter Joe Short!

Joe has already given an account of his introduction to the group and that first practice session we had with him on bass guitar was a revelation. The difference in our sound was fantastic, especially after having played so long without a bass, and we realised that it would soon be possible for us to attempt a lot of material that so far we had avoided. Joe now had to develop further his playing skills and learn a lot of songs very quickly. He also had to adapt to playing bass whilst singing, either as part of the backing vocals or as a solo voice - not always a straightforward feat to pull off. However, to his great credit, he managed to achieve a high performance standard in a very short time. A little while later, the bass guitar that he had originally borrowed from Pete, which Joe found quite awkward to play because of its high action, was replaced by a Hofner 185, a similar shaped instrument to a Fender Precision bass, but a fraction of the price!

At this point we felt that, as the group now had a new line-up and a different sound, we should make a complete break from the past and start afresh with a change of image. We decided to call ourselves 'The Notions', picking up on a song by Mary Wells entitled 'I've Got A Notion'. Now the group was more than ready to take to the stage anywhere, especially the Cavern and, to capitalise on the situation, my father sent out flyers to all the venues we had previously played at (and a few others besides) and to the local newspaper (the 'Crosby Herald') who covered the story in their music pages.

Joe's first gig was at the Local Government social club, known as the NALGO club, in West Derby, Liverpool, on 25th September 1963. Having played there only the previous week, under a different name and with a different sound, we particularly enjoyed the new feel of the performance and realised that the group had advanced significantly. Joe's debut was a success and we looked forward to re-visiting the many other venues where we had previously appeared as a trio to demonstrate what we were now capable of as a four-piece outfit.

My father must have felt that the time was now right for the group to raise its game and responded by seeking out even more bookings, seventeen in October alone, including a very special one on 27th October – the Cavern! At last we were to have the chance of performing on the same stage where the Beatles had played so many times. They had been practically resident there for the previous couple of years but were soon to make their final appearance at the club as their worldwide fame was taking off in a big way. Unfortunately we never did manage to appear on the same bill as the Beatles despite playing at many of the same venues in and around Liverpool.

Prior to our first Cavern date, there were a number of gigs, which were particularly memorable. 'Lowlands', a club in the West Derby area of Liverpool, was a popular venue because it often showcased groups from other parts of the country. The night the Notions played there the Barron-Knights were topping the bill – and rightly so. They were a terrific act, the first group I had ever seen that fully entertained its audience with a clever mix of music and comedy. The group deservedly went on to achieve great success nationally. Another venue in West Derby, the C.I. Club, was becoming a key place for us, as we had already played there three times. The building was basically a large, old Nissen hut with tiny, dust-filled 'dressing rooms' at either side of the stage. It was one of my favourite places to play despite the dust and dirt, such things being of little consequence when you are young and enthusiastic, the atmosphere being the most important attribute of the place. We were looking forward to playing there again, as we seemed to have developed something of a following and were eager to see how the crowd would react to our new sound and line-up. The October 11th gig gave us that opportunity and it turned out to be a really great night, which rewarded us with several more bookings at the club.

Finally, the eagerly-awaited day came for our very first gig at the Cavern. In those days there was only one way into the club, for public and groups alike, and that was down a steep flight of narrow stone steps, which were well-worn and quite slippery. Nobody gave it a second thought at the time but nowadays the 'Health and Safety' crowd would have a field day over such a hazard. In fact, on a later gig, I had cause to become intimately acquainted with those steps. I was making my way down, with my Vox amp needing both of my outstretched arms to carry it, when the heel of my Cuban-style boot came off and sent me bouncing down to the foot of the steps on my backside. I remember with absolute clarity the pain of that experience, fortunately with no lasting consequences. Of course the important thing was that the amp was still in one piece!

The steps led down into the cellar with its three arched tunnels, the centre one of which had the wooden stage at the far end. As everyone who visited the Cavern in those days will remember, on reaching the bottom step the first thing that hit you was the smell – a heady mixture of disinfectant and stale sweat, evidence of which could be seen all over the flaking brick walls and ceilings of the tunnels. To the left of the stage was the band room, piled high with amps and drums, with just enough room for the group members to hang out whilst waiting their turn to go on.

We were the 'newbies' and hence the first group to play that night. Having managed to carry our equipment down into the place, we set up on the stage and waited in the band room to begin our set. We were duly introduced to the audience by Bob Wooler, the well-known Cavern DJ, and on we went. Unsurprisingly, it took a few numbers to settle our nerves and get used to the sound on the stage. I can remember that although the combined noise of the backline sounded pretty good to me, I was less certain about the quality of our vocals due to the position of the Cavern's PA speakers, which meant that you couldn't hear the singing from the stage – a particular problem if you were trying to harmonise with another singer. However, encouraged by the friendly audience, we played our hearts out and seemed to go down quite well. To our delight Bob Wooler was sufficiently impressed to declare over the PA system: "I have a notion that this bunch of youngsters is going to be Big, Big, Big in 1964" and wrote it down for us on a signed piece of paper to use as we wished. He then offered us five further bookings on the spot. I'm pleased to say that I still have that piece of paper!

From that first gig onwards we knew that we would enjoy playing at the Cavern and we went on to perform there over one hundred times during the following years, headlining on quite a few occasions. That total was surpassed by only a couple of other groups – one of which was the Beatles!

Although our first Cavern gig was the highlight of the year for me, we continued to play at an increasing number of venues in and around Liverpool and the North West of England, many of which gave us the opportunity of coming into contact with famous names of the time. One of our first gigs at a major venue in Cheshire was at Northwich Memorial Hall on 2nd November 1963. There was a dance held there every Saturday night and Tom McKenzie, the manager and MC at the hall, always arranged for a top national recording artist to appear, usually with one or two local groups such as ourselves in support. Top of the bill on the first of our many Northwich gigs were the Hollies, who already had hit records to their name. What made that gig so memorable for me, besides the thrill of playing on the same bill and meeting that great group, was that I saw and touched Eric Haydock's Fender 6-string bass for the first (and only) time in my life! Well, why wouldn't a seventeen-year-old be impressed by that?

In the last two months of 1963 the Notions played a total of forty-nine gigs, six of them at the Cavern where we supported and enjoyed some of the most popular Liverpool groups of the day. We were in awe of these outfits, the members of which were generally two or three years older than us. They had been in the 'first wave' of the Mersey Beat phenomenon and we were just catching the tail end of it. The list included, amongst others, the Merseybeats, the Big Three, the Roadrunners, the Escorts and the Dennisons. They were extremely accomplished groups, all of which eventually made excellent records, but only one of them really hit the big-time and remarkably has endured to this day – the Merseybeats. Another group that we got to know at the Cavern in 1963 was a German outfit called 'The Rattles', who by chance we also played with at Northwich at a later date. They were a great bunch and a couple of them spoke fairly good English. It was quite amusing to hear them checking the microphones before the start of their set with the words: "Testing… eins, zwei, drei"!

During this same period the Notions played on several occasions at the Blue Angel club in Seel Street and also commenced a regular Monday night residency at the Jacaranda club in nearby Slater Street. Initially we found the Jacaranda to be a rather weird place. We played in the almost-dark cellar, hemmed into a corner by big oil drums belonging to a Jamaican steel band and surrounded by ghostly murals reputedly painted by John Lennon and Stuart Sutcliffe a couple of years previously. As a gig it was a real killer – 8pm until 1am with a half-hour break – but the biggest problem was getting up for school or work having not arrived home until well after 2am. However, despite its drawbacks, it was a great place to play and also to practise, something we were always able to do as no-one ever turned up until after 10pm. It turned out to be a great training ground for the group – it allowed us to hone our playing skills, extend our repertoire and increase our powers of endurance. Our residency continued every week from November 1963 until July 1964, a total of 31 appearances. The 'Jac' experience undoubtedly helped us to mature musically, but by the time we played our final gig there, we felt we had definitely served our sentence.

Of the many other venues that we played in late 1963, the Iron Door was one that most Liverpool groups wanted to play. It had atmosphere and was frequented by rising stars of the Mersey Beat growth period - Cilla Black often appeared there. It was located in Temple Street, a stone's throw from the Cavern, and because of its proximity many groups undertook double bookings, which involved playing at both clubs on the same night. This arrangement served to boost the meagre earnings associated with playing in a Liverpool group in those days, mainly because there were minimal transport costs incurred for the second gig. However, it was hard graft, requiring unloading of the van at the first venue, setting up the equipment, playing for an hour, breaking the kit down, loading the van again, driving around the corner and then repeating the entire process. The Notions did this a number of times but I really hated it – it was all too rushed and not at all enjoyable. We played at the Iron Door several times in 1963 and supported some great acts, including Rory Storm and the Hurricanes (post-Ringo) and King Size Taylor and the Dominoes.

1964

As 1963 gave way to 1964, the bookings for the Notions seemed to become more and more numerous. The gig list shows that we played twenty-one times in January, twenty-four in February and twenty-two in March. Our manager, my father, certainly seemed to be getting the hang of it! I have no idea how this compared with other groups in Liverpool at the time, but we must have been one of the busiest on the scene. Needless to say, with all this activity on the music front, my sixth form schoolwork was starting to feel the effects. I had somehow managed to keep my head above water during the previous year but now it was becoming ever more difficult to find the time to catch up on homework. Of course, as playing in the group far outweighed the 'joys' of studying, unsurprisingly I found it much more fun to do the former than to toil over the latter.

In those days the paltry fees that we played for meant that there was very little to distribute amongst the group members after the transportation costs had been deducted, and so for the group's first year it was decided that we should pool whatever money was left over. By doing this and with the benefit of our heavy programme of gigs, we were able to upgrade and pay for our equipment whenever needed and as a result, in January, I was able to replace my trusty Stratorama with a better quality instrument. I had to make a choice between the two guitars that I liked the most – the long coveted Fender Stratocaster and the more recent Gibson ES335. After deliberating for days I finally decided on a cherry red Gibson, which firmly severed any distant ties with our earlier Shadows influence. I remember that this new guitar cost the princely sum of £168, a lot of money in those days. At around the same time, Joe traded in his red Hofner 185 for a pale-blue Fender Precision bass. We found that these new instruments added more weight and tone to the sound of the group. Nonetheless, looking back, I wish I had held on to my Stratorama as, being partly home-made, it was one of the only two in existence and was a pretty reasonable guitar to play.

In the first three months of 1964 we performed twenty times at the Cavern, playing with well-known groups such as the Escorts, the Mojos, the Remo Four, Chick Graham and the Coasters, the Chants and many others. At our first session of the new year Bob Wooler told us that we were to be the 'Cavern's Choice for 1964' which for us was a tremendous honour - it seemed that 1964 was shaping up to be an exciting year. Then on 1st February we had the special privilege of headlining the first Cavern Saturday afternoon juvenile session, as well as several of the normal evening gigs. Later the same month, on 21st February, we were chosen to take part in a live recording to be made by Oriole at the Cavern, along with Herman's Hermits from Manchester and a few other local groups, although sadly nothing ever came out of it.

In April 1964, after we had been operating with the original Notions' line-up for over six months, a school friend of Joe's, Dave McCarthy, took over the rhythm guitarist slot from Keith. Dave possessed an exceptionally good voice, was a good guitarist and could add harmonies into any song instantly. My father felt that he would not only enable the group to extend its musical range but also help to take some of the pressure off me, as at this stage I was doing most of the singing and guitar arranging whilst still trying to cope with the ever-increasing load of school-related work.

After only a few practice sessions, Dave was fully up to speed with the Notions' material and made his first appearance with the group at the Jacaranda on 20th April 1964. His first Cavern gig was on 24th April when the Notions were top of the bill and just a few days later on 28th April the group was the subject of a recording session for the Radio Luxembourg programme 'Sunday Night at the Cavern'. This was a new experience for us and was quite nerve racking, as it was a live recording in front of a full audience. If we were to make any mistakes, they would be there for posterity. We had to play half a dozen numbers, which were interspersed with records by various artistes, selected and played by Bob Wooler. Bob compèred the show and managed the timing of the whole operation with practised ease.

The radio programme was actually broadcast a month later on 24th May but, as the group was playing in Litherland that evening, we missed out on hearing it. Unfortunately, at that time I had no means of recording a radio programme at home and to this day I have still not heard it, so I have no idea what the group sounded like on the night. However, I clearly remember the reaction from my schoolmates the next morning – I was ribbed mercilessly but fortunately the comments were positive, so I assume that it must have sounded okay.

Throughout May, June and July the Notions were continually busy, playing sixty-nine gigs in total. In this period we again played with many of the top local groups - the Dennisons, the Escorts, the Roadrunners, the Clayton Squares, the TT's, the Kirkbys, the Hideaways and Herman's Hermits to name but a few - and at most of the popular venues. As well as the Cavern, we had repeat bookings at the Plaza Ballroom in St Helens, the C.I. Club and Northwich Memorial Hall. We played three gigs at Northwich where we supported the Hollies for a second time, the Rattles and Lulu and the Luvvers. We always looked forward to the Northwich gigs as we were able to chat with the big recording stars of the day and hear about their own experiences.

At a Cavern gig on 26th May we supported a new Liverpool group, the Kinsleys, formed by Billy Kinsley soon after he quit the Merseybeats. I remember asking him why he had pulled out just as the group was enjoying its first hit record and was on the cusp of fame and fortune. He replied that it was an issue with the group's management, but didn't expand on it and I didn't query it further. Being such a talented musician, Billy went on to greater things anyway, subsequently finding success with Tony Crane as the Merseys and with Liverpool Express some years later.

One of the most unusual engagements that we undertook in 1964 was to play at a private cocktail party hosted by Lord Derby at his stately home, Knowsley Hall, on 30th June. We were asked to initially provide light background music whilst the guests were arriving and chatting, then to ramp it up a little if anyone wanted to dance. To fulfil the request for the early part of the evening we chose our 'gentlest' vocal numbers and liberally spaced them out with some much-elongated 12-bar blues that we made up as we went along. It appeared to work well and all the guests seemed very happy, probably more to do with the cocktails than the music! At the end of the evening, as a special thank you from Lord Derby, we were given a conducted tour of the hall by his butler. Apparently, we were the first rock group ever to play there – and possibly the only one? We were even provided with a police motorcycle escort on our way to the gig, which made us feel like we were famous celebrities, albeit briefly. It was certainly an unforgettable evening for us and probably for Lord Derby as well.

One gig that was unforgettable for an entirely different reason was at the Carlton Ballroom in Rochdale on 9th July. While we were playing our first set, high up on the ballroom stage, we could see a gang of thugs, led by a scruffy young lad, moving around the dance floor and randomly attacking blokes who were simply enjoying dancing to our music with their girlfriends. I watched this mob launch into different groups of people several times during the forty-five minutes we played. When the set was finished we left the stage and went down into the band room. A few minutes later I set off for the bar to fetch us all some food and drinks. On my way back and with a tray full of glasses in my hands, I was suddenly set upon by this same bunch and collected a full-on head butt from the scruffy ringleader. As the whole pack started to close in around me for the 'kill', I recall thinking that this was not looking too good and that some drastic action was needed on my part to defend myself. I quickly decided that I would heave the whole tray of glasses at the leading yob to create a bit of chaos and hopefully make my escape in the confusion. However, before I could move, and at the best possible moment, another group of lads came charging out of nowhere in a blur of arms and legs and piled straight into the first lot. An almighty fight immediately ensued leaving me standing to one side still holding the tray, whereupon I made a rapid exit from the carnage and slipped quietly back to the band room.

During the second set, there was no sign of the yobs and I consoled myself with the thought that they had been given a good pasting and had slunk off. At the end of the night, despite a burning desire to find and take my revenge on the ringleader, I was sensibly persuaded to climb into the van and head for home, nursing an increasingly colourful lump on my forehead. Amazingly, in the almost one thousand gigs that we played in the sixties, I saw only one other incident of blatant aggression, which I'll describe a little later.

Thankfully, after such a busy half-year in which we had played a total of one hundred and thirty-six gigs, the last two weeks in July and the first two weeks of August were kept free of bookings to allow for everybody's holidays – and boy, did we need them!

When the holidays were over and we were back together again, our first gig after nearly a month's break was at the Cavern on 12th August where we were top of the bill with the Hideaways and the Mighty Avengers. After that session we played every single night to the end of the month, seven of the dates being at the Cavern and a further one at Northwich supporting Manfred Mann. The Manfreds were riding high in the charts at the time and put on a great performance. I remember being very impressed by their musicianship and particularly by Paul Jones's harmonica skills – he was a maestro of the blues harp.

When Dave McCarthy first joined the Notions he was using an old Hofner President guitar, a large, semi-acoustic model which, although a fine instrument, had rather a 'Bert Weedon' look about it and a sound that was more suited to jazz than rock n' roll. Consequently, shortly after joining, he switched to playing my old Stratorama, which looked and sounded better for our purposes. However, just as I had found, even that guitar was not the best for the job and, towards the end of August, it was Dave's turn for an upgrade. After a bit of deliberation he went for a cherry red Gibson ES335 like mine and so now we had a full complement of top quality gear to help us deliver a good, solid sound and keep us on a par with the professional outfits that we were encountering more and more.

On 31st August the Notions played at the Plaza in St Helens with Herman's Hermits. We had appeared with them a number of times previously, mostly at the Cavern, and we often seemed to go down even better than they did with the audiences there, probably because we were the 'locals' and they were the 'foreigners' from Manchester! However, on this occasion, the situation was very different. Peter Noone (alias Herman) and his group had obtained a recording contract and had released a cover version of 'I'm Into Something Good', a catchy song written by the American songwriter Carole King. On the day of the Plaza gig, the record had reached number nine in the national charts. The difference that their new-found success made was amazing – girls rushed to the stage and screamed wildly whenever Pete so much as blinked an eye. To be fair to him, he was just as astonished at the reception as we were but, as things turned out, Herman's Hermits went on to fame and fortune and eventually conquered America. Such was the effect of their first hit record that we decided that we too had to try to get a recording contract. However, we knew that it would be no easy matter, as the emphasis in the music scene was just beginning to shift away from Liverpool even at that stage.

With such frequent appearances throughout 1964, especially at the Cavern, the C.I. Club, Northwich and certain other venues, we found that we had built up quite a following of faithful fans. We even had a fan club, which was run for us by two girls, Pat and Maureen, who had started it just after the Notions first appeared at the Cavern. From about the same time a number of other girls had been coming regularly to see us, sometimes two or three times in one week, which must have taken a lot of their hard-earned cash. On a few occasions 'Big Ian' took it upon himself to arrange coach trips to provide them with transport to some of our out-of-town gigs. It was a great boost for us, knowing that we had friends in the audience. They often used to hand us written requests to play particular songs and many of these were extremely inventive and cleverly made. Because of the effort that had gone into making them, they were not simply left behind after a gig. They were saved and became part of the collection of Notions' memorabilia that my father assembled.

Some of the gigs we played in the next few months involved travelling greater distances than usual, to such 'far-flung' places as Kendal in Cumbria, Much Wenlock in Shropshire, Huddersfield in Yorkshire, Ruthin in North Wales and Salop, also in Shropshire, as well as Stockport, Chester and others not quite so far away. For a fully professional group, travelling to distant gigs would have been quite normal and probably would have included overnight stays away from home. However, for the Notions, a non-professional outfit with jobs and school commitments to be met every day, such gigs were a lot more demanding as we had to travel back in the early hours and often had to make do with only a few hours sleep before getting up again. In fact the list for the last quarter of 1964 shows that we played sixty-nine gigs, including five doubles in December, which was probably as many as, if not more than, some of the fully professional groups and, of these gigs, ten were well outside our normal range of travel. It must have been adrenaline that kept us going at the time - we certainly didn't get much sleep!

In this same period some the gigs gave us the opportunity to support national recording artistes. On 10th October, at Mersey View in Frodsham, we were billed with Dave Berry and the Cruisers, who had recently had a big hit with 'The Crying Game'. At the time this was one of my favourite pop records, mainly because the Cruisers' lead guitarist had created an interesting and distinctive sound effect using a volume control pedal. It was great to watch him recreate the sound live on stage, which he did perfectly. A month later, at the same venue, we supported Jimmy Nicol and the Shubdubs. Jimmy Nicol was the drummer who substituted for Ringo when he fell ill just before the Beatles' tour of Australia back in June. After that experience he had formed his own outfit and attempted to capitalise on his brief period of extreme fame.

On a couple of occasions in November and December, the Notions provided the instrumental backing for a new Liverpool vocal group called the Excelles - a five-piece outfit consisting of both male and female members. Their voices blended perfectly and they were able to create some superb harmonies. They were just starting out and were being promoted enthusiastically by Bob Wooler. We backed them as a favour to Bob to help them get their musical career moving but unfortunately, despite their considerable talent, this appears to have been relatively short-lived.

Overall 1964 had been a pretty hectic year for the Notions. We had played a total of two hundred and seventy four gigs and to round off the year with a flourish we played at the Cavern on Christmas Eve,

Boxing Day and New Year's Eve. It all felt like quite an achievement, given that the group had only been in existence for a little over a year.

1965

With my father's now well-honed skills for obtaining bookings, we left 1964 behind and started into the New Year with gusto. Of course, we could no longer make use of Bob Wooler's much-appreciated words 'The Cavern's Choice for 1964', but although we were now past that 'sell-by date', we had high hopes that 1965 would turn out to be an even better year for us. The diary was filling up rapidly and the first three months were going to be as busy as ever. We were looking forward to playing at our favourite venues and some new ones, but for me there was an inescapable black cloud looming on the horizon. I was definitely not looking forward to the summer, as this was going to be my 'A' level final year. I really wanted to succeed in these exams, mainly because I had put in a lot of effort to get as much work done as I possibly could in the circumstances and also because having them under my belt gave me some degree of backup for the future, in case it was needed. To add to my worries and workload, the mock exams were scheduled to take place in February, which meant my life was going to be pretty damn busy all round for the next six months. However, on the bright side, I would be finishing my schooling in July and from then on there could be new possibilities open to me regarding future group-related activities. Every cloud has a silver lining!

During those first few months we played many times at the Cavern, the C.I. Club, St Helens Plaza and other venues, along with local groups including the Roadrunners, the Hideaways, the St Louis Checks and Earl Preston's Realms. A further gig at Mersey View in Frodsham on 30th January saw us supporting the Fortunes who had just had a major hit with 'You've Got Your Troubles'. They were a really good band, with great vocal harmonies, and went on to make several more hit records. One of the Cavern gigs, on 20th February, was an all-nighter — we took part in a few of these Cavern 'specials' over the years that we played there – and on this particular evening Alexis Korner topped the bill. Alexis was one of the 'greats' of the R&B scene in Britain during the sixties and was received enthusiastically by the blues fans in the Cavern audience

It was around this time that Joe decided to swap his Fender bass for a Gibson model. He had found the Fender to be quite a heavy instrument and also a little unbalanced, and so having tried a few others, he decided on a cherry red Gibson EB-0. This meant that we now all had Gibsons, all cherry red ones! I imagine that people probably thought that we had planned to achieve a matching line-up, but in fact it just happened that way. Nonetheless, it actually looked pretty good.

The following month, for the first time ever, we experienced the making of a recording in a proper studio. We had previously attempted to make recordings ourselves, but these were typically done in an empty room somewhere, using a basic tape recorder and a single microphone. Consequently the results were always poor, with a total lack of balance and usually a hollow, clattery sound representing the drums. In complete contrast, the Radio Luxembourg recordings were professionally executed but, as these were done in front of a live audience, they were a once-only 'take' with no opportunity for us to influence the final output or even retain a copy of the proceedings. However, next door to the Cavern, in the adjacent tunnels, a fully-equipped studio had been set up as a business venture under the name 'Cavern Sounds' and we were one of the first groups to be invited to record there. This was our first experience of 'laying down' backing tracks and dubbing vocals on top and we learnt a lot about the techniques and equipment involved in engineering a recording. I still have copies of some of the tapes which were made at that session – these include Dave McCarthy and I singing an Everlys-style arrangement of 'Memories Are Made Of This' and Joe performing 'Go On Home Girl', a song originally recorded by Arthur Alexander. The engineers at Cavern Sounds created an acetate disc of 'Memories' for us which Bob Wooler played a number of times over the Cavern PA system. It was great to hear it in that setting and it even felt like we had a real record out.

Later that month, on 22nd March, we played for the first time at Parr Hall in Warrington. Like Northwich Memorial Hall, this venue held weekly dances featuring groups from all over the country, many of whom were recording artistes with hit records to their credit. Parr Hall was located in the town centre, about twenty miles from Liverpool and, unlike Northwich Memorial Hall, it was a grim-looking, soot-blackened, Victorian edifice containing an enormous ballroom with a high, old fashioned, theatre-style stage. The building functioned as a social venue for weddings, conventions, meetings, and in the mid-sixties, rock concerts. On this occasion we were booked to support a group called 'The Who' and, at that time, they were a virtually unknown band in the North of England. We didn't know it before the start of the evening, but we were going to be treated to a very different sort of performance to any we had previously experienced.

Dave McCarthy recalls a great story about that gig:

'The headline artists were already unloading their gear when we arrived at around four-thirty on a sunny afternoon. We were fascinated to observe that their mode of transportation was an enormous converted furniture removal van, customised to include bunk beds, a kitchen, a bathroom and a small shower, with ample room to store and transport all of their personal stuff and musical equipment. There was a lad sitting on a large speaker cabinet on the tailgate of the van when we arrived, and I walked over to say hello. He broke out the fags and offered me a 'Senior Service' from a packet of twenty no less! I observed that it must be nice to have a hit record and be able to afford expensive un-tipped fags, coincidentally of the same brand that I would regularly and surreptitiously nick from my dad's packet when he wasn't looking. We exchanged a bit of the usual Cockney and Scouse banter and had a crack while we sat on his amp and finished our smoke, after which I gave him a hand to carry a large speaker cabinet inside the building. He had introduced himself as Pete. Nice to meet you Mr. Townsend!

We had left Liverpool as early as possible that day in order to beat the traffic and, as a result, we had about two and a half hours before we were due to open for the Who. This was a plus, since the place was deserted when we arrived, allowing both bands plenty of time and space to load all of their gear onto the stage, and get set up without getting in each others way. The only problem was that the place stayed virtually deserted! As show-time approached there were exactly two people in the enormous hall, a young lad and his girlfriend sitting at a small table at the back, which was so far away from the stage that you would have needed binoculars to discern any further details.

With about ten minutes to the curtain, Roger Daltrey walked up to me and asked if we would mind letting their band open the show. He explained that they had a fair distance to travel to their next job, and since the Parr Hall appearance was a last minute addition to their itinerary, and had obviously not been well promoted, he suggested that we would really be doing them a favour if they went on first and third in the running order, rather than second and last as originally planned. Of course we agreed, and I used the unexpected delay to retire to the spacious dressing room at the side of the stage, and continue working on a letter I had been writing.

I heard the band kick off with their first number, the sound incredibly loud as it reverberated unobstructed around the walls of the cavernous mausoleum. After only a few minutes, Dave Delaney came into the room and insisted I accompany him.

"You've got to see this," was all he said.

As I came into the wings, the Who were in already full flight. Dave told me to keep an eye on the lead guitarist, whom he informed me had already smashed the head of his guitar into his speaker cabinet, and the drummer, who had taken about three minutes of hysterical flailing to perforate the head of his bottomless Ludwig snare drum before grabbing Dave Armstrong's drum from where it was stacked with the rest of our gear, and to Dave A's horror, began to batter his beloved drum with the same insane violence.

"Don't worry...I've got spares," roared Mooney in our direction, his voice barely distinguishable over the deafening sound emanating from the stage.

Sure enough within a few minutes, the quiet, unassuming manner that Pete Townsend displayed during our earlier meeting underwent a radical metamorphosis as, to my dismay, he violently and sacrilegiously impaled his speaker cabinet upon the head of his sunburst Les Paul Deluxe, stabbing the speaker in a frenzy to the accompaniment of a piercing shriek of feedback, until the fabric ripped and a couple of the speakers imploded.

Meanwhile, between song lines, the lead singer Roger Daltrey, was feverishly whirling the microphone cable around his head like a lassoo in the hands of a demented cowboy, before allowing centrifugal force to send the device sailing high over the dance area to land in the middle of the deserted floor with a sickening thud, then reeling the mic back in for a repeat performance. I honestly did not know whether to laugh or run! It was by far the most shocking performance I had ever seen and yet even then, I instinctively realised this to be a quantum leap in the evolution of popular musical entertainment, from which there could be no going back.

Our early arrival in Warrington, had afforded us ample to time to fraternise and compare notes with our fellow musicians. I remember the members of the Who as extremely likeable and personable lads, with the exception of John Entwhistle who remained a bit more reserved and aloof from everyone around him. Apart from that, they were all very down-to-earth and, like ourselves, from a similar working-class background. I remember saying to Roger Daltrey that the London bands we had previously met were all hairy, dishevelled, hippie types. Daltrey responded that their group was from the Shepherds Bush area of London, a bastion of the 'Mod' movement, and advised us:

"If you walk around like that down our way mate, you'll get your faaackin' head cut off."

I also had the opportunity to ask Pete Townsend about the origin of the band's unusual name. He explained that they started out, unbelievably, as a Beach Boys cover-band called 'The High Numbers'. Punters would come up to them at various venues around London and enquire:

"What's the name of the band mate?"
"The High Numbers."
"The who?"
"The High Numbers mate."
"The WHO?"

Well, if you can't beat 'em, join 'em, although I did suggest to Townsend's amusement, that in the interest of English grammar, the band should really have been entitled 'The Whom'!

With the exception of a relatively small number of people, the huge ballroom remained largely empty all evening. Nonetheless, the Who successfully maintained, throughout their sets, an anarchistic, high-energy cacophony of conflicting frequencies and deconstructive vandalistic theatre - a remarkable feat made even more unique by virtue of being performed in an almost empty room. To say I enjoyed them is a stretch, as I don't think enjoyment is the right word, but I was certainly excited and profoundly affected by their performance, the natural reaction, perhaps, of someone witnessing an original art form for the first time?

There was more opportunity for socialising as the soon-to-become-legendary band broke down their equipment during an extended break in order for them to get back on the road, before our final set concluded the evening as agreed. We asked them how much equipment they needed to compensate for this kind of technical attrition on a nightly basis. They informed us that the replacement and repair of their gear, all of which was top-of-the-line Marshall amps and Ludwig drums, with no stage props, was a continuous and ongoing process completely covered by their management and sponsors. I can only assume that there must have been big money behind them from the outset. Even so, we now understood the necessity for the furniture removal van!

With the hype from their high-energy performance, no doubt fuelled by a few 'prellies', their cosmetically confrontational style of banter continued while they broke down and packed up their stuff.

"What are you faaackin' looking at you kaaant*?" Keith Moon asked Pete Townsend, who immediately responded by violently kicking Mooney's bass drum across the dressing room floor.
The drummer got right up in Townsend's face and said, 'Oi....you don't faaaackin' kick a kit of Ludwig around like that you kaaant*, you kick it around like this," and he aimed a violent kick at the offending bass drum, sending it bouncing down the two flights of stairs leading from the dressing room. This was not as shocking as it would otherwise have been, as it was the method he had used to end their final number and remove the drums from the stage in the first place.

*(Of course during this discourse, Dave Delaney and myself naturally assumed that the band members were referring to the German philosopher, Immanuel Kant. It was only later we realised this to be an anatomical reference!)

The global success of The Who and their subsequent influence upon the evolution of popular music, as effectively forerunners of the Punk Rock movement, is literally history. I will always consider this circumstantial encounter, during which the Notions effectively topped the bill over the legendary Who, as one in a long list of musical privileges exclusively attributable to membership of my first tremendous young band – 'The Notions'.

Joe remembers that night vividly, partly because of the Roger Daltrey 'incident' he described earlier. Fortunately no fisticuffs ensued and everyone parted amicably. Joe has also related his impression of Lulu whom he met a few weeks later, on 17th April, when we were the supporting group for 'Lulu and The Luvvers' for the second time at Northwich. After their set I had the opportunity to chat with the fiery pocket-rocket, Lulu, myself and my recollection is that, although I decided that she was genuinely very nice, I too was quite glad that I wasn't one of her 'Luvvers'.

At the beginning of May, the Notions played on the same bill as the Abstracts, whose rhythm guitarist was Dave McClure. This was the first of three occasions when the paths of the two groups crossed, the other dates being in August and October of 1965, all of them at the Plaza ballroom in St Helens. In fact Dave McCarthy had met Dave McClure and his group before joining the Notions, almost becoming a member at one stage. Fortunately for us, he didn't!

A week later, on 8th May, we were back at Mersey View in Frodsham, this time supporting Johnny Kidd and The Pirates. 'Shakin' All Over' was the song they were most famous for, but they had recently had a big hit with 'I'll Never Get Over You'. I had been a Pirates fan for a long time, mainly because I really liked the playing style of their lead guitarist, Mick Green. He managed to get a superb, twangy sound out of a single pick-up Gibson Junior that somehow swelled to fill the sound voids that can sometimes occur with a three-piece guitar, bass and drums line-up. They put on a great show all dressed up in their pirate gear and featuring Johnny, complete with eye-patch, prancing around the stage slicing up imaginary foes with his evil-looking cutlass, a real one not a stage prop. Afterwards, when we were chatting, we were quite surprised to find that he was a really friendly and quite gentle guy!

Later that same month we were back at Parr Hall in Warrington to support a London band called 'The 'Pretty Things' who, it has to be said, didn't quite live up to their name! They had just had a major chart success with 'Don't Bring Me Down' and attracted a big crowd. Their lead singer was Phil May, who was known for his near waist-length hair and somewhat provocative singing style. The lead guitarist was Dick Taylor, who had previously played bass for the embryo Rolling Stones, subsequently being replaced by Bill Wyman. In complete contrast to Johnny Kidd's group, we felt that the Pretty Things were a rather unfriendly bunch, particularly their drummer, Viv Prince, who seemed to be totally spaced-out during their performance and very aggressive towards his bandmates.

Afterwards I felt a bit disappointed that, although our performance that night had been good, we didn't register particularly well with the audience, perhaps because it seemed to consist mainly of out-and-out blues fans — I suppose you can't win 'em all.

Looking back, the summer of 1965 was a particularly testing time for me personally. I was heavily involved with the group, playing a lot of gigs and not getting much sleep and as a consequence I managed to do only the bare minimum of studying in the weeks leading up to my 'A' levels. Amazingly, I had done pretty well at 'O' level, mainly because of the amount of work that I had done long before the group's activities became so hectic, but 'A' levels were going to be another story. Anyone who was in a Sixth form during that era will tell you that there was a very big difference between 'O' and 'A' level standards and that the two years of study required between the corresponding exams was pretty heavy going, particularly for science students like myself. In those same two years I had played over five hundred gigs, which clearly didn't leave a lot of time for anything else. As a result my revision timetable was very simple – a day or two manically cramming before each exam and that was it! Despite my earlier desire to make a success of them, as the exams approached I resigned myself to doing badly, but somehow I managed to get through them, although with lower grades than I might have otherwise achieved. However, when all the exams were over and I had effectively finished my schooling, I felt a great weight had been lifted off me and I could savour a wonderful feeling of freedom. I was so wrapped up in playing in the group that I wasn't greatly concerned about my results, as at that stage I believed that my future was going to be in music. The idea of ever being in a 'normal' job was a very long way from my mind!

In the middle of this period, on 25th June, we hit a major milestone in the Notions' journey – we played our one hundredth Cavern gig. On that night we were billed with the Hideaways, one of the very few other groups eventually to play more than one hundred times at that hallowed venue. Strange as it may seem, I don't think we were aware at the time that we had reached such a significant total and, as far as I can remember, we didn't rush off to celebrate afterwards. I'm pretty sure that none of us would have had any idea about how many gigs we had performed there or anywhere else for that matter. I can only imagine that my father might have been a bit behind with his record keeping at that point and forgot to mention it to us, hardly surprising with everything that was going on. The fact that he documented the Notions' progress in such great detail is the only reason that I am now able to recall anything at all about where, when and with whom we played so many gigs.

Our next trip to Northwich, on 24th July, saw us supporting the Animals. At this particular point in time, the Animals were at their peak of popularity, with a number of great records under their belt. They had recently enjoyed a big success with 'We Gotta Get Out Of This Place' and all of the original band members were still present in the line-up, including keyboard player Alan Price, who later left the group to become a successful recording artist in his own right. As with the vast majority of the big name groups that we encountered, despite their fame they were usually open, friendly and ready to chat. Coming from Tyneside, the Animals and Eric Burdon in particular, had a great northern sense of humour, one that coming from Liverpool we could readily appreciate.

By the autumn of 1965 we had had a busy and eventful year and we were by that time a well-established outfit in and around the Liverpool area, with a solid and still growing following. We were good friends, we fitted together well musically, we enjoyed playing and our line-up had not changed for eighteen months, so no-one in the group foresaw the bombshell that was about to happen. One day in August my father gathered us together and quietly informed us that Joe was leaving the group! We were dumbstruck to say the least at this sudden news and then dumbstruck even more when we learnt the reason why – he had decided to become a priest! Well, we certainly didn't see that one coming and initially it just seemed a complete impossibility - a quantum leap from rock musician to 'man-of-the-cloth'. However, Joe explained that it was something he really wanted to do, even though it meant quitting the group and, although the rest of us were extremely disappointed at the thought of losing him, we had to respect his decision. Unfortunately, it meant that we now had to find a replacement bass player in double-quick time in order to honour our heavy schedule of bookings.

Then, while we were still reeling at this unexpected state of affairs, Joe played his trump card! He had already primed his older brother, Kevin, to take over his role in the Notions and asked us if we would be happy with that arrangement. He planned to work with Kevin, who was already playing in another local band, to rehearse the material in our repertoire such that he could slip into the Notions seamlessly. Although neither Dave A nor I knew Kevin, Dave Mac had been at school with him and was aware that he was already an experienced band member. To me it sounded like it could work out and when Joe subsequently brought Kevin round to meet the rest of us, I began to feel that it was going to be a good solution for the group. Kevin was instantly friendly and likeable and, although he was not currently a bass player, he demonstrated that he could readily adapt to the role, and so the decision was made – Kevin was in!

Of course, as far as the press was concerned, the story was a great piece of news - it wasn't every day that a member of a rock n' roll band quit to become a priest. Consequently when the news got out, reporters started ringing up my father wanting to know the full details. The story was covered in all the local papers – the Crosby Herald, the Liverpool Echo and the Liverpool Daily Post – and also in several of the national dailys. A journalist from the Daily Mirror even staged a 'ceremonial handover' between Joe and Kevin for the purpose of getting some photos to support his write-up. The shots were taken in the journalist's back garden and appeared in the paper the following day.

So it transpired that Joe played his final gig with the Notions on 5th September 1965 and Kevin made his first appearance a few days later at the NALGO Club, the very same venue where Joe had played his first gig with the group almost two years previously. As I'd expected, Kevin slotted in quickly and easily, thanks to his 'training' from Joe. A couple of practice sessions with the band and we were ready to pick up from where we'd left off. By and large, it felt like nothing had really changed for the rest of us, which was all to the good as we already had bookings taking us up to the end of the year. During the next few months Kevin had to shift up a gear to meet the demands of the Notions' bookings schedule, having not been used to playing so frequently. I think it came as a bit of a shock to the system, but he managed to cope with it all and rapidly developed his bass playing and singing skills to suit his new role.

A week or two after Kevin's inaugural performance, the group played a truly memorable gig supporting the Walker Brothers at Northwich. The Walkers were at the height of their fame at this time and the place was packed, mainly with very excited young girls! Scott Engel, the trio's main singer, was their idol and their anticipation of seeing him in the flesh was building up long before he set foot on the stage. Fortunately for us the 'Engel effect' rubbed off, which meant that when we played our set, just before the Walkers went on, there was a lot of screaming from the girls in the audience, which wouldn't normally have happened. This was an unexpected but very pleasant experience for us and it encouraged us to play even more enthusiastically. Then when the Walkers came on, along with their ten-piece orchestra, the place erupted - you couldn't hear yourself think. We watched from the wings as they played a terrific set, wondering if we could ever reach the same dizzy heights of fame that they had achieved. We were all on a high going home in the van that night, still buzzing from the thrill of being part of such a great event.

Over the next few weeks we played at a number of local venues, including the C.I. Club, the Peppermint Lounge and the Gartan Club, plus the St Helens Plaza (with the Abstracts) and the Lion Hotel Ballroom in Warrington (with Ian and the Zodiacs) which were both a little further out of the city.

On 16th October the Notions took part in an all-night session at the Cavern with the Merseybeats topping the bill. This was a marathon session for the Merseybeats who were attempting to play non-stop for 24 hours for charity. Then a little over a week later we were on the Cavern again, this time with the Big Three. What a fantastic sound they made with just a guitar, bass and drums. Griff, Johnny Gus and Hutch were seasoned professionals and they put on a great performance that night. Griff's guitar playing was streets ahead of anyone else on the Liverpool scene at the time.

The following month, on 6th November, the Notions were back at Northwich, this time supporting PJ Proby. It turned out to be another unforgettable night at the Memorial Hall, but not for the same reasons as our previous date there. As with the Walker Brothers gig, we benefited from being on the same bill as this hugely popular singer, who by that time had a couple of major hit records to his name and was a great crowd-puller. As a result, our first set went down really well and once again we experienced similarly wild treatment from the girls in the audience. Without having a hit recording of our own, that kind of reception didn't happen very often for us, which made it all the more exciting.

Jim's (PJ's) show started off as expected, with lots of girls crowding around the front of the stage eagerly waiting for him to make his grand entrance. His backing outfit, a 10-piece band similar to the Walker Brothers ensemble, struck up and the screaming began in earnest. Jim then appeared from the wings and the noise level ramped up as he launched into his first number. Being the great showman that he was, he powered into his set with great style and stage presence. We were watching the show from the wings, as we often did at the Memorial Hall and then, about halfway through, we noticed a tall, black guy working his way towards the front of the crowd. As he reached the second row of girls he started spitting at Jim, repeatedly and aggressively. He must have had a lot of practice, as he was hitting the front of Jim's stage outfit every time. At first Jim stoically refused to be distracted by this lowlife's actions and carried on regardless, but by the time the set was reaching its climax, he was covered in slime and was clearly getting very angry. In the end, with his patience exhausted and the final chorus of 'Hold Me' tailing off, Jim launched himself off the stage and dived right on top of the black guy, whereupon an almighty fight broke out just below the front of the stage. Several burly bouncers quickly ran from the wings and threw themselves into the fray and then, to our dismay, the curtain came down blocking our view of the rest of the action.

When we followed on with our last set, feeling somewhat apprehensive about what might happen, there was no sign of trouble and everything was back to normal. As it happened the set went particularly well, despite it being the end of the evening, and most of the audience had stayed on, seemingly unfazed by the earlier disruption. We never found out what it was all about, whether it was a spontaneous dislike of Proby on the part of the guy or if there had been some earlier altercation that had subsequently sparked off the attack. However, it all made for an 'interesting' gig and gave us our second experience of senseless violence in a dance hall.

The next gig we played at Northwich, on 4th December was, for me personally, the most unforgettable of all our appearances there. It is emblazoned on my mind right to this day. On that occasion we were supporting the Hollies (our third gig with them), who were at their peak at the time with a lot of major hits behind them. At Northwich, two support groups were always booked to play along with the main act, and most often the Notions played the set immediately before the star attraction's performance as well as the closing set of the evening (aka the 'graveyard shift').

When the Hollies went on, I noticed that Graham Nash was using a weird-looking black guitar with long curved horns, shaped a little like an instrument from an earlier century. I hadn't seen one like it before and was keen to get a closer look, so in the few minutes gap before our final set, I asked Graham if I could have a quick play of it. He willingly obliged and I thought it was such a cool-looking piece that I asked him if he wanted to sell it. He responded by offering to swap it for my Gibson and I suggested that I would need to try it out first before deciding. To help me make up my mind I used it during the first few numbers of our set and, on the spur of the moment, still swayed by the sexy styling, I agreed to the swap. At that moment, my Gibson went out of the stage door of Northwich Memorial Hall with the Hollies as they headed straight back to Manchester.

Clang! That was my worst-ever decision, one which I have regretted ever since. My Gibson was a much more refined instrument than a Danelectro Longhorn Guitarlin, even if it didn't look as cool. I definitely got the worst of the deal, but it was my own silly fault and I had to live with it. The next night the Notions played at the C.I. Club, where I used my 'new' guitar, hoping to impress any guitar buffs in the audience with my unusual acquisition. Instead, by the end of the evening, I had found that I couldn't get on with it at all. It was a very different guitar to play and I was too used to my good old '335'.

The next morning I rang Graham and asked him if he would consider swapping back and offered to meet up with him to effect the handover. His reply shocked me to the core - he said that he no longer had the guitar as he had sold it to a music shop in Manchester. So that was it, gone, my lovely Gibson. I was distraught and I felt I had been rather shabbily treated by someone I held in great esteem, who was a lot more wealthy than I was and who surely didn't need the money so desperately that he would instantly sell the guitar. Admittedly, I only had myself to blame for being too hasty, but of course it then left me with the problem of how to cope with my new guitar for the foreseeable future. Fortunately, Dave Mac came to my rescue by offering to let me use his Gibson, leaving him to play the Danelectro. As I did most of the lead guitar work, Dave only needed to play rhythm with it, so that provided an immediate solution to the problem, albeit a temporary one. A month later I bought a second-hand, 1962 fiesta red Fender Stratocaster from Cranes music shop in Hanover Street. This guitar was to be my permanent replacement, so I was able to return Dave's Gibson to him, to his great relief. (I'm happy to say that after all the years since those halcyon days, I still have that same Stratocaster - and the Danelectro!)

The rest of December 1965 was a really busy time for the group, mainly playing at local venues with other Liverpool groups. We played twenty-two gigs in the month, culminating in a double on New Year's Eve which involved dashing between Liverpool Student's Union and the C.I. Club - a hectic way to see in the New Year!

1966

The list of bookings that we were committed to even at the beginning of 1966 was pretty impressive for a non-professional outfit. My father had yet again been busy selling our souls to venues and promoters all over Merseyside and the North West. His efforts resulted in us playing fifty-seven gigs in the first three months of the year. In particular, he had secured a string of dates at Northwich Memorial Hall going forward well into the year. We were to play there as the main support group for famous bands of the day, including the Kinks (in January), the Drifters (also in January), the Mindbenders (in February), the Small Faces (in March), the League of Gentlemen (in April), Manfred Mann (also in April), the Cryin' Shames (in June), the Troggs (in August), and a few more stretching into 1967. I'm sure we could have become the resident support group at Northwich had we not already been booked on the other Saturday nights.

Occasionally an incident took place at a gig which has remained very clear in my mind. I remember the night we supported the Kinks and we were getting ready to start our usual warm-up slot just before their set. We decided we would try to fool the audience into thinking that the Kinks were starting ahead of schedule, by launching into the opening riff of 'You Really Got Me' just as the curtains began to open. It seemed to work initially but, unfortunately, as the curtains swept fully to the side to reveal just the Notions, they also knocked over our microphone stands and dragged them into the wings. At that point we had no choice but to abandon the song and try to make light of the situation. Disappointingly, our attempt at a joke had somewhat backfired, but I think we just about got away with it, probably because a lot people in the crowd knew us quite well from our previous gigs there. We always enjoyed playing at the Memorial Hall because it gave us the chance to meet top artistes on the national music scene and to watch and learn from their performances. By this time we also felt quite at home there, as there were always friendly, familiar faces in the audience.

Some of our other gigs were memorable for quite different reasons, particularly when we played for charities and for the sick or disabled. On 5th April we joined in with a number of other Merseyside groups to support a charity event entitled 'A Night For Mike' at the Grafton Rooms in Liverpool, which was a tribute to Mike Millward of the Fourmost who had recently died of cancer. The Fourmost themselves gave a great performance, with Mike's replacement filling his slot in their line-up. Other local acts that gave their services that night included the Escorts, the Dennisons, the Remo 4, Earl Preston's Realms, Silkie and Billy J Kramer and the Dakotas. It was a terrific session and I'm sure Mike himself would have enjoyed it immensely.

As well as playing at the numerous clubs and halls in and around Liverpool, we started picking up bookings for events being promoted by the students of Liverpool University. Dances were held at various halls belonging to the University and, quite often, in the Students Union building itself. We really looked forward to these gigs because, just like at Northwich, we found ourselves alongside the big names of the day, such as Sounds Incorporated, the Big Three, the Who and several others. Disappointingly, at the Who's gig, neither Pete Townsend nor Keith Moon seemed to remember us from Warrington Parr Hall and, unlike that occasion in the Who's early career, they made no effort to speak to us. I suppose it had been a long gap since then, during which time they had played all over the world and no doubt had encountered many, more high-profile people, but I always say it doesn't cost anything to be friendly.

Right at the start of 1966 we had promised ourselves that this was going to be our year for bringing out a record and making a real stab at fame and fortune. Other Liverpool groups had done it, so why couldn't we? We had already written several songs which we had performed on stage and which had gone down well with our faithful fans, so we considered that we were in a good position to interest a record company sufficiently to offer us a trial recording session. Also, we felt strongly that the window of opportunity was beginning to close for Merseyside groups and we wanted to make a name for ourselves before it vanished altogether. In order to achieve this goal my father approached several record labels armed with tapes of our own songs, which we had recorded some months earlier at the Cavern Sounds studio. To our surprise and delight, Polydor Records called us for an audition on 22nd April at Advision Studios in Wardour Street, in the heart of London. We were also required to attend a rehearsal session the day before at the famous Marquee Club, the very same place where the Rolling Stones, the Yardbirds, Alexis Korner and other famous names had cut their teeth. To say we were excited would have been a massive understatement - we were over the moon. In our mind's eye we were already on our way to musical fame; we would be on television, on 'Top of the Pops'; we would play concerts at big venues around the country or perhaps the world - and at last we would top the bill at Northwich Memorial Hall! Finally, it was all happening for us - only of course, it didn't!

Fred Lloyd was the guy who was to record us at Advision. He was an A&R man working for Polydor and came across as very friendly and pleasant. He had written a song, which he had sent on a demo tape for us to learn prior to going down to London for the rehearsal. Well, we had a go at it but, to be honest, we didn't actually like it very much. It was the sort of song that would have suited the popular 'Eden Kane' or 'John Leyton' type of solo artiste, not a group like the Notions. As a result we probably didn't put as much effort into it as we should have. We were quite confident that when we started playing at the rehearsal, we would be able to persuade Fred to record our own material instead. How naive can you get?

At the rehearsal, we went through Fred's song several times and didn't get a chance to play any of our own numbers. That should have been warning enough, but despite that, we still felt that Fred would change his mind and use our songs when we got into the studio.

When we entered the studio the next day, Fred immediately told us that he would only be recording us playing his song. That was a bit of a shock and it meant that we weren't quite as well prepared as we should have been to make a really good job of it. Although we cut a couple of takes, Fred wasn't totally happy with the outcome and so, as a final take, the song was recorded with Fred singing the lead as he wanted it sung and with the Notions providing the backing. I still have that recording now and, to be fair, the song now doesn't sound all that bad. Maybe if we had approached the whole affair a bit more positively from the outset, things may have worked out quite differently. As it was, we realised that we had probably blown it with Fred and we would have to look elsewhere for a second bite at the cherry!

Unfortunately, at the time all this happened, we were completely unaware of the similar situation experienced by the Beatles when they made their first recording for Parlophone. By all accounts, it seems they had been scheduled to record the Mitch Murray song 'How Do You Do It' but eventually managed to persuade George Martin that it didn't suit their style and it was passed on to Gerry and The Pacemakers. Apparently, at that first encounter, George Martin was not quite as receptive to their views as he subsequently became and had initially resisted their objections but, unlike the Notions and Fred, they soon got their own way.

Not long afterwards, in May, the Notions suffered a huge setback. Dave McCarthy told my father that he was leaving the group to take up an offer from the League of Gentlemen, which they had made to him when we had supported them at Northwich a month earlier. Dave had been very disappointed by the outcome of the recording session, as we all had, and had come to the conclusion that it was now less likely that the Notions would ever become fully professional. By this stage in his personal development he had decided that he wanted to pursue a full-time career as a musician and that he would not be able to do so by remaining in a non-professional group. Although I had to respect his decision and the reasons for it, for me it was a particularly hard blow, mainly because I felt that not only were we good friends having played together for such a long time but also I considered that Dave's singing voice was exceptional and would be a major loss to the group. The fact that all our voices blended so well for singing in close harmony was a significant aspect of the success of the group. I especially enjoyed performing Everly Brothers numbers with Dave and I was disappointed that I would no longer have that opportunity. I was pretty cut-up about it for a while but eventually I realised that had I been in Dave's shoes myself, I probably would have done the same thing.

Dave's departure from the band on May 26th left us with the problem of whether to try to recruit a replacement or stay as a trio, a configuration that Dave A, Keith and I had experienced back in the old Phantoms' days. As we were facing a heavy schedule of some fifty-seven gigs over the next three months, we realised that it would be quite difficult to find the time for rehearsals with a new member, even if we could quickly find someone suitable. We came to the conclusion that remaining a trio was the only option, at least in the short term. Carrying on with the same line-up, albeit with some appropriate adjustments to the singing arrangements, would enable us to fulfil our forthcoming commitments and give us a chance to seek out a replacement under less pressure. So the Notions became a trio and, as it turned out, that's the way we stayed until our very last gig.

Our first date without Dave Mac was on the very next night at the C.I. Club, one of our most frequented venues. It felt strange performing on that familiar stage with one member missing and it was quite difficult having to make changes to song arrangements on the fly in order to plug the gap in the voices. However, although we managed to get through the evening, we came away thinking we had a lot of work to do to get into better shape for dealing with the large number of forthcoming gigs. Many of these were venues within the immediate Liverpool area at clubs where we had played before, such as the Downbeat, the Peppermint Lounge, the Mardi Gras and NALGO, and I remember feeling that we needed to make a big effort to re-establish the group with the people we knew at these places. The same was true for out-of-town venues such as Northwich where we were by now well known. It was a lesser problem at places where we had played only once or twice before and others, which were completely new to us. Some of the gigs we played subsequently were with significant names of the time, such as the Mojos (Liverpool University's Roscoe Hall), the Herd (Lion Hotel Ballroom in Warrington), the Crying Shames (Northwich), David Bowie (Lion Hotel, before he became really famous) and the Troggs (Northwich). We also played with a number of top Liverpool groups, many of whom we knew very well, including the Cordes, Cy Tucker's Friars, the Kirkbys, the Escorts and the Hillsiders, to name but a few.

As the summer of '66 rolled on into autumn, I started to think seriously about my own future prospects as a full-time musician. I felt that we had probably missed out on our opportunity to break into the big time and, with the emphasis on the music scene slowly but surely shifting away from Liverpool, I decided that perhaps it would be sensible to have a second string to my bow, just in case it all fell apart at the seams and I had to resort to a 'proper' job. I came to the conclusion that the best option for me was to try to follow a further education route whilst also carrying on with the group. Of course, having experienced during my schooldays, the difficulty of mixing the very same activities, I knew that I would not be able to study successfully and still play as many gigs as the group had undertaken continuously for the last few years.

With this in mind, I applied to Liverpool Polytechnic and got a place on an engineering 'sandwich' course, starting in September. This meant working in industry for six months of each of four successive years and studying at college for the other six months - all a bit of a shock to the system after having spent almost a year solely involved with playing in a band! For the first industrial period, scheduled to last until January 1967, I was going to be working as a student trainee for the English Electric Company based at Kirkby on the East Lancs Road just outside Liverpool, not a very easy place to get to from where I lived in Waterloo. I would have to be there for eight o'clock in the morning, which meant leaving home before seven and catching two buses. I could see that this was going to be a test of endurance from the very start, whether I was playing in the group or not.

The job with English Electric commenced almost immediately but despite the new demands on my time and energy, the group continued with a full list of around seventy-five engagements from the beginning of September through to the end of the year. However, although it was sometimes a struggle to get up for work in the morning after arriving home in the small hours, I was still enjoying playing too much to worry about being tired and so for the next few months everything continued just as before. As well as playing with many of our contemporaries, such as the Escorts, the Kirbys, the Undertakers, Howie Casey and the Seniors, and others, we also supported a few big names like the quirky Temperance Seven, Sounds Incorporated, and even the BBC Dance Orchestra (under Ronnie Aldrich) at St George's Hall. Eventually we rounded off what had been a very eventful year for the group by playing for the New Year's Eve party of the South Shore Tennis Club in Blackpool. It turned out to be a really good night and went on well into the early hours.

1967

January 1967 kicked off with a New Year's Day gig at the Casino Club, also in Blackpool. This was one of the rare occasions when we stayed overnight after playing at an away gig, but given that we needed to be in Blackpool again for the following night's performance, it was a much easier option than going home and coming back to virtually the same place. This first gig of the year was followed by another fourteen dates in the same month, only a slightly reduced number compared with previous months! As a result I discussed with Dave A and Kevin about cutting down further on the gig rate to allow me to get stuck into the academic part of my engineering course, which had now started at the Polytechnic. Having obtained their agreement I spoke to my father to ask him to ease off a little on dates for the next few months owing to the pressure created by the 'Poly' throwing a shedload of work my way. Of course many of the gigs were already booked for months ahead, so all he could do was not go looking for any more. As it turned out, there were almost as many in February and more in March than there were in January, a grand total of fifty-seven. As, at this stage, I was still enjoying being in the group, I just carried on with both activities as best I could.

During those first few months of 1967, we played at various venues in Blackpool a further eight times and at the Mardi Gras in Liverpool no less than eleven times. Of the other venues we played, the gig at Liverpool University Salisbury and McNair students' hall of residence was particularly memorable, as the group topping the bill on 20th January was Tony Rivers and the Castaways. They were masters of three and four-part harmonies and their repertoire consisted almost entirely of Beach Boys' covers. They were so good that it was almost like the real Beach Boys were in the room. Another gig we played for the University, on 24th February, was at the main Students Union building and featured the Alan Price Set. Alan Price had been the keyboard player in the Animals when we played with them at Northwich and had been a founder member of that by then world-famous group. After leaving the Animals he had shown that he also had a great, bluesy singing voice. He had a very big hit with 'I Put A Spell On You' which, of course, was his finale on the night.

By April we had picked up several more bookings for the Mardi Gras and the Downbeat Club in particular and it was looking like we were going to continue being very busy for the next few months. On May 6th we had a gig at the Manchester University Faculty of Technology supporting for a third time, Manfred Mann, now with Mike D'Abo as their frontman following the departure of Paul Jones. Although they played a good set, I couldn't help feeling that they had lost a certain something that only the presence of Paul Jones could provide. Certainly his superb harmonica skills were no longer a feature of the band. Nevertheless they went on to produce several more major hit records, so clearly not everyone in the world felt the same as I did.

A week later we were surprised to receive a call from Granada Television inviting us to audition for a programme called 'First Timers' produced by Johnny Hamp. This was a show with a similar format to Bill Grundy's 'Look North', which had given the Beatles such fantastic exposure a few years earlier. We were to go to Manchester to meet Johnny and to perform a song of our choosing whilst being filmed. So on 17th May we went to the Granada studios and set up our gear on the small stage being used for the audition. We had chosen to play a number called 'Voice Your Choice', which had unusual harmonies in one or two parts and hopefully would enable us to show what we were capable of. However, we hadn't expected to be working with a sound system that had no foldback facility for the performers, meaning that we couldn't hear what we were each singing individually or, worse still, what the other person was singing. This made it virtually impossible to ensure that our harmonies and timing were correct and tight. Under the circumstances and with our choice of material, the likelihood of our performance doing us justice was pretty low and so we weren't surprised that nothing came of the exercise, other than the experience of being in a TV studio.

Before long it became obvious that my father's reaction to my plea for some free time had started to take effect, which meant that May, June and July were going to be quite unlike any month we had experienced since the Notions first started - in fact the bookings in June and July were down to single figures in each case. This meant that I now had a reasonable chance of getting through the first year exams of my course - for which no re-sits were allowed - and, as it transpired, I got through them all without too much trouble. However, whilst this was a happy state of affairs for me, the other side of the coin was that as the group's level of activity wound down, the others began to realise that the situation was likely to remain that way for another three years.

Looking back now I believe that, during those early summer months of 1967, I reached a turning point. I had spent the last four years playing in probably one of the busiest groups in Liverpool and had finally reached the conclusion that our prospects of becoming really successful were fading. We had not achieved the goal of seeing a record released and we had been unsuccessful at our one-shot TV audition. We had had our chances but we had not been able to capitalise on them. Furthermore, I felt that we were no longer playing to our full potential and that we would now have to make some serious changes in order to improve the situation. From my previous experience I knew that if I was going to stick with my engineering studies, I would not have time to be involved in a major re-development of the group. To be totally honest, by this stage I also felt a little jaded, my zest for playing was beginning to falter and it was probably affecting the other group members. Eventually we talked through the whole issue at length and reluctantly agreed that the best course of action was to disband the group when we had fulfilled all of our existing engagements.

We played our last gig at the Downbeat Club on July 21st 1967, almost four years after the first public appearance of the Notions in September 1963. We had played at venues all over Liverpool and the North West, we had met and performed alongside many famous names in the music business, we had achieved a fair degree of acclaim and popularity, we had enjoyed ourselves enormously and overall I had played almost one thousand gigs.

It was time to take a break - which I did, for thirty years!

THE STORY OF THE 'NOTIONS' AS REPORTED BY THE LOCAL AND NATIONAL UK NEWSPAPERS

FOCUS on YOUTH
BY CLUBMAN

No First Night Jitters For 'Teenage Group Who Win 300 Hearts

FOR them it was the supreme test. Atmosphere was so electric it could have charged their three guitars. Nearly 300 critical teenagers waited for the curtains at St. Faith's Church Hall to open and reveal Crosby's newest instrumental group—The Phantoms.

The pop records stopped . . . all eyes switched to the stage . . . and to the sound of hot guitars and pulsating drums they were ON. This was their first big engagement.

What followed was a swinging, beat-filled performance that had the cats mesmerised and even the sternest Crosby teenager critics snapping fingers.

Remarkable feature of the group—they have only been playing together for six weeks, and even then practising for a few hours at the week-ends.

Fifteen-year-old leader, David Delaney, of Ferndale Road, Waterloo, said they played for St. Faith's Youth Club on October 7. This was their first official engagement.

On Saturday they were booked to support the Black Velvets in a dance organised by 18-year-old John Goodwin.

BIG BOOM

So great was their success that they were asked to play for the youth club the following evening. They did and attendance was threefold. A big boom for St. Faith's. Most Sundays the Phantoms have a regular date at the club.

The group started casually. Sixteen-year-old David Armstrong, of Rockland Road, Waterloo, who left school last summer, together with David Delaney on guitar and D. Armstrong, the drummer, tried their skill.

Two other boys joined, and after limited practice, put on their first performance. Peter Little, bass guitar, didn't know how to play six months ago. Peter, of Walton, is oldest in the group, at 18. Rhythm comes from 16-year-old David Powell, of Eshe Road, Blundellsands.

Said leader David: "We are not going for the 'big time.' We just like to play locally. I take nine G.C.E.'s next year and I'm studying hard. My father sees that the playing doesn't interfere with school work."

CROSBY HERALD
FRIDAY, NOVEMBER 9, 1962

FLAGS OF ALL NATIONS

Dances with an international flavour will be organised by St. Nicholas' Youth Club.

April 19 sees the first dance in the series and France, the country chosen.

Les Phantoms (Waterloo's own Phantoms for the non-linguist) are playing and les billets sont deux nouveaux francs (for those with rusty French, tickets are 3s.).

French style decorations will add that authentic touch and nobody will object if two French-speaking girls call in.

CROSBY HERALD
FRIDAY, APRIL 12, 1963

Phantoms - First Line Up:
David Delaney – Lead Guitar
Dave Armstrong - Drums
Peter Little – Bass Guitar
Dave Powell – Rhythm Guitar

The 'Phantoms' first official engagement at St. Faiths referenced in this Friday, November 9, 1962 clipping from the Crosby Herald was on Sunday, October 7, 1962.

Their St. Faiths engagement supporting the **Black Velvets** was on Saturday November 3, 1962.

The St. Faiths Youth Club engagement was the following evening Sunday, November 4, 1962.

While it is not officially documented, it seems likely that **Peter Little** left the group on April 15, 1963. This is based on Frank Delaney's letter of September 30, 1963 (referring to a change of the group's name) that the Phantoms had been a trio since the April 15 date. In addition, **Keith Balcomb** recalls that **Peter Little** was no longer with the 'Phantoms' when he joined. (see below).

Phantoms - Second Line Up:
David Delaney – Lead Guitar
Dave Armstrong - Drums
Dave Powell – Rhythm Guitar

The 'Flags Of All Nations' clipping from the Crosby Herald dated Friday, April 12, 1963 referenced the 'Phantoms' engagement at St. Nicholas Youth Club the following Friday, April 19, 1963. This was also the first appearance of **Keith Balcomb** who replaced **Dave Powell** on rhythm guitar.

Phantoms - Third Line Up:
David Delaney – Lead Guitar
Dave Armstrong - Drums
Keith Balcomb – Rhythm Guitar

The 'Over The Top' clipping from the Crosby Herald dated Friday, April 19, 1963 referenced the 'Phantoms' engagement at St. Faiths the following evening Saturday, April 20, 1963

The clipping below from the Crosby Herald dated Friday, April 26, 1963 is a retrospective review of the 'Phantoms' engagement at the St. Nicholas 'French Night' Youth Club dance the previous Friday, April 19, 1963.

OVER THE TOP

Ready to top the £100 mark with his third rock dance is 19-year-old John Goodwin, of Mornington Avenue, Crosby.

Answering the call of his church, John is doing all he can to raise money for St. Faith's new vicarage. Not only has he raised over £80 in two successful dances—he has also provided many rocking hours for local teenagers.

Next dance in the series is to-morrow night at St. Faith's Hall, when the very popular "Flintstones"—favourites at the Cavern—couple with the Black Velvets and the Phantoms to make it a really swinging evening.

Co-partner in this venture is 17-year-old Colin Ryan, of College Avenue.

CROSBY HERALD
FRIDAY, APRIL 19, 1963

The clipping below from the Crosby Herald dated Friday, May 17, 1963 references the fact that while the Phantoms had made it to the semi-finals of the 'Lancashire and Cheshire Beat Group Competition' they unfortunately lost out to the ultimate winners – the **Escorts** from Allerton, a suburb of Liverpool.

✂ ✂ ✂

Mesdames . . Messieurs . . . and all that jazz. If you wanted to go French on Friday night, St. Nicholas' Church hall was the place to be, when the youth club held the first in a series of international style dances.

Take Les Phantoms . . . add three coats, three hats and three pipes and ola, you have Maigret three times.

The three man rock group opened their act with this mysterious gimmick but after the first beaty number it was back to Britain.

Atmosphere was just right and a lot of hard work had been put in by club members to create that Continental atmosphere. Lighting was effective (about 20 candle power), and the stage was ooo la la.

Next in this series is on June 7 when the club present an American type Barn dance.

Latest news from the Phantoms brings a change of personnel. Dave Powell had to put down his rhythm guitar a few weeks ago to go to Germany on the education exchange system.

BIG CHANCE

And big chance presented itself for keen follower Keith Ballcomb, of St. John's Place, Waterloo.

A friend and biggest fan, 16-year-old Keith stepped in at rhythm and is keeping up to par.

Dave Powell returns in a few days' time and one of the boys will have to revert to bass guitar. Just who, is being kept a secret.

When the Phantoms began their rock career, they were instrumental.

To provide a change, lead guitarist Dave Delaney now sings and, Dave told me, they have just learnt 45 numbers in one month. Some going. But when school comes round again — its back to the books for these boys. G.C.E. in less than two months.

Another successful rock dance was held the following night at St. Faith's Hall. The Flintstones joined with the Phantoms and the Black Velvets to make it a swinging evening.

CROSBY HERALD
FRIDAY, APRIL 26, 1963

Crosby's Phantoms Star In Beat Competition

IT was a disappointed group of Crosby fans who went home from the Philharmonic Hall, last Friday, after the Phantoms, Crosby's own rhythm and blues group, had been knocked out of the Lancashire and Cheshire Beat Group competition semi-finals.

The Phantoms had put up a wonderful show during the first day of the competition and were chosen to appear in the semi-finals from 56 entrants which included top groups from all parts of the north-west.

A tough set of adjudicators included Peter Sullivan, recording manager for Decca records, Tony Osborn, Jimmy Watson, editor of the New Record Mirror, and Franklyn Boyd of the Aberhach Music Company.

The lucky winners, chosen by the adjudicators in a thrilling final on Friday evening, were the Escorts, a group from Allerton, who received a recording contract, among other prizes. Second and third respectively were the Mersey Beats and, Derry and the Pressmen, who also received recording contracts.

BEATLES SURPRISE

Present to hand over prizes were two members of the Beatles making a surprise visit.

A special 20-minute performance was staged by Freddy Star and the Midnighters.

The Midnighters had been given a recording contract after their first appearance in the competition, and their first record, "Who Told You," is to be released on May 23.

They gave such an exciting example of their talent, that they raised a storm of enthusiasm from all the beat fans that packed the hall.

The whole competition was organised by Harry Lowe, one of the earliest promoters of Merseyside talent, and was compered by Bob Wooler.

CROSBY HERALD
FRIDAY, MAY 17, 1963

**THE REPORTER,
FRIDAY, 7th JUNE, 1963**

SUCCESS STORY

A success story began at St. Mary's social club Northwood on Sunday night, when three young lads known as the "Phantoms," played their first date in Kirkby.

The group, from Crosby, was formed in April. Their date went down extremely well, and as a result, landed several other engagements.

The group's manager, Mr. F. Delaney, told Teen Topics: "There was a fantastic attendance at the club for our first appearance."

Youth Chatter

The Phantoms local rock group won through to the second round of a Liverpool talent show last week.

**CROSBY HERALD
FRIDAY, AUGUST 2, 1963**

The clipping from the Kirkby Reporter dated Friday, June 7, 1963 references the Phantoms engagement at the St. Mary's Social club the previous Sunday, June 2, 1963.

The 'Youth Chatter' clipping from the Crosby Herald dated Friday, August 2, 1963 references the Phantoms participation in the 'Frankie Vaughn Talent Contest' held at Crane Hall, Liverpool. The preliminary round was held on Wednesday, July 24, 1963 and the Finals on Friday, July 26, 1963.

Keith Balcomb recalls that while the Phantoms were warming up backstage for their Tuesday, September 3, 1963 performance at Southport's Floral Hall, **Tony Jackson**, the bass guitarist for the **Searchers**, sat in with them. This Impromptu jam session reinforced the fact that they still needed to fill the bass guitarist position in their line up.

> Tuesday's midnight dance will feature The Searchers, the Liverpool group, with their hit recording, " Sweets For My Sweet." Helping to ensure four beat-packed hours will be The Phantoms.

CROSBY HERALD - FRIDAY, AUGUST 30, 1963

A minor piece of history of the era is documented in the Crosby Herald clipping dated Friday, September 20, 1963 titled 'Sprightly Coach'. It is included here for the obvious reference to the Phantoms and **Keith Balcomb**.

Wednesday, September 25, 1963 brings another change to the lineup with the addition of **Joe (Alec) Short** on bass guitar.

Phantoms - Fourth Line Up:
David Delaney – Lead Guitar
Dave Armstrong - Drums
Keith Balcomb – Rhythm Guitar
Joe Short – Bass Guitar

Sprightly Coach

SPRIGHTLY 72-year-old sales representative Paul Rochford, of Manor Road, Crosby, has an unusual part-time hobby — he coaches beat groups.

Mr. Rochford — stage name Percy Pryde — claims to be the man who dressed Crosby group the Black Velvets in black velvet.

A one-time performer in the old time music halls and theatres, Mr.

Paul Rochford

Rochford told me " This modern stuff is fantastic -- fabulous. Elder people nowadays want to go back to the good old days. I want to look at the present and into the future."

Mr. Rochford — he plays five musical instruments—teaches teenagers how to get the best out of their guitar and how to present their music. Rhythm guitarist, Keith Balcomb of the Phantoms is on Mr Rochford's books.

To all teenagers who think adults are against them — remember Mr. Paul Rochford!

**CROSBY HERALD
FRIDAY, SEPTEMBER 20, 1963**

As documented by manager Frank Delaney in a letter (below) dated September 30, 1963, a change of name for the group from the Phantoms to the Notions becomes effective on Tuesday, October 1, 1963. On the following page there are two undated clippings and a Crosby Herald clipping dated Friday, October 25, 1963 also announcing the new name.

Telephone : WATerloo 6023.

THE NOTIONS

22, Ferndale Road,
Waterloo,
Liverpool 22.

30th September, 1963.

Dear

In view of the fact that there are now several groups playing under the name of "The Phantoms", at least three in the greater Liverpool area and one from the Isle-of-Man, which is about to record for Decca, it has been decided to re-name the group "THE NOTIONS" as from 1st October, 1963.

The group, which has been a threesome since 15th April, 1963, always warmly acclaimed for its zest and presentation, has just acquired a fourth member, Bass-guitarist, 16 years old Alec Short, and the line-up is now as follows :-

David Delaney, 16, Lead-guitarist and Vocals.
Keith Balcomb, 17, Rhythm-guitarist and supporting Vocalist.
Alec. Short, 16, Bass-guitarist.
David Armstrong, 17, Drummer and supporting Vocalist.

We should like to take this opportunity of thanking all our friends for their most valuable support, bookings and recommendations, and to assure you of our very best efforts to entertain you in the future.

Yours faithfully,

(F.E.DELANEY.)
Manager.
" THE NOTIONS ".

NEW NAME FOR PHANTOMS
Liverpool's **Phantoms** have now changed their name to **The Notions**, due to the fact that there were so many groups throughout the country who use the former name.

Notions - First Line Up:
David Delaney – Lead Guitar
Dave Armstrong - Drums
Keith Balcomb – Rhythm Guitar
Joe Short – Bass Guitar

Quote . . .
"I've a notion this bunch of youngsters is going to be big, big, big, in 1964. A very promising new group indeed," Bob Wooler, manager of the world famous Caven, as he passed over five bookings on Monday, to Waterloo group "The Notions."

SAME SOUND: NEW NAME

BECAUSE there are at least three groups in greater Liverpool and one in the Isle of Man called "The Phantoms" the popular Waterloo group with the same name have changed to "The Notions."

The group, which has been a zestful threesome since April, recently welcomed a fourth member, bass guitarist Joe "Alec" Short. The line-up now reads (left to right): Keith Balcomb (rhythm), David Armstrong (drummer), "Alec" Short (bass), and David Delaney (lead).

With an impressive list of bookings in front of them, "The Notions" is a name fated to become a high-ranking sound on the Liverpool scene.

CROSBY HERALD - FRIDAY, OCTOBER 25, 1963

Northwich Beat

THE NOTIONS (formerly the Phantoms) are booked to appear at the Memorial Hall, Northwich, on November 9, supporting Shane Fenton. Recently they were on the same bill as the Searchers and Duke D'Mond and the Baron Knights.

**PUBLICATION UNKNOWN
UNDATED BUT REFERENCES
SATURDAY, NOVEMBER 9, 1963
ENGAGEMENT**

The 'Northwich Beat' clipping references the Notions appearance at the Memorial Hall in Northwich on Staurday, November 9, 1963. However, **Shane Fenton** did not appear his replacement was the **Hollies**.

> **"CAVERN'S CHOICE" NOTIONS ON RECORD**
>
> The Notions, claimed to be Bob Wooler;s Cavern choice for 1964, are the youngest group to play regular dates at the Cavern.
>
> This popular group which became the Notions only last October has such a demand for its services that it has already been booked for a date on New Year's Eve.
>
> On Monday the four boys, Dave Delaney, lead, Keith Balcomb, rhythm, Joe "Noddy" Short, bass, and Dave Armstrong, drums will be appearing at the St. Helens Theatre Big Show compered by Ken Dodd.
>
> This show features top-name entertainers invited for their name, and the Notions have been asked along as a known Cavern group.
>
> The Notions will also be featured on Oriole's third Mersey Sound LP.
>
> **COMBO - WEDNESDAY, FEBRUARY 19, 1964**

The importance of the 'Caverns Choice' clipping from the Combo newspaper dated Wednesday, February 19, 1964 is the mention that the Notions will be featured on **Oriole's** third 'Mersey Sound' LP. There is significant mystery surrounding this statement as will be explored below. In addition, it is a fact that only two recordings in that series were ever released under the title 'This is Merseybeat Volume 1 & 2' and those albums were recorded at the Rialto Ballroom in 1962 by **John Schroeder**, Oriole's leading A&R man. Both volumes were released in 1963.

> **Cavern L.P. To-night**
>
> WATERLOO beat group "The Notions" have been chosen with several other Liverpool groups to play on a new L.P. which is to be recorded at the Cavern to-night.
>
> Details of the recording are still vague and groups chosen do not know how many numbers they will have on the L.P. The Notions have had a tune specially written for them and it is believed they will feature it to-night.
>
> Manager, Mr. Delaney, told me yesterday: "We had an offer to back a London singer the other day. It would probably mean a recording contract, but we decided to turn it down."
>
> **CROSBY HERALD**
> **FRIDAY, FEBRUARY 21, 1964**

The Crosby Herald clipping 'Cavern LP To-night' dated Friday, February 21, 1964 reinforces a recording session to take place at the Cavern that same evening. Unfortunately, there is an obvious 'vagueness' included in the report.

However, the Notions manager Frank Delaney's copious notes include the following statement *"Oriole live recording at the Cavern. Present - Canadian Broadcasting Corporation film unit - The Notions, Herman & the Hermits, the Markfour, Chris & the Autocrats, Bobby & the Batchelors"*. Unfortunately, there is no information on this session in Spencer Leigh's book 'The Cavern' or the 'Cavern Diary' section of Phil Thompson's book 'The Best of Cellars, just this minor reference in the 1964 chapter *"Two record companies Decca and Oriole, determined to try and capture the unique Cavern atmosphere, recorded a variety of local groups for LP release"*.

> ... THE NOTIONS recorded 14 tracks with Oriole when their mobile unit was at The Cavern.
>
> **FRIDAY, FEBRUARY 21, 1964**
> **(PUBLICATION UNKNOWN)**

It is unfortunate that the source of the Friday, February 21, 1964 clipping is unknown as it obviously adds support to the fact that there was an **Oriole** recording session at the Cavern and that the Notions recorded 14 tracks.

> **Snap Cavern**
>
> NOEL WALKER (Decca) has just completed an LP at the Cavern. D-J Bob Wooler introduced the groups. Now John Schroeder (Oriole) is making an L.P. Possible groups to be featured include The Notions, The Secrets, The Roadrunners, and Ricky Gleason and the Top Spots.
>
> **CROSBY HERALD**
> **FRIDAY, FEBRUARY 28, 1964**

The Crosby Herald clipping 'Snap Cavern' dated Friday, February 28, 1964 goes a step further and identifies not only **Oriole**, but also **John Schroeder's** participation. However in a 2014 phone call to John, he was unable to recall a recording session at the Cavern that included the Notions, so the mystery deepens. None of the 'Mersey Sound' historians document the session and **John Schroeder**, Oriole's top A&R man could not confirm if it ever happened.

There were a number of articles in the Liverpool Echo, Mersey Beat and Combo newspapers announcing that a photograph, to include 'all' of the current Liverpool groups, was scheduled to be taken on Sunday, March 22, 1964 at ten o'clock in the morning on the steps of St. George's Hall, Liverpool. The photograph had been commissioned by the German magazine 'Stern' and the photographer was **Astrid Kirchherr**. Unfortunately, as the clocks had been adjusted forward by one hour (to summertime) at midnight on Saturday many of the groups that had played a late night booking on Saturday failed to show. Regardless, it was estimated that 200 groups were represented in the photo and it is probably one of the most iconic photographs documenting the era. A Liverpool Echo photographer also recorded the image and it was subsequently published in a number of local and national publications owned by the 'Mirror Group' of newspapers.

Dead center of the Echo photograph **Dave McCarthy** can be seen standing in front of **Derry Wilkie,** sandwiched between **Joe Short** (with bass guitar) and **Dave Armstrong.** To their left **Keith Balcomb** can be seen standing in front of **Rory Storm**. Unfortunately, due to copyright restrictions it was not possible to obtain permission for the use of the image in this publication.

The Notions—heading for the top

by PAUL REED

"THE Cavern's Choice for 1964"—that's what Bob Wooler said of The Notions, when they first performed at the Cavern in November last year.

Since their appearance at the Cavern, the boys have become practically unbookable, and are probably the youngest group to make regular appearances at the club.

The Notions were formed at the beginning of October, 1963. Up to that time David Delaney, David Armstrong and Keith Balcombe made up the Phantoms but when Joe Short joined the group as bassist things started moving.

Thumb nail run down on the boys from left to right:

Keith Balcombe, rhythm guitar; 17; apprentice paint sprayer; brown hair; blue eyes; playing guitar 18 months; likes Beatles, Searchers, Chuck Berry, Arthur Alexander and girls.

David Armstrong, drums; apprentice motor mechanic; learnt drums at Masonic School, Bushey Hall, Watford; brown hair; blue eyes; likes Beatles, Searchers, Cilla Black, Arthur Alexander, Tony Meehan and playing drums.

Joe Short, bass; 16; playing bass nine months; inland revenue (foreign branch); dark brown hair; blue eyes; likes Beatles, Searchers, reading, sleeping. Still studying.

Dave Delaney, lead; 17; sixth form boy; playing 18 months; fair hair; blue grey eyes; likes the Beatles, the Searchers; Little Richard, Arthur Alexander; dislikes unkind people.

The Notions—going from strength to strength.

LIVERPOOL WEEKLY NEWS - WEDNESDAY, MARCH 25, 1964

The Notions appearance at the Jacaranda Club, Liverpool on Monday, April 20, 1964 brings about another change in their line up as **Dave McCarthy** replaces **Keith Balcomb** on rhythm guitar and vocals. (See the 'Kirkby Reporter' clipping of May 8, 1964 below).

Notions - Second Line Up:
David Delaney – Lead Guitar
Dave Armstrong - Drums
Dave McCarthy – Rhythm Guitar
Joe Short – Bass Guitar

THE NOTIONS OUT TO CONQUER

The Notions, voted one of Liverpool's top groups, are to make a determined bid to conquer Kirkby's teenagers.

This month the group have several bookings arranged in Kirkby, including one at St. Kevin's on 20th May and another at the Labour Club on the 14th.

Recently the group recorded a track for an Oriole LP, cut "live" at The Cavern. They are eagerly awaiting the release of this number, and are hopeful it may lead to a contract.

The boys have also recorded at The Cavern for the Sunday Night programme from the club. This will be broadcast on 24th May.

Since their last appearance locally, a new rhythm guitarist has been playing with the group. He is Dave McCarthy. The other members are Dave Delaney (lead), Dave Armstrong (drums) and Joe Short (bass).

Keith Balcomb, the former rhythm guitarist is still with the group as "a floating reserve"

**KIRKBY REPORTER
FRIDAY, MAY 8, 1964**

THREE DAVES IN NOTIONS

Youngest group playing regularly at Cavern evening sessions are THE NOTIONS, whose average age is 17.

When they first formed they encountered the usual difficulty groups find – that of choosing a suitable name. After referring to Chambers' 20th Century Dictionary, they decided on THE NOTIONS.

DAVID DELANEY (lead), DAVID McCARTHY (rhythm), DAVID ARMSTRONG (drums) and JOE SHORT (bass) have no less than five changes of stage dress.

AGENCY

Strange to think that after all these years when groups toddled down to The Cavern after a job it's only just gone into business as an agency.

The new agency started last week and groups on the books include THE CLAYTON SQUARES, THE KIRKBY'S THE HIDEAWAYS and THE NOTIONS.

Says BOB WOOLER: "We're only including on our books what we call 'Cavern endorsed groups,' which means groups who've played here and on whom we can rely."

NOTIONS FOR LUX

THE NOTIONS can be heard on "Sunday Night At The Cavern" on May 24. The group, who were taped recently for a Swedish radio programme, tells us that they are sending tapes to New York for "Movie Life Magazine" radio programme.

**PUBLICATION UNKNOWN
UNDATED BUT LIKELY
MID MAY 1964 AS IT
REFERENCES THE SWEDISH
RECORDING SESSION OF
WEDNESDAY, MAY 6, 1964**

Bob has a pretty good say in the Cavern show productions. His velvet voice introduces the discs and his vast knowledge of the Mersey Sound and the groups in it, helps him pick the records he is going to play.

"I insisted that I picked the records", he said. "Of course I try and keep the Liverpool flag flying but groups on the show come from all over the country. Liverpool were featured well last Tuesday when the Dennisons, Notions, and Fortunes did their stuff."

I asked Bob what sort of record he liked to play on the show. That he told me, was the hardest part. "The show is squeezed between two pretty good shows on a Sunday and the last thing I want to do is play the same material as them.

"We play some way-out tunes at the Cavern but it's very hard to find the right thing for the radio shows. I'm always on the look-out for good material from these groups".

COMBO comment: Let's hope the powers that be take notice of Bob's plea. What teenagers want is the REAL Cavern produced on these shows - not a poor imitation whipped up by the radio technicians in a quick-fire session.

The Notions - pictured rehearsing at the Cavern for the 208 show which will be broadcast next Sunday.

COMBO NEWSPAPER W/E MAY 28 1964

The clipping from the 'Combo' newspaper references the Radio Luxembourg show 'Sunday Night at the Cavern' which was recorded on Tuesday, April 28, 1964 and broadcast on Sunday, May 24, 1964. **Bob Wooler** can be seen in the background sandwiched between **Dave McCarthy** (partially obscured by **Joe Short**) to the left side of the photo and **Dave Delaney** to the right.

Beat Group At Knowsley

The Notions, From Waterloo

A beat group who have played at the Cavern Club last night found another venue—Knowsley Hall, the home of Lord Derby, Lord Lieutenant of Lancashire.

The Notions, the youngest group to appear at the Cavern, provided background music at a cocktail party given in honour of Lieutent-General Sir Edward Howard-Vyse, G.O.C., Western Command, who is leaving.

Some months ago Lord Derby paid a surprise visit to the Cavern, though the Notions were not playing there then. "The idea to have a beat group at Knowsley may have arisen from that visit," a spokesman at the hall said to-day.

DELIGHTED

Highly delighted at being the first group to play at Knowsley were the four members of the Notions, all 17 years of age, and from Waterloo.

They are: David Delaney (lead guitar), a Merchant Taylor's sixth former, 22 Ferndale Road; Joseph Short (bass guitar), inland revenue foreign branch employee, 5 Woodlands Road; David McCarthy (rhythm guitar), who works in the Ministry of Aviation and lives at 21 Curzon Road; and David Armstrong (drums) clerk in a city office, 17 Rockland Road.

They formed the group in October last year.

The Liverpool group, the Notions, who played at Knowsley Hall last night. They are (left to right): David Delaney, of 22 Ferndale Road; David McCarthy, of 21 Curzon Road; Joseph Short, of 5 Woodlands Road, and David Armstrong.

LIVERPOOL ECHO - WEDNESDAY, JULY 1, 1964

Extract from Liverpool Echo, 25 July, 1964

THE NOTIONS

The four 17-year-olds who form one of the busiest groups on Merseyside—the NOTIONS, were recently chosen to play for Lord Derby at Knowsley Hall-the first beat group to play there.

The line up is Dave Delaney (lead guitar), Dave Armstrong (drums), Joe Short (bass guitar) Dave McCarthy (rhythm guitar) They all sing, and the two Daves frequently combine to perform many of the Everley Brothers' numbers.

Being the proud owners of five different stage outfits, the Notions (who picked their name at random from the dictionary) are always very smart and well-dressed. Each member of the group reads music, and they're all very intelligent lads. Dave Delaney is in the sixth form of a public school studying for his "A" levels, and the other three have good day-time occupations.

They play regularly at the Cavern and the management speak highly of them.

Originally doing the rounds as a threesome called The Phantoms, they changed their name to The Notions last October when Joe Short joined them. In February this year they recorded for the long awaited L.P. which is tentatively titled "Cavern Alive," and looks like being released at last. In May they broadcast on the Radio Luxembourg show "Sunday night at the Cavern."

The Notions are managed by the lead guitarist's father, Frank Delaney, who tells me the lads are shortly to go to Scotland for a few days, fitting in the playing with their holidays. (His son Dave, by the way is an expert marksman with the rifle, and won a trophy at Bisley last year).

With their looks, smartness and ability this young group, billed as "the Cavern's Choice," look like having a bright future—GEOFF LEACK.

(SEE FOLLOWING PAGE FOR ACTUAL NEWSPAPER ARTICLE)

Liverpool Echo
and Evening Express

The boys with the beat

The Notions

The four 17-year-olds who form one of the busiest groups on Merseyside—the NOTIONS, were recently chosen to play for Lord Derby at Knowsley Hall—the first beat group to play there.

The line up is Dave Delaney (lead guitar), Dave Armstrong (drums), Joe Short (bass guitar), and Dave McCarthy (rhythm guitar). They all sing, and the two Davids frequently combine to perform many of the Everly Brothers' numbers.

Being the proud owners of five different stage outfits, the Notions (who picked their name at random from the dictionary) are always very smart and well-dressed. Each member of the group reads music, and they're all very intelligent lads. Dave Delaney is in the sixth form of a public school studying for his "A" levels, and the other three have got good day-time occupations.

They play regularly at the Cavern and the management speak highly of them.

Originally doing the rounds as a threesome called The Phantoms, they changed their name to The Notions last October when Joe Short joined them. In February this year they recorded for the long awaited LP which is tentatively titled "Cavern Alive," and looks like being released at last. In May they broadcast on the Radio Luxembourg show "Sunday night at the Cavern."

The Notions are managed by the lead guitarist's father Frank Delaney, who tells me that the lads are shortly to go to Scotland for a few days, fitting in the playing with their holidays. (His son Dave, by the way is an expert marksman with the rifle, and won a trophy at Bisley last year).

With their looks, smartness and ability this young group, billed as "the Cavern's Choice," look like having a bright future.—GEOFF LEACK.

LIVERPOOL ECHO - SATURDAY, JULY 25, 1964

A feature of many of the top groups to-day has been that their talent has been recognised in its early stages by BOB WOOLER and they have been given a residency at The Cavern. THE BEATLES, GERRY & THE PACEMAKERS, BILLY J. KRAMER and THE SWINGING BLUE JEANS have all held resident spots and THE NOTIONS are now one of the current regulars. In fact, Bob has even gone as far as to refer to them as "The Cavern's Choice for '64." The Notions have been featured on Sunday Night at The Cavern, and they also have three tracks on the second LP. In addition, two of Liverpool's most prolific and talented song writers, MIKE BATESON and CARL HAWKINS who hitherto have devoted their talent to cabaret and musical comedy, have decided to launch themselves into the "pop" music world and have especially asked that they may write for The Notions. This obviously could result in a single record release in the very near future.

Recently they had the honour of playing at the Knowsley home of Lord Derby, Lord Lieutenant of Lancashire, the first time a group has been so privileged.

Because of the lead guitarist's school commitments and examinations, this group cannot at the moment turn fully professional and have unfortunately had to turn down extensive tours of Norway, Sweden and Scotland.

The very attractive style, and the clever harmony work of The Notions, makes them a group that it is always a pleasure to watch and listen and unlike many groups they can always be relied upon to give a complete and lively show.

PUBLICATION UNKNOWN - DATED THURSDAY, NOVEMBER 5, 1964

THE NOTIONS

WHO was the mystery group in last week's "Focus On Youth"? It was the Phantoms, a group which added another member and became the Notions. Here's a more recent photograph of the group with (left to right) Dave McCarthy (17), rhythm guitar, vocals; Dave Delaney (17), lead guitar and vocal; Dave Armstrong (18), drums; and Joe Short (17), bass and vocal.

The Notions are, of course, "The Cavern's Choice" and are well known for their presentation and their first-class harmony numbers.

CROSBY HERALD - FRIDAY, NOVEMBER 13, 1964

THE BOYS (and girls) WITH THE BEAT

The Excelles pictured with Long John Baldry (bottom left) at the Cavern. Left to right: Paddy McHugh, Carroll Carter, Vicky Bird, Frank Collins. Bottom right: Maureen Collins.

The Excelles

A brand new vocal act hit the scene last week, and immediately caused a storm of interest.

They're called the EXCELLES, and people who have already heard them perform are predicting big things for them.

I haven't heard Bob Wooler quite so ecstatic about an act for a long time, and he's gone as far as saying: " I've never been so knocked out with an act since I introduced the Beatles to the scene four years ago. They're going to be very, very big."

The Excelles, three girls and two boys, were heard singing in a social club by the Cavern's office boy, who was so excited he immediately got Bob Wooler to listen to them.

Bob signed them up at once and is now in the process of getting a backing group for them. " We're going to have just piano, bass and drums behind them," says Bob, " and we've almost got this organised. We just need a pianist, and then we can really get started."

Although they only came to notice a week or so ago, the Excelles have already been offered a TV appearance, and will be on " Scene at 6.30 " on Monday night. The number they will be performing will in all probability be " Nitty Gritty," and they will more than likely be doing it live, with no instrumental backing.

For the bookings they've already done they've been backed by the St. Louis Checks and the Notions.

Britain hasn't really got any answer to the American vocal groups, and the Excelles are hoping to fill this gap.
GEOFF LEAK.

The publisher of this clipping is unidentified. However, **Geoff Leak** did many of the reports on the local music scene for the Liverpool Echo. In addition, the byline on the clipping is one that was used by him for that newspaper so it's possibly an Echo clipping.

The photo offers a clue to the date, as both **Long John Baldry** and the **Excelles** were on the same bill at the Cavern on Saturday November 7, 1964. In addition, as the **St Louis Checks** were also on the same bill it's possible that they backed the **Excelles** for that performance.

The Notions and the **St Louis Checks** also appeared on the same bill with the **Excelles** at the Cavern on Sunday, November 15. Unfortunately, it is not known which of those two groups backed the **Excelles**.

However, in his notes, Notions manager Frank Delaney specifically states that the Notions backed the **Excelles** at the Cavern on Sunday, November 29, 1964 (the **St. Louis Checks** were not on the bill that night).

As the clipping also states that the **Excelles** had been backed by the Notions on a previous appearance this would date the clipping to late November or early December 1964.

What is more significant is the fact that the Sunday, November 29, 1964 appearance of the **Excelles** backed by the Notions was recorded for the Radio Luxembourg show 'Sunday Night at the Cavern'. The recording session is confirmed by both **Spencer Leigh** in his book 'The Cavern' and **Phil Thompson's** book 'The Best of Cellars'.

Focus On Youth 1965 Popularity Poll Results

THE Music Students, the Notions and the Jensons are tops ! That is the verdict of the youth of Crosby,

There was a fantastic response to the poll, the first to be staged by Focus on Youth. Most voting was thoughtful, though we did receive some peculiar votes.

Voting was for the top local rhythm and blues group; the top local beat group; the top local instrumentalist; the top local singer; the top Liverpool group not yet had a record in the top 50; the artiste or group most deserving success in 1965; and for the best single record of 1964.

For top local rhythm and blues group, the youth of Crosby picked the Music Students, followed three votes behind by the Earthlings.

NECK AND NECK

Neck and neck for top local beat group were the Notions and the Jensons. These and the other results are published in this issue.

We also asked the local beat promoters to nominate their choices, and their votes can be found under " promoters' poll." My own choices and those of my colleague Teenpager, of the Bootle Herald, are published under " writers' poll."

who over the past weeks " went to the polls " and voted in the Focus on Youth 1965 Popularity Poll.

Next year we hope to widen the scope of the poll, to include Merseyside artistes. Such groups as Rhythm and Blues Incorporated, from Southport, got many votes, but unfortunately these had to be discounted as they are not a local or Liverpool group.

Among the strange votes were the Merseybeats for success in 1965; and the Grimbles for top local rhythm and blues group, top local beat group, top Liverpool group and group most deserving success in 1965.

The most difficult category proved to be the choice of 1964 record. Almost everyone voted for a different record, from James Brown's " Night Train " to P. J. Proby's " Walkin' The Dog" (I must be ignorant, didn't even know he'd recorded it).

However some votes tallied and we had three neck and neck winners of this part of the poll.

The Roadrunners were the overwhelming favourites and they had the top Liverpool group category all their own way. For those of you who voted: thanks. For those who voted too late: sorry. Here's hoping for an even bigger response next year.

CROSBY HERALD - FRIDAY, JANUARY 15, 1965

READERS' POLL

Votes received from readers were as follows:

A—Top Local Rhythm and Blues Group:
The **Music Students** beat the **Earthlings** by two votes. No other local rhythm and blues group got more than one vote.

B—Top Local Beat Group:
The **Notions** had this category beaten hands down in the first few days of the poll, but then further votes for the Jensons poured in and the two groups finished neck and neck.

C—Top Local Instrumentalist:
Billy Lovelady, lead guitarist of the Music Students, beat **Bryan Dodson**, drummer of the Earthlings, by two votes. Billy also won some votes as a singer.

D—Top Local Singer:
Johnny Almond, vocalist with the Music Students, had an easy victory in this part of the poll. Twelve local singers were voted for—a rather unexpected amount.

E—Top Liverpool Group not yet had a record in the Top 50:
This left lots of scope and a total of 15 talented groups were voted for, some, however, a good deal more talented than others. The winners — as most people agree, I think—deserved to be and were the **Roadrunners**.

F.—Artiste or Group most deserving success in 1965:
I had expected voters to look a little further over their garden wall when making a choice here. The winners were again the **Roadrunners**, but as this category was international I think I can say that a lot of people used little imagination and votes included some for Crosby groups.

G—Best Single Record of 1964:
The three records which tied for this category were "**A Hard Day's Night**" (Beatles), "**She's A Woman**" (Beatles) and "**It's All Over Now**" (Rolling Stones). For a time it looked as though everyone would vote for a different record! These votes only just tied.

Writers' Poll

TEENPAGER, Focus on Youth, Bootle Herald voted:
MUSIC STUDENTS, as top local rhythm and blues group.
THE NOTIONS, as top local beat group.
THE ROADRUNNERS, as top Liverpool group yet to have top 50 success.
ALEXIS KORNER, as artiste most deserving success in 1965.
"**DIMPLES**" by John Lee Hooker, as the best single record of 1964.

CLUBMAN voted:
MUSIC STUDENTS, as the top local rhythm and blues group.
THE NOTIONS, as top local beat group.
BILLY LOVELADY, lead guitarist with the Music Students as top local instrumentalist.
JOHNNY ALMOND, vocalist with the Music Students, as top local singer.
THE ROADRUNNERS, as top Liverpool group yet to have top 50 success.
LONG JOHN BALDRY, as artiste most deserving success in 1965.
"**WHO'S AFRAID OF VIRGINIA WOLF?**" by Jimmy Smith as the best single record of 1964.

**CROSBY HERALD
FRIDAY
JANUARY 15, 1965**

Focus On Youth
1965 Pollwinners' Poll

NOW the poll-winners go to the polls! As an interesting follow-up to the Focus on Youth 1965 Popularity Poll I asked some of the poll-winners to express a few of their own opinions, likes and dislikes.

So this week here are the results of the 1965 Poll-winners Poll—their own favourites in 10 different categories.

The two poll-winners who replied to my request were the **Notions** (joint winners of the "Top local beat group" category) and, on behalf of the Roadrunners, ("Top Liverpool group" and "Group most deserving success in 1965"), their leader, Mike Hart.

Mike Hart—voting as leader of the Roadrunners and not for the group—wishes it to be made clear that his votes consist of his opinions and these, he writes, are definitely not those of the rest of the group.

A NEW picture of top Crosby beat group, the Notions. Next week they will make another demo-disc to add to the two already out.

This time it will be a number they have written themselves called "Another Time." Dave Delaney (lead guitar) and Dave McCarthy (rhythm guitar) started the composition while the group was on its way home in their van from Frodsham, and afterwards the others fitted in their own parts.

The group votes for its favourite artistes in this week's Focus on Youth Pollwinners' Poll.

How The Winners Voted

A—Liverpool's top rhythm and blues group:
Mike Hart chose the GRIMBLES.
The Notions chose the CLAYTON SQUARES and the ST. LOUIS CHECKS.

B—Liverpool's top beat group.
Mike Hart chose the BEATLES.
The Notions chose the ESCORTS.

C—Semi-professional Liverpool group most deserving success this year:
Mike Hart chose the CORDES.
The Notions made no choice.

D—Professional Liverpool group most deserving success this year:
Mike Hart chose the UNDERTAKERS.
The Notions chose the ESCORTS.

E—Liverpool's top instrumentalist:
Mike Hart chose GEORGE HARRISON (Notes: for taste and interest, not technique).
The Notions chose NICK CARVER (tenor saxophone, Roadrunners) and BRIAN GRIFFITHS (lead guitarist, Johnny Gus Set).

F—Liverpool's top vocalist:
Mike Hart chose JOHN LENNON.
The Notions chose EARL PRESTON.

G—Top artiste or group in Great Britain:
Mike Hart chose the BEATLES.
The Notions chose the BEATLES. Snap.

H—Top artiste or group of 1964 (any nationality):
Mike Hart chose the BEATLES.
So did the Notions.

I—Best single record of 1964:
Mike Hart chose "CAN'T BUY ME LOVE" (Beatles).
The four Notions chose "CRYING GAME"; "THAT'S WHAT LOVE IS MADE OF"; "HARD DAY'S NIGHT"; "CAN'T BUY ME LOVE."

J—Best long-playing record of 1964:
Mike Hart chose "A HARD DAY'S NIGHT.
The Notions did likewise.

CROSBY HERALD - FRIDAY, JANUARY 29, 1965

The clippings on this page and the previous page are all related to a 'popularity poll' conducted by the Crosby Herald newspaper. As there were seven categories in the poll the chances of an outright winner were somewhat slim!

Pollwinners' Dance

ANOTHER Pollwinners' Dance, featuring some of the winners of the Focus on Youth, 1965, Popularity Poll, is to be held. Last time it was Brian Kelly, of Bee-Kay promotions, who held a dance featuring the Music Students and the Jensons; this time it is English Martyrs, Litherland, who will be staging the Roadrunners, the Music Students, and the Notions, on April 11.

The Crosby Herald followed up on that 'poll' by asking the Notions to cast their own personal votes in a number of similar categories. Ultimately, the poll resulted in a series of dances featuring the winners.

Sunday, September 5, 1965 was a memorable day in the story of the Notions, the venue was St. Anne's Social Club, Marmaduke Street, Liverpool (the Crosby Herald clipping incorrectly identifies the day). It was the last appearance of bass guitarist **Joe Short**, who had announced his intention to leave the group to enter the priesthood. His place in the Notions was filled by his brother **Kevin Short**, former bass player for the **Jokers** from Southport. Kevin's first appearance with the Notions was Wednesday, September 8, 1965 at the N.A.L.G.O. club in West Derby.

GUITARIST TO ENTER PRIESTHOOD

Joseph Short, aged 18, guitarist and vocalist with the Notions, a Mersey beat group, gave his last performance last night and is preparing to enter the priesthood.

Joseph, an income tax clerk, of Woodland Road, Seaforth, near Liverpool, who

Joseph Short

has played 100 times at the Liverpool's Cavern Club, will study for two years at Osterley, the Roman Catholic training college.

He said last night "I have enjoyed my time with the group immensely, but I feel the call to enter the Church."

LIVERPOOL DAILY POST MONDAY, SEPTEMBER 6, 1965

POP SINGER TO BECOME A PRIEST

POP group guitarist and singer Joe Short yesterday turned his back on the beat world to become a priest.

When the 18-year-old income tax clerk, of Woodlands Road, Waterloo, Liverpool, broke the news to the group, The Notions, they thought it was a joke.

But Joseph, the quiet one of the quartet, had already confided

JOE SHORT
Doing the right thing

his secret ambition to the Archbishop of Liverpool, and been accepted as a trainee.

Yesterday he left the stomping world of beat and screaming fans for the cloistered quiet of Austerley College, in Middlesex. He will spend the next two years there training for the priesthood.

For the last few years Joseph and The Notions have played the best known places on the beat scene. They were regulars at Liverpool's Cavern and played for Lord Derby at a house party at Knowsley Hall.

Joseph said: "I cannot explain why or how this has happened, but the feeling that I wanted to enter the priesthood has been with me for a long time."

UNDATED - PUBLICATION UNKNOWN - POSSIBLY THE DAILY MAIL

Boy leaves beat world to be priest

BEAT group guitarist Joe Short, 18, yesterday left the world of clubs like Liverpool's famous Cavern to train to be a priest.

"It may seem a big change," he said, "but it's something I have always wanted to do."

For two years Joe, a clerk, of Woodland-road, Waterloo, Liverpool, played bass guitar with the semi-professional Merseyside group, The Notions.

Four months ago he saw the Archbishop of Liverpool, the Most Rev. George Beck.

Now Joe is bound for a Roman Catholic training college at Osterley, Middlesex.

Said Joe: "The Archbishop seemed surprised that I played with a group. But I enjoyed every minute."

DAILY MIRROR MONDAY, SEPTEMBER 6, 1965

NEW NOTIONS

The "new" Notions: left to right, Kevin Short (new boy, on bass guitar), Dave Delaney (lead guitar), Dave McCarthy (rhythm guitar), and rear, Dave Armstrong (drums).

Local beat guitarist will be priest

NOTIONS' bass guitarist Joe Short left the group last Saturday ... to change from beat to the Church and train as a priest.

Joe, aged 18, of 5 Woodland Road, Seaforth, is a former St. Bede's School pupil, and has been working since he left school as an income tax clerk. He has been in the Notions—Crosby's most successful group—since they formed over two years ago.

His last engagement with the group was a booking at a social club in Kensington, Liverpool, on Saturday. Among parting gifts he received were a travelling clock, a pen, and several books from fans. From the Notions—Dave Delaney, Dave McCarthy and Dave Armstrong—he received an electric shaver. Now he leaves for a Middlesex training college.

Joe will be replaced in the group by his 19-year-old brother Kevin, formerly of the Jokers. Kevin made his debut with the Notions last Wednesday at West Derby N.A.L.G.O., coincidentally the same venue that Joe first appeared with the group two years ago.

Manager of the group, Mr. Frank Delaney, of Waterloo, tells me that the group will be going "full steam ahead" this winter, as his lead-guitarist son Dave has left school. Bookings and publicity had to be held under a tight rein while Dave was still at Merchant Taylors' School, because of the young guitarist's studies.

A week on Saturday the group appears at Northwich with the Walker Brothers, and three weeks after—also at Northwich—on the same bill as Chuck Berry. Mr. Delaney also hopes to get some recording done with the boys, and they have already made several demo-discs.

Bookings are going very well, he informs me. They are very popular at both English Martyrs' and St. Elizabeth's Youth Club dances in Litherland, and have a large number of dates up to the end of December. The Notions fan-club is reported to be 300-strong, with several fans following the group round on nearly every booking.

CROSBY HERALD - FRIDAY, SEPTEMBER 10, 1965

Leaves Group To Enter Priesthood

Bass guitarist and vocalist Joseph Short made his last appearance with the Mersey beat group, The Notions, last night. He is leaving them to prepare for entry into the priesthood.

Joe, who is 18, is an income tax clerk and lives at Woodland Road, Seaforth. He has appeared at the Cavern scores of times and he said

Joseph Short

last night: "I have enjoyed my time with the group immensely, but I feel the call to enter the Church."

Joe will prepare for his new life at Osterley, the Roman Catholic training college. His place in the group will be taken by his brother, Kevin.

LIVERPOOL ECHO MONDAY, SEPTEMBER 6, 1965

OFF-BEAT NOTION

TAKING the place of bass guitarist Joe Short in Liverpool beat group The Notions this week is Joe's elder brother Kevin.

For Joe, who lives at 5, Woodland Road, Seaforth, has just left the group to become a priest.

A parishioner of St. Thomas of Canterbury, Waterloo, Joe was due to leave Merseyside for Osterley yesterday (Saturday, September 11), to begin his studies.

Youngest of three docker's children, Joe has worked for three years as a tax officer playing with The Notions in his spare time.

Now his problem is to learn as much Latin as possible quickly since he's never studied it before — while Kevin, 19, fits into his place with the group.

UNDATED & PUBLICATION UNKNOWN

BUT LIKELY SOMETIME SHORTLY AFTER SEPTEMBER 8, 1965 AS THAT WAS THE DATE OF KEVIN'S FIRST APPEARANCE WITH THE NOTIONS AND THE CLIPPING REFERENCES THAT HE TOOK JOE'S PLACE IN THE GROUP 'THIS WEEK'.

It is somewhat apparent that the newspapers of the day went out of their way to sensationalize the fact that a former 'beat group' member was leaving to join the church. However, Liverpool has always been a deeply religious city, predominantly Catholic and Church of England. There is both a Catholic and an Anglican cathedral in the city and it was not unusual in the 60's for teenagers of either sex to pursue a religious career. The fact that **Joe Short** was a former beat group member was obviously more newsworthy than the many other teenagers that devoted themselves to a religious calling.

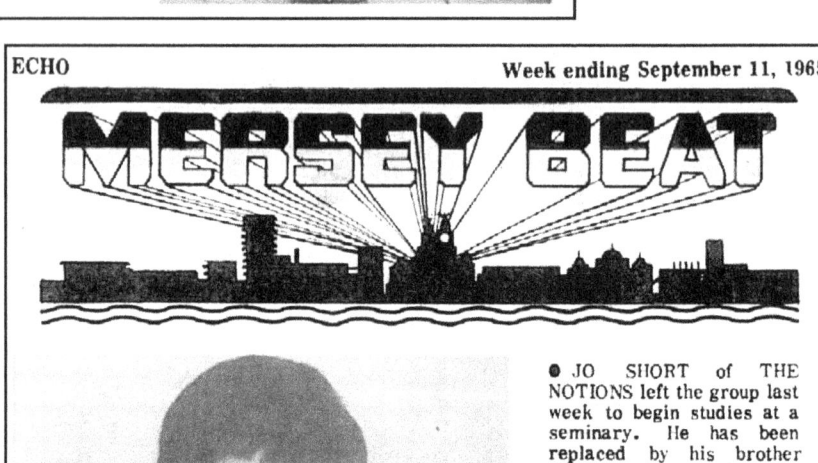

ECHO — Week ending September 11, 1965

THE NEW NOTION

● JO SHORT of THE NOTIONS left the group last week to begin studies at a seminary. He has been replaced by his brother KEVIN, who for the past two months has been learning bass guitar with the help of his brother. The group made their debut last Wednesday at N.A.L.G.O.

LIVERPOOL ECHO W/E SATURDAY, SEPTEMBER 11, 1965

ECHO — Week ending October 16, 1965

● The bass guitarist from THE BUMBLIES, BRIAN NORRIS, has replaced JOHN CAULFIELD in recording group EARL PRESTON'S REALMS. Apart from playing bass guitar, Brian will be taking the lead vocal on some numbers and harmonising on others.

● THE NOTIONS forthcoming dates include appearing on the same bills as P. J. PROBY, MANFRED MANN and THE HOLLIES.

LIVERPOOL ECHO W/E SATURDAY, OCTOBER 16, 1965

Notions - Third Line Up:
David Delaney – Lead Guitar
Dave Armstrong - Drums
Dave McCarthy – Rhythm Guitar
Kevin Short – Bass Guitar

All of the clippings on this page are undated and none of the publications are identified. However, based on Frank Delaney's notes the dates can be approximated.

THE Notions, certainly the most popular of Crosby's beat groups, made their first appearance in the borough for two years on Wednesday.

They topped the bill at St. Luke's Hall, and re-established their reputation as a swinging outfit with local teenagers.

Although the group has appeared regularly in Litherland, at St. Elizabeth's and at English Martyrs', they have not managed to fit in a date over the borderline. Pictured left to right above are: Dave McCarthy, Dave Armstrong (rear), Kevin Short (front) and Dave Delaney.

THE NOTIONS 'RETURN' TO St LUKE'S WAS ON WEDNESDAY, NOVEMBER 17, 1965

Pop news and views from . . . . . . TONY VARNEY

■ The Notions are becoming an increasingly active group. I've got one of those feelings - that they will make their mark on the national pop scene in the very near future. This is an outfit that is greeted with a tremendous reception wherever they appear.

Their manager, Frank Delaney, is a shrewd and capable business man, and he has great faith in the Notions' talent and ability. Frank tells me that the boys "will be making a recording in the near future. The numbers have not been decided on yet, but if all goes well, we should have a record on the market early next year. Let's hope it's a big success for them.

DECEMBER 1965

Notions: high hopes

THE Notions, Crosby's top beat group, are currently recording six numbers for demonstration to a London record company.

One of the numbers, lead guitarist Dave Delaney told me this week, is their famous "Another Time," which like the other tunes to be recorded, is one of their own compositions.

"We've got high hopes," said Dave. "At the moment things are going fine. We're out four or five nights a week on bookings."

He and the other Notions — Dave McCarthy (rhythm), Kevin Short (bass) and Dave Armstrong (drums) — will be appearing at English Martyrs' Youth Club dance on Sunday, and at St. Elizabeth's in Litherland the following week.

THE NOTIONS PLAYED THE ENGLISH MARTYRS' ON SUNDAY FEBRUARY 13, 1966 AND St ELIZABETH'S ON SUNDAY FEBRUARY 20, 1966

ATTRACTIONS AT WHIT WEEK-END GALA

LITHERLAND'S 21st Gala is to take place at the Moss Lane Sports Ground, Litherland, between Saturday, May 28, and Whit Monday, May 30.

Among the many attractions will be the 1966 Gala Queen, Judith Williams, and her retinue, plus the Dowager Queen, Jennifer Ashdown. It is also hoped to have as many of the past queens present as possible.

The programme on Saturday includes morris dancing, the crowning of the Gala Queen, and the grand parade of Queen and retinue. On Monday there will be an entertaining groups competition, a darts competition and a ladies' football match. During the afternoon "The Notions," a top Liverpool group, will perform, as also will "The Efforts." Also, for the first time, Litherland residents and other visitors will have the opportunity of seeing "Augusto's Miniature Circus."

THE NOTIONS APPEARANCE WAS MONDAY, MAY 30, 1966

PRIOR TO THIS BOOKING ANOTHER SIGNIFICANT CHANGE HAD TAKEN PLACE IN THEIR LINE UP (SEE FOLLOWING PAGE)

> **NOTIONS**
> Rhythm guitarist DAVE McCARTHY has quit Liverpool group the NOTIONS to join London-based LEAGUE OF GENTLEMEN. The Notions are now operating as a threesome.

MAY 1966
PUBLICATION UNKNOWN

This insignificant clipping announces another major change in the Notions line up with **Dave McCarthy** leaving to join the London Based group **The League of Gentlemen**. Unfortunately, neither it nor the other newspaper clippings on this page, or the following page, are dated and none of the publications are identified. While Frank Delaney's notes help approximate the date of these clippings he does not make any reference in his notes regarding **Dave McCarthy's** departure. However, **Dave McCarthy** is certain that his last appearance with the Notions was at the Mardi Gras on May 26, 1966.

Notions – Fourth & Final Line Up:
David Delaney – Lead Guitar
Dave Armstrong - Drums
Kevin Short – Bass Guitar

SOMETHING FOR THE YOUNG PEOPLE TOO

Just wait – the big beat starts at eight

If you are the kind of person who would rather dance to the music of a beat group on show day than look at flowers, cattle and horses—wait patiently. Your turn comes at 8 p.m., when the big beat session starts in the main tent.

Two top groups are appearing at the session: the Notions and the Country Rhythm Boys.

Popularity poll winners the Notions are still riding very high. Big favourites at the Mardi Gras and Peppermint Lounge in Liverpool, they have very recently topped the bill at the famous Mr. Smith's Club in Manchester, the Casino Club, Blackpool, Casino Club, Bolton, the Marine Hall in Fleetwood and many other venues, and are acclaimed from Cumberland to Derbyshire.

They have been operating as a threesome for over a month following the departure to London of their rhythm guitarist. The present line-up is Dave Delaney—lead guitar and vocals, Kevin Short—bass guitar and vocals, and Dave Armstrong—drums.

This clipping for the Notions appearance on Saturday, July 9, 1966 at the Formby Flower Show also notes that the group has been performing as a trio for over a month.

Another 'Notion' goes

"... and then there were three." As is now the case with semi-professionals "The Notions," since they lost their fourth member. I asked manager Frank Delaney if they were looking for a replacement, but he thought they probably wouldn't bother—their popularity has increased.

All aged 19, the group now consists of David Delaney, lead guitar; Kevin Short, bass guitar and David Armstrong, drums. Some numbers are going to be arranged so that the drumming David has a chance to vocalise; the other two are the singers at the moment.

"The Notions" played at Formby Flower Show and are just completing a week in and around Blackpool. Although the boys come from Crosby, they don't appear much locally. They're too much in demand in other parts of the country, like from Shrewsbury to the Lake District. They have to find time to go down to London again, to put the voices to an already-recorded backing.

NEW - "IN" - "WITH-IT"
DINING — WINING — DANCING
GAMING
ENTERTAINMENT — GROUPS
RECORDS — MUSICIANS
ATMOSPHERE — SENSATIONAL
DECOR POLYNESIAN
MEMBERS — GUESTS
8 P.M. to 2 A.M. NIGHTLY
except MONDAYS
Your Host: LEN McMILLAN
56 SEEL ST. LIVERPOOL 1
Telephone Royal 6788
Membership: Personal applications only.

THIS CLIPPING MENTIONS THE APPEARANCE OF THE NOTIONS AT THE FORMBY FLOWER SHOW ON SATURDAY, JULY 9, 1966 AND IT ALSO INCLUDES AN ADVERTISEMENT FOR THE 'BEACHCOMBER' CLUB WHICH THEY PLAYED ON TUESDAY, AUGUST 23, 1966

WHERE THE FOURTH "NOTION" WENT

WE now know where that fourth "Notion" went. A Mr. Dave McCarthy by name, who resigned from a worthy Civil Service position in the Ministry of Transport (comforting to know that the Civil Service is worthy) to throw in his lot and his rhythm guitar with the London-based "League of Gentlemen." Of which he is also the singer. The group has just appeared in Germany—first in Frankfurt for two weeks, then for a further two weeks in Cologne. Back in England looking for a new manager, the group is holidaying while waiting for completed bookings.

★ ★ ★

AUGUST 1966 - PUBLICATION UNKNOWN

THIS CONCLUDES THE STORY OF THE 'NOTIONS' AS REPORTED BY THE LOCAL AND NATIONAL UK NEWSPAPERS

2336 Cherry St
Denver, Colo.
Nov. 4, 1965

To The Notions —

I'm writing this note to thank you for the lovely autographed photo you sent me. I was thrilled to receive it, and appreciated deeply your thoughtfulness in sending it.

Are you still performing at the Cavern? It was quite an experience for me, an American, to be there, and hearing your great group made it complete. I enjoyed very much hearing you perform and wish you much luck and success always — you're deserving of the best.

Sincerely,
Joanne D'Amato

FANMAIL FROM THE U.S.A.

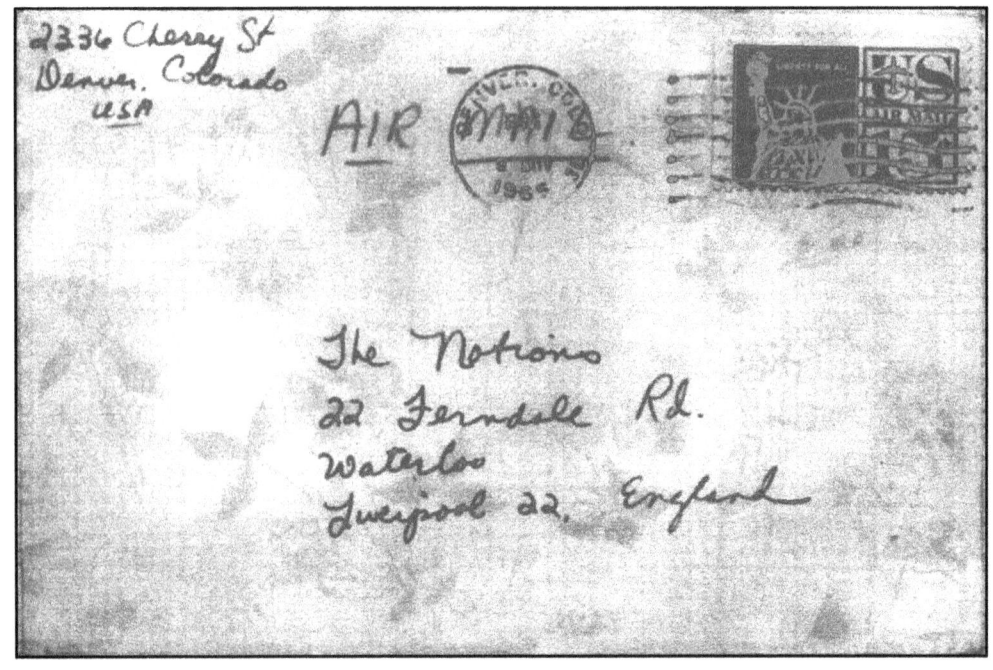

THE 'NOTIONS' BOOKING/ENGAGEMENT/GIG LIST

OCTOBER 7, 1962
TO
JULY 21, 1967

Bookings/Engagement/Gig List

Commonly known as 'Bookings or Gigs' most groups of the sixties normally kept a handwritten diary in which they recorded their current and future bookings. However, Frank Delaney, the Notions manager, went a step further and recorded the information on neatly typewritten sheets.

In addition, he also included details that most other groups and/or managers failed to keep. In many cases he included the names of other groups that appeared on the same 'gig' along with the Notions. He also added notes for events or occurrences he considered to important enough to be documented.

Reproductions of these typewritten sheets are included in this chapter and significant dates are identified by the addition of a rectangle to the right hand side of the page which may also contain information not included in the original typewritten documents.

In addition to documenting the Notions 'Bookings' Frank Delaney went a step further and created separate alphabetized lists of 'other' groups that the Notions had appeared with and the venues that they played at. Those lists are also included at the end of this chapter.

Bookings/Engagement/Gig List - General Statistics

The Notions first official 'gig' was on October 7, 1962 at St. Faith's Youth Club in Great Crosby. Their last documented gig was on July 21, 1967 at the Downbeat Club, Liverpool. During that 4 year 10 month period they played a total of 986 bookings, including 103 appearances at the Cavern Club, the first on October 27, 1963 and their 100th appearance on June 25, 1965.

Their first documented double booking was on August 25, 1963 when they played both the St. Peter & Paul Youth Club in Crosby and the Merseyside Artists Club in Sheil Road, Liverpool. Their last double booking was on July 15, 1967 when they played both the Lion Hotel in Warrington and the Kabel Club in Prescot. This brought their total number of 'doubles' to 59 during that 3 year 11 month period.

Their average 'booking ratio' was 17 per month or a little over 4 per week, including an average of 5 double bookings for each 4 month period from August 25, 1963 onwards, a somewhat demanding schedule for a non-professional group.

Bookings/Engagement/Gig List - Group Member Statistics

The list that follows identifies all of the individual group members, their time with the group and the number of appearances or 'gigs' at which they performed.

Dave Delaney – Lead Guitar & Vocals   October 7, 1962 – July 21, 1967 – 986 gigs

Dave Armstrong – Drums & Vocals   October 7, 1962 – July 21, 1967 – 986 gigs

Pete Little – Bass Guitar   October 7, 1962 – March 28, 1963 – 34 gigs

Dave Powell – Rhythm Guitar   October 7, 1962 – April 18, 1963 – 36 gigs

Keith Balcomb – Rhythm Guitar & Vocals   April 19, 1963 – April 19, 1964 – 211 gigs

Joe Short – Bass Guitar & Vocals   September 25, 1963 – Sept 5, 1965 – 505 gigs

Dave McCarthy – Rhythm Guitar & Vocals   April 20, 1964 – May 26, 1966 – 525 gigs

Kevin Short – Bass Guitar & Vocals   September 8, 1965 – July 21, 1967 – 391 gigs

ENGAGEMENTS.

1962.

Date	Venue	Acts
Oct. 7.	St. Faith's Youth Club.	
Oct. 14.	St. Faith's Youth Club.	
Oct. 25.	Congrgational Youth Club. Crosby.	
Nov. 1.	Congregational Hall. Dance.	"Citadels".
Nov. 3.	St. Faith's Hall. Dance.	"Black Velvets".
Nov. 4.	St. Faith's Youth Club.	
Nov. 10.	Christ Church Hall. Dance.	"Black Velvets".
Nov. 11.	St. Faith's Youth Club.	
Nov. 15.	Congregational Youth Club.	
Nov. 21.	St. Luke's Hall.	"Undertakers". "Four Mosts". "Classics".
Nov. 22.	Litherland Labour Club.	
Dec. 2.	St. Faith's Youth Club.	
Dec. 14.	St. Nicholas Youth Club Dance.	"Falcons".
Dec. 15.	Southport Technical College Dance.	
Dec. 22.	St. Faith's Hall. Christmas Dance.	"Black Velvets".
Dec. 23.	St. Faith's Youth Club.	
Dec. 27.	Litherland Labour Club.	"City Kings".
Dec. 28.	Norman's Cafe. D.I.Wright's Dance.	
Dec. 31.	St. John's Bootle.	"Memphis Three" "Earl Preston & T.T's." "City Slickers".

1963.

Date	Venue	Acts
Jan. 3.	Litherland Labour Club.	
Jan. 10.	Litherland Labour Club.	
Jan. 21.	St. Helen's Youth Club. (Vocals).	
Feb. 9.	St. Peter & St. Paul. Dance.	
Feb. 10.	St. Peter & St. Paul. New Youth Club Opening.	
Feb. 14.	Congregational Hall. Crosby.	
Feb. 16.	St. Peter & St. Paul. (Ursuline College Dance).	
Feb. 17.	St. William of York Youth Club.	"Sabres".
Feb. 18.	St. Helens Youth Club.	
Feb. 25.	St. Thomas of Canterbury.	
Mar. 2.	St. Peter & St. Paul. Dance.	
Mar. 3.	St. Peter & St. Paul. Youth Club.	
Mar. 17.	St. Peter & St. Paul. Youth Club.	
Mar. 24.	St. William of York. Dance.	
Mar. 28.	Merchant Taylor's Girls School (Freedom from Hunger Campaign).	"Falcons". ← PROBABLY THE LAST APPEARANCE BY PETE LITTLE
Apl. 15.	St. Peter & St. Paul. Dance.	"Memphis Three" "Top Spots" "Lee Eddy Five".

A DANCE
featuring
THE BLACK VELVETS and THE PHANTOMS
WILL BE HELD IN
ST. FAITH'S HALL, WATERLOO,
ON SATURDAY, 3RD NOVEMBER, 1962,
AT 7-45 P.M.

ADMISSION 3/6

SATURDAY, NOVEMBER 3, 1962

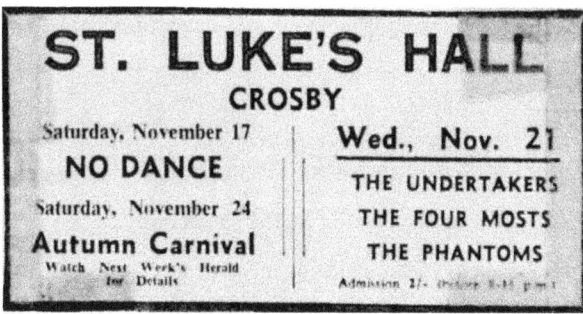

ST. LUKE'S HALL
CROSBY

Saturday, November 17
NO DANCE

Saturday, November 24
Autumn Carnival
Watch Next Week's Herald for Details

Wed., Nov. 21
THE UNDERTAKERS
THE FOUR MOSTS
THE PHANTOMS

Admission 2/-

WEDNESDAY, NOVEMBER 21, 1962

THE BLACK VELVETS

SS. PETER and PAUL'S YOUTH CLUB
LIVERPOOL ROAD, CROSBY

Would you like to go to a REAL
DANCE THIS WEEK-END?
Then come along
EASTER MONDAY EVENING
at 7-30, for a Real BIG Show, Featuring

The Fabulous Top Spots
The Lee Eddie Five
The Memphis Three
The Phantoms

Admission 5/- Refreshments

S.S. Peter and Paul Youth Club
(Liverpool Road)

La Danse Magnifique
(In Association With A.M.E.)
To Be Held On

Easter Monday Evening
7.30 p.m. — 11.30 p.m.

★ The Top Spots ★ The Lee Eddy Five
★ The Memphis Three ★ The Phantoms

ADMISSION 4-6 REFRESHMENTS

MONDAY, APRIL 15, 1963

ENGAGEMENTS (CONTINUED).

1963.

Apl. 18. Congregational Hall. Dance. ← **PROBABLY THE LAST APPEARANCE BY DAVE POWELL**

Apl. 19. St. Nicholas Youth Club Dance.   (French Night). ← **FIRST APPEARANCE OF KEITH BALCOMB**

Apl. 20. St. Faith's Dance.   "Flintstones". "Black Velvets"."Tributes"

Apl. 27. St. Peter & St. Paul.

May. 4. Our Lady, Queen of Peace.

May. 9. Philharmonic Hall.   Liverpool Beat Competition.

May. 11. David Scott's Birthady(21st). West Derby.

May. 13. St. Thomas of Canterbury.

May. 18. G.P.O.Social Club. Liverpool.

June. 1. All Saints. Forefield Lane. Crosby. (Stuart).

June. 2. St. Mary's Social Club. Kirkby. (Berge. Litherland).

June. 6. Norwest Construction Club.

June. 8. St. Katharine's Technical College. Childwall. "Some People"
                                                    TOP BILLING.

June. 9. Pemketh & Sankey Social Club.   (Jimmy Vance).

June. 10. St. Thomas of Canterbury.

June. 11. Our Lady, Queen of Peace. New Youth Club.

June. 23. Gilmoss Labour Club.

June. 29. English Electric Social Club. East. Lancs. Road.

July. 1. Litherland Labour Club.

July. 4. Norwest Construction Club.

July. 5. Stephen Du Cros. 21st Birthday. Alexandra Hall. "Black Velvets"

July. 6. Maghull Institute. Barbecue.   "Clansmen". "Futurists".

July. 7. C.I.Club. Sandfield Park. West Derby.

July. 8. Norman's Cafe. Waterloo.

July. 12. Savoy. Waterloo.   "Escorts". "Triumphs".

July. 13. Norwest Construction Club.

July. 14. The Temple Restaurant. Dale Street. Liverpool. "Chessmen".
                                                         TOP BILLING.

July. 19. Mayfair. A.B.C. Knowsley Road. Bootle. "Pawns". "Cracksmen".
                                                         TOP BILLING.

July. 20. English Electric Social Club. East. Lancs. Road.

July. 21. Litherland Labour Club.

July. 24. Crane Hall. Liverpool.   Frankie Vaughan Talent Contest.

July. 26. St. Nicholas Youth Club.

July. 26. Crane Hall. Liverpool. Frankie Vaughan Talent Contest-FINALS.

Aug. 17. Yeowart's 21st. Birthday. R.C.M.P.Mess. Seaforth Barracks.

Aug. 18. Our Lady, Queen of Peace. Senior Members.

Aug. 23. C.I.Club. West Derby.

Aug. 24. Litherland British Legion Club.

J. AND C. present
THE BLACK VELVETS
THE FLINTSTONES
THE PHANTOMS
at S. FAITH'S HALL, WATERLOO,
on SATURDAY, APRIL 20TH, 1963
at 7-30 p.m.

ADMISSION 4/-   (In advance 3/6)

SATURDAY, APRIL 20, 1963

Crosby Young Conservatives
(Headquarters Branch)
SATURDAY NIGHT HOP
ALL SAINTS' HALL
Forefield Lane
Saturday, June 1st
— 8 p.m. —
Dancing to the PHANTOMS
Admission 3/-
Ring GRE 2784 or at Door

SATURDAY, JUNE 1, 1963

CROSBY HEADQUARTERS BRANCH
YOUNG CONSERVATIVES

SATURDAY NIGHT HOP

to be held at
All Saints' Hall, Forefield Lane,
on ......JUNE 1ST......
from 7-30 p.m. to 11-0 p.m.
(8-0)

Admission : 3/-   Refreshments

SATURDAY, JUNE 1, 1963

St. Thomas of Canterbury, C.O.M.
TWIST & ROCK DANCE
on MONDAY, JUNE 10th
THE PARISH HALL, QUEEN STREET
WATERLOO
Dancing to the Phantoms — Tickets 2/6
Dance 7-30 to 10-30 p.m.   Refreshments

MONDAY, JUNE 10, 1963

LITHERLAND TRADES & LABOUR CLUB
LIMITED
★ — ★

Rock, Beat and
Twist
to
THE PHANTOMS

★ — ★

MONDAY,
1st JULY, 1963   8 p.m.

COMPLIMENTARY
TICKET

MONDAY, JULY 1, 1963

ENGAGEMENTS. (CONTINUED).

1963.

- Aug. 25. St. Peter & St. Paul. Crosby Youth Club.
- Aug. 25. Merseyside Artist's Club. Sheil Road.
- Aug. 27. Our Lady, Queen of Peace. Youth Club.
- Aug. 30. C.I.Club. West Derby.
- Aug. 31. Hamilton Hall. Prescot.
- Sept. 1. English Electric Club. East Lancs. Road.
- Sept. 2. Empress Ballroom. Wigan.
- Sept. 3. Floral Hall. Southport. "The Searchers".
- Sept. 5. St. Mary's Old Boys. Moor Lane. Crosby.
- Sept. 7. St. Edward's Old Boys. R.U.F.C. C.I.Club. West Derby.
- Sept. 8. Merseyside Artist's Club.
- Sept. 13. M.A.N.W.E.B. Club. Thingwall.
- Sept. 14. Lewis's Hall. Beach Road. Litherland. 21st Birthday.
- Sept. 15. Jacobs. Long Lane. Aintree. Lunch Time Concert.
- Sept. 16. Temple Restaurant. Dale Street. Liverpool.
- Sept. 18. N.A.L.G.O. Club. Alder Road. West Derby.
- Sept. 20. M.A.N.W.E.B. Club. Thingwall. Wavertree.
- Sept. 21. Lewis's Hall. Beach Road. Litherland. Wedding. Miss Box.
- Sept. 25. N.A.L.G.O. Club. Alder Road. West Derby. Joe Short - First appearance. **← FIRST APPEARANCE OF JOE SHORT**
- Sept. 27. M.A.N.W.E.B. Club. Thingwall. Wavertree.
- Sept. 28. State Cafe. Dale Street. Liverpool. "Laurie Lee Dance Band".
- Sept. 29. New Bear's Paw. Lord Street. Liverpool.
- Oct. 4. St. Edmund's Youth Club. Waterloo.
- Oct. 5. Sankey & Penketh Conservative Club.
- Oct. 6. Lowlands. West Derby. (Dixon). "Duke D'Mond and the Barron Knights"
- Oct. 11. C.I.Club. West Derby.
- Oct. 12. St. Edward's Old Boys. R.U.F.C. C.I. Club. West Derby.
- Oct. 14. Nashville Tennessee Club. Redcross Street. Liverpool.
- Oct. 18. The Ramp. Low Hill. Liverpool. (Woltman).
- Oct. 19. Nashville Tennessee Club. Redcross Street. Liverpool.
- Oct. 25. Liverpool College Crafts & Catering. Colquitt Street. L'pool.
- Oct. 26. Blue Ball Hotel. Prescot Street. Liverpool.
- Oct. 26. H.M.S. "Eaglet". Salthouse Dock. Liverpool.
- Oct. 27. The CAVERN. ("Jimmy Powell & the 5 Dimensions" "Del Remos" "The Zenith 6"). **← FIRST CAVERN APPEARANCE**
- Oct. 27. Nashville Tennessee Club. Redcross Street. Liverpool.
- Oct. 28. Freshfield Winter Sports Club. Formby Ice Rink.
- Oct. 30. Majestic Ballroom. Birkenhead.

```
FLORAL HALL

Tuesday 3rd Sept. 1963.

PLAYING TIMES

8.0  -  9.0  p.m.   EDWIN HARPER
9.0  -  9.30 p.m.   THE PHANTOMS
9.30 - 10.0  p.m.   THE SEARCHERS
10.0 - 10.45 p.m.   EDWIN HARPER
10.45 - 11.15 p.m.  THE SEARCHERS
11.15 - 12.0 Mid.   THE PHANTOMS
```

TUESDAY — MIDNIGHT DANCE featuring
"Sweets For My Sweet"
★ THE SEARCHERS
Also THE PHANTOMS
TICKETS: 5/6 advance   6/6 At Door

**FRANK DELANEY'S SET LIST FOR THE 'PHANTOMS'
TUESDAY, SEPTEMBER 3, 1963
SUPPORTING THE 'SEARCHERS'**

SUNDAY, OCTOBER 6, 1963

ENGAGEMENTS. (CONTINUED).

1963.

Oct. 30. Freshfield Winter Sports Palce. Formby. Ice Rink.

Oct. 31. Nashville Tennessee Club. Redcross Street. Liverpool.

Nov. 1. Blue Ball Hotel. Prescot Street. Liverpool. "Clayton Squares"
TOP BILLING. "Vara Sounds".

Nov. 2. Palais de Danse. Wigan. "Lee Castle and the Barons".

Nov. 3. N.A.L.G.O. Alder Road. West Derby.

Nov. 4. Jacaranda Club. Slater Street. Liverpool.

Nov. 8. St. Gerrard's Club. Boundary Street, Liverpool. 5. "Dominators"
TOP BILLING.

Nov. 9. Memorial Hall. Northwich. "Hollies". "Jeannie and the Big Guys"

Nov. 10. Blue Angel Club. Seel Street. Liverpool.

Nov. 11. Jacaranda Club. Slater Street. Liverpool.

Nov. 13. St. Mary's Social Club. Kirkby. "Mr. Smith & Sum People"

Nov. 15. Freshfield Winter Sports Club. Ice Rink. Formby.

Nov. 16. Chester College. Chester.

Nov. 17. Blue Angel Club. Seel Street. Liverpool.

Nov. 18. Jacaranda Club. Slater Street. Liverpool.

Nov. 22. Derby Cinema. Burscough.

Nov. 23. Durning Road Conservative Hall. (Kensington Methodist Youth Club)

Nov. 24. The CAVERN. ("The Big Three". "Merseybeats". "Road Runners"
"Escorts". "Astrals". "Panthers" "Derry & the Pressmen"

Nov. 24. C.I. Club. West Derby.

Nov. 25. Jacaranda Club. Slater Street. Liverpool.

Nov. 26. St. George's Hall. Liverpool. "Laurie Lee Dance Band".
(Canadian Pacific Railways Staff Dance).

Nov. 27. Freshfield Winter Sports Palace. Formby Ice Rink.

Nov. 29. Prescot Cables F.C. Social Club. Prescot.

Nov. 30. State Cafe. Dale Street, Liverpool. (Eric Bemrose). Laurie Lee
Dance Band.

Dec. 1. Walkers Brewery Social Club. Warrington.

Dec. 2. Jacaranda Club. Slater Street. Liverpool.

Dec. 4. The CAVERN. ("Dennisons". "Dean Stacey & the Detonators").

Dec. 5. Peppermint Lounge. Fraser Street. Liverpool.

Dec. 6. IRON DOOR CLUB. Temple Street. Liverpool. ("Vic & the "Spidermen"
TOP BILLING. " Danny Havoc & the Secrets").

Dec. 7. Gilmoss Labour Club. East Lancs Road, Liverpool.

Dec. 8. The CAVERN. ("Vic & the Spidermen". "The Panthers". "The Red
"THE RATTLES". River Jazzmen").

Dec. 9. Jacaranda Club. Slater Street. Liverpool.

Dec. 11. The CAVERN! ("The Big Three"."The Roadrunners"."The Mafia".)

Dec. 12. Blundellsands Hotel. (Associated Re-Deffusion)."Tom Hughes
Dance Band".

Dec. 13. Automatic Telephones Laboratories. St. Mary's Hall. Pownall Sq.
Liverpool.

Dec. 14. Penketh & Sankey Conservative Club. Warrington.

JAZZ

BLUE BALL HOTEL,
PRESCOT STREET.
Anfield 2332.

TO-NIGHT:
THE FOUR DIMENSIONS
THE CITY BEATS
THE DOWN AND OUTS
WEDNESDAY:
THE DELMONT FOUR
THURSDAY:
THE FOUR DIMENSIONS, Also
THE CHEVRONS
FRIDAY:
THE NOTIONS. Plus
THE CLAYTON SQUARES
SATURDAY:
THE DOMINATORS

FRIDAY, NOVEMBER 1, 1963

SATURDAY, NOVEMBER 2, 1963

Come Dancing at the EMPRESS SUPER BALLROOM
STATION ROAD, WIGAN. Tel. 3501

J. E. and A. Farrimond, Proprietors present
The Resident Musician :

Bill Unsworth and his Empress Orchestra

FRIDAY, 1st NOVEMBER :
WIGAN BOROUGH POLICE BALL : 8 p.m. — 1-30 a.m. 6/6

SATURDAY, 2nd NOVEMBER :
SATURDAY SPECIAL
In the EMPRESS BALLROOM : BILL UNSWORTH AND HIS EMPRESS ORCHESTRA, playing the music you want ; also LEE CASTLE AND THE BARONS in the PALAIS-DE-DANSE : By popular request featuring every week a different group. This week : THE NOTIONS. Also Top Records for Dancing.

7-30 p.m. to 11 p.m.
Admission ... 4/6

St. Mary's Club, Northwood

A Grand Dance
(FOR MEMBERS AND THEIR FRIENDS)

in ST. MARY'S CLUB,

on Wednesday, 13th November, 1963

Dancing from 8-30 to the Music of

Mr. SMITH AND "SUM PEOPLE" also "THE NOTIONS"

TICKETS 2/- each   Bar extension applied for
(Limited Number)

WEDNESDAY, NOVEMBER 13, 1963

KENSINGTON METHODIST YOUTH CLUB

"Twitch"
with
the
"Notions"
(Phantoms!!)

CONSERVATIVE HALL
Durning Road   . . 3/- . .
8 to 11 p.m.   Saturday, 23rd November, 1963

SATURDAY, NOVEMBER 23, 1963

THE BIG ONES ARE
AT THE CAVERN
BUT OF COURSE!
The Most "With It" Beat Music Centre in Great Britain.
NOTE THESE THREE
MIGHTY MIDWEEK SESSIONS
FOR YOU AND YOUR FRIENDS!

1
To-night TUESDAY To-night
THE ROAD RUNNERS
CHICK GRAHAM AND COASTERS
THE MIGHTY AVENGERS
ROY AND THE DIONS
Definitely the best Tuesday show in Town!
Members 3/- Visitors 4/-

2
To-morrow WEDNESDAY To-morrow
They're With Us Again!
YOUR ALL TIME FAVOURITES
THE DENNISONS!
Plus The Cavern's Choice for '64:
THE NOTIONS!
Plus THE CITY BEATS and
DEAN STACEY & THE DETONATORS
PLEASE BE EARLY—7.15 p.m. START
Members 3/6. Visitors 4/6 That's All!

WEDNESDAY, DECEMBER 4, 1963

THE PEPPERMINT LOUNGE
FRASER STREET (OH LONDON ROAD).
TO-NIGHT   TO-NIGHT
ORIOLE RECORDING ARTISTS
THE BLUE MOUNTAIN BOYS
Plus
THE STEREOS
THE NOTIONS
ADMISSION ONLY 5/-
New Members Welcome.

THURSDAY, DECEMBER 5, 1963

IRON DOOR CLUB,
13 TEMPLE STREET (OFF DALE ST.)
TO-NIGHT!   TO-NIGHT!
VIC AND THE SPIDERMEN
They're Great! They're Going Places
And They Are Appearing at —
THE IRON DOOR CLUB —
THE NOTIONS
Also
DANNY HAVOC AND THE SECRETS
TO-MORROW (SATURDAY):
THE FABULOUS
RICKY AND THE DOMINANT FOUR
IAN AND THE ZODIACS
THE TALISMEN
SUNDAY:
Oriole Recording Artistes
RORY STORM AND THE HURRICANES
From Chester: Decca Recording Artistes
THE EXCHECKERS
Also
JOHNNY TEMPLER & THE HI-CATS

FRIDAY, DECEMBER 6, 1963

67

E N G A G E M E N T S.   (CONTINUED).

1963.

Dec. 15. Blue Angel Club. Seel Street. Liverpool.

Dec. 16. Jacaranda Club. Slater Street. Liverpool.

Dec. 17. The CAVERN. "The RATTLES". "The MERSEYBEATS". "The MARKFOUR".

Dec. 18. Sandfield School for Spastic Children. West Derby.

Dec. 18. Freshfield Winter Sports Club. Formby Ice Rink.

Dec. 21. Dunlop Sports & Social Club. Speke.

Dec. 22. C.I.Club. West Derby.

Dec. 23. Jacaranda Club. Slater Street. Liverpool.

Dec. 24. English Electric Club. East Lancs. Road. Liverpool.

Dec. 26. The CAVERN. "Riot Squad". "Liver Birds". "Escorts". "Pawns"

Dec. 28. Vaughan's. Prescot Road. Liverpool. "The Barneybeats".

Dec. 28. IRON DOOR. "King Size Taylor & Dominoes". "Centremen". "Rory Storm & the Hurricanes"

Dec. 29. Blue Angel. Seel Street, Liverpool.

Dec. 30. Jacaranda Club. Slater Street. Liverpool.

Dec. 31. Freshfield Winter Sports Club. Ice Rink Formby.

1964.

Jan. 1. The CAVERN. "The Escorts"."Gerry De Ville & the City Kings" "Shondells".

Jan. 3. The CAVERN. "The Escorts"."The Casuals"."Herman & the Hermits" (M/C).

Jan. 4. H.M.S."Eaglet".   (Mrs. Barnes - 21st Birthday).

Jan. 5. The CAVERN. "The Mojos". "Ian & the Zodiacs". "Panthers". "Shondells".

Jan. 6. Jacaranda Club. Slater Street. Liverpool.

Jan. 8. Island Road Methodist Church Hall. Garston.

Jan. 10. The CAVERN. "The Markfour". "The Rainmakers"(M/C). "Pawns".

Jan. 11. Memorial Hall, Northwich. "Karl Denver Trio"."Bruce Harris and the Cavaliers".

Jan. 12. Tudor Rooms. Prescot Road. Liverpool. (21st Birthday).

Jan. 13. Jacaranda Club. Slater Street. Liverpool.

Jan. 17. C.I.Club. Sandfield Park. West Derby.

Jan. 18. St. Edwards R.U.F.C. @ C.I.Club. Sandfueld Park. West Derby.

Jan. 19. The CAVERN. "Denny Seyton & the Sabres". "The Cresters" "The Mafia".

Jan. 20. Jacaranda Club. Slater Street. Liverpool.

Jan. 21. Floral Hall. Southport. "Screaming Lord Sutch & the Savages" "Denny Curtis & the Renegades".

Jan. 22. Freshfield Winter Sports Club. Formby.

Jan. 24. M.A.N.W.E.B. Thingwall Road. Wavertree.

Jan. 25. The CAVERN. "Escorts".

Jan. 26. Gilmoss Labour Club. Sovereign Rd. Gilmoss.

Jan. 27. Jacaranda Club. Slater Street. Liverpool.

Jan. 31. The CAVERN. TOP OF THE BILL. "Spidermen". "The Riot Squad" "Cordelles".

WEDNESDAY, January 1st—

THE ESCORTS
THE SHONDELLS ★ THE NOTIONS
GERRY DEVILLE AND THE CITY KINGS

WEDNESDAY, JANUARY 1, 1964

FRIDAY, January 3rd—

THE ESCORTS
THE NOTIONS ★ THE BEATCOMBERS
THE CASUALS

FRIDAY, JANUARY 3, 1964

SUNDAY, January 5th—

IAN AND THE ZODIACS
THE PANTHERS ★ THE SHONDELLS
THE NOTIONS

SUNDAY, JANUARY 5, 1964

THE CAVERN

```
The Notions

              MEMORIAL HALL, NORTHWICH (Saturday, January 11th)

        7.30p.m.  to  8.00p.m.    Records
        8.00p.m.  to  8.35p.m.    The Notions
        8.40p.m.  to  9.15p.m.    Bruce Harris and the Cavaliers
        9.20p.m.  to  9.40p.m.    The Karl Denver Trio
        9.45p.m.  to  10.30p.m.   The Notions
       10.35p.m.  to  10.55p.m.   The Karl Denver Trio
       11.00p.m.  to  11.45p.m.   Bruce Harris and the Cavaliers

DRESSING ROOM:     Situated to the right of the stage door entrance.
                   Shared with Bruce Harris and the Cavaliers.
EQUIPMENT:         Must be stored in dressing room.
STAGE ARRANGEMENTS: Check with the electrician and M.C. (Tom McKenzie).
GUESTS:            Not permitted back-stage without permission of the Management.
```

FRANK DELANEY'S SET LIST FOR THE 'NOTIONS', SATURDAY, JANUARY 11, 1964

Southport Corporation Attractions

FLORAL HALL

"SATURDAY NIGHT OUT," to 11-45 .... 5/6
Licensed Lounge Bar
MONDAY to 10-30.—OLD TIME and MOD. SEQ ... 2/6
Licensed Lounge Bar

TUESDAY (JANUARY 21) to Midnight—

LORD SUTCH AND THE SAVAGES
Plus DENNY CURTIS and THE RENEGADES
THE NOTIONS

5/- in advance   6/- at door

TUESDAY JANUARY 21, 1964

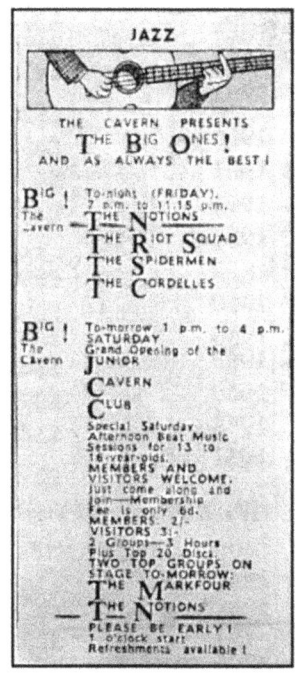

WEDNESDAY JANUARY, 1, 1964

FRIDAY JANUARY 31, 1964

ENGAGEMENTS. (CONTINUED).

1964.

Feb. 1. Majestic Ballroom. Birkenhead.

Feb. 1. The CAVERN. FIRST SATURDAY AFTERNOON JUVENILE SESSION **[INAUGURAL JUNIOR SESSION AT THE CAVERN]**
"The Markfour". TOP BILLING.

Feb. 5. Freshfield Winter Sports Club. Formby Ice Rink.

Feb. 6. Gilmoss Labour Club. Teenage Dance.

Feb. 7. The CAVERN. "The Remo Four". "The Georgians".

Feb. 8. Majestic Ballroom. Birkenhead. "J.J. & the HiLites"
"The Five Shillings"

Feb. 8. H.M.S. Eaglet. Dance. "Earl Scott & his Talismen" TOP BILLING.

Feb. 9. Blue Angel Club. Seel Street. Liverpool.

Feb. 10. Jacaranda Club. Slater Street. Liverpool.

Feb. 12. N.A.L.G.O. Club. Alder Road. West Derby.

Feb. 13. Waterloo. R.U.F.C. Blundellsands. "Forgers" TOP BILLING.

Feb. 14. C.I.Club. Sandfield Park. West Derby.

Feb. 16. Plaza Ballroom. St. Helens. "R.& B. Inc". "Nocturnes"

Feb. 16. The CAVERN. "Escorts" "Billy & the Tuxedos"."Bobby & the Bachelors"

Feb. 17. Jacaranda Club. Slater Street. Liverpool.

Feb. 19. Freshfield Winter Sports Club. Formby Ice Rink.

Feb. 20. Litherland Town Hall. "The Remo Four". "The Secrets".

FEB. 21. THE CAVERN. ORIOLE RECORDING "LIVE" AT THE CAVERN **[RECORDING SESSION WAS 'DISPUTED' IN A 2014 PHONE CALL TO JOHN SCHROEDER (ORIOLE RECORDS). IT'S ALWAYS POSSIBLE THAT THE C.B.C. FILM STILL EXISTS]**
Present - CANADIAN BROADCASTING CORPORATION FILM UNIT
"Herman & the Hermits"."The Markfour"
"Chris & the Autocrats"."Bobby & the Bachelors".

Feb. 22. Memorial Hall. Northwich. "The Merseybeats". "The Hi-Five".

Feb. 23. N.A.L.G.O. Alder Road. West Derby.

Feb. 24. Jacaranda Club. Slater Street. Liverpool.

Feb. 27. Prescot Cables Football Club. (Social).

Feb. 28. Strand Hotel. Liverpool. Law Students Dance.

Feb. 29. The CAVERN. Juvenile Afternoon Session. "The Dions".
TOP BILLING.

Feb. 29. The CAVERN. "Sonny Webb & the Cascades". "Panthers"."The Riot Squad".

Mar. 1. C.I.Club. West Derby.

Mar. 2. Jacaranda Club. Slater Street, Liverpool.

Mar. 4. The CAVERN. "Chick Graham & the Coasters". "The Kubas"
"The Georgians".

Mar. 6. Peppermint Lounge. Fraser Street. Liverpool."The Commancheros"
"Billy Butler & the Tuxedos". TOP BILLING.

Mar. 7. The CAVERN. "The Spidermen". "The Georgians" "The Huntsmen".
TOP BILLING.

Mar. 8. The CAVERN. "The Mastersounds". "The Markfour".
TOP BILLING. "Gerry Deville & the City Kings"."Vic & the T.T.'s"

Mar. 9. Jacaranda Club. Slater Street, Liverpool.

Mar. 10. The CAVERN. "The Chants"."The Harlams"."The Caverners".

Mar. 11. N.A.L.G.O. Alder Road. West Derby.

Mar. 12. Waterloo. R.U.F.C. Club House. Blundellsands.

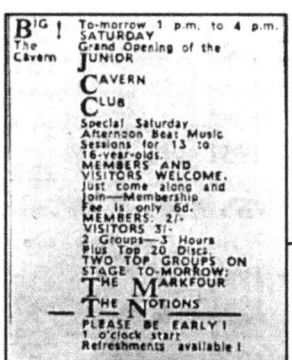

GRAND OPENING OF THE 'JUNIOR CAVERN CLUB'

SATURDAY FEBRUARY 1, 1964 'NOTIONS' PERFORM

500 Queue At The Cavern

Police There For Juvenile Session

Ten Liverpool policemen were rushed to Mathew Street at lunchtime to-day to control a crowd of more than 500 schoolchildren queuing for the first juvenile session at the Cavern Club.

When the doors opened at 1 p.m. there was a surge forward, and the organisers decided to admit only about 250 youngsters—aged between 13 and 16—at first. An hour later, a further 150 were admitted.

Said a spokesman: "It's much safer to do it this way. For one thing, the youngsters are strange here, as this is the first time we've admitted the under 16's. But it's obviously a great success."

BEAT MUSIC MATINEE

EACH SATURDAY AFTERNOON: 1 p.m.—4 p.m.
13—16 YEAR OLDS ONLY

SATURDAY, FEBRUARY 1st—

BIG OPENING SESSION

THE MARKFOUR
THE NOTIONS

SATURDAY, FEBRUARY 8th—

THE ESCORTS

Admission:
MEMBERS - - - 2/-
VISITORS - - - 3/-

Gillmoss Labour Club F.C.
present
A Twist & Jive Session
at
GILLMOSS LABOUR CLUB
Sovereign Road
by kind permission of the Gillmoss Management Committee

THURSDAY 6th FEBRUARY 1964

8 p.m. to 11 p.m.   TICKETS 3/- each

Dancing to **THE NOTIONS**

No Tickets to be sold to persons under 18 years of age

THURSDAY FEBRUARY 6, 1964

S & S ELECTRICAL & WRENS BRANCHES

MISCELLANEOUS

Dance

on Board H.M.S. EAGLET
Salthouse Dock Liverpool 3

Saturday 8th February 1964

DANCING TO

Earl Scott & his Talismen

The Notions

FROM 2000 hrs. TO 2330 hrs.   TICKETS 5/- EACH
2 BARS   INCLUDING LIGHT REFRESHMENTS

SATURDAY FEBRUARY 8, 1964

The Notions

MEMORIAL HALL, NORTHWICH (Saturday, February 22nd)

```
7.30p.m. to  8.00p.m.   Records
8.00p.m. to  8.30p.m.   The Notions
8.35p.m. to  9.05p.m.   The Hi-Fives
9.10p.m. to  9.40p.m.   The Merseybeats
9.45p.m. to 10.20p.m.   The Notions
10.20p.m. to 10.30p.m.  Records
10.30p.m. to 11.00p.m.  The Merseybeats
11.05p.m. to 11.45p.m.  The Hi-Fives
```

DRESSING ROOM: Situated to the right of the stage door entrance. Shared with the Hi-Fives.

EQUIPMENT: Must be stored in dressing room.

STAGE ARRANGEMENTS: Check with the electrician and M.C. (Tom McKenzie).

GUESTS: Not permitted back-stage without permission of the Management.

FRANK DELANEY'S SET LIST FOR THE 'NOTIONS'

SATURDAY FEBRUARY 22, 1964

ENGAGEMENTS. (CONTINUED).

1964.

Mar. 13. The CAVERN. "Roadrunners". "Mersey BlueBeats". "Georgians" "Conchords".

Mar. 14. Chester College. Students Dance. Chester College.

Mar. 15. Peppermint Lounge. "Karacters". "Blackwells".

Mar. 16. Jacaranda Club. Slater Street. Liverpool.

Mar. 18. Freshfield Winter Sports Club. Formby Ice Rink.

Mar. 19. Island Road Methodist Church. Garston.

Mar. 20. Peppermint Lounge. Fraser Street. "Lee Eddy & the Chevrons" "Bobby & the Hailers".

Mar. 27. The CAVERN. GOOD FRIDAY MARATHON. "The Hideaways". "The Kirkbys" "The Chants". "The Road Runners". "The Master Sounds" "The Kubas". "Vic & the T.T.'s". "The Markfour" "Billy Butler & the Tuxedos". "The Harlems" "Russ & the V-Tones".

Mar. 28. Reece's. Parker Street. Liverpool. **"Freddie Corbett's Band"**.

Mar. 29. C.I.Club. Sandfield Park. West Derby. "The Chessmen". TOP BILLING.

Mar. 30. Jacaranda Club. Slater Street. Liverpool.

Mar. 31. The CAVERN. "The Feelgoods". "The Liverbirds". "The Green Beats". TOP BILLING.

Apr. 1. Freshfield Winter Sports Club. Formby Ice Rink.

Apr. 3. The CAVERN. "Chants". "Four Pennies". "The Clayton Squares" "The Kubas". "Group One". "The Harlems".

Apr. 4. Floral Hall. Southport. "Kirklands Dance Band".

Apr. 5. N.A.L.G.O. Alder Road. West Derby.

Apr. 6. Jacaranda Club. Slater Street. Liverpool.

Apr. 7. The CAVERN. "The Five Embers". "The Rattles". "The Feelgoods".

Apr. 8. N.A.L.G.O. Alder Road, West Derby.

Apr. 9. The CAVERN. Lunch Time Session. "The Five Embers".

Apr. 10. Savoy. Bath Street. Waterloo. "Lenny & the Teammates". TOP BILLING.

Apr. 11. The CAVERN. "Millie". "The Five Embers". Billy Butler & the Tuxedos". "The Clayton Squares". "Bobby & the Batchelors"

Apr. 11. Henderson's Stores Staff Dance. Henderson's Restaurant. Church Street. Liverpool.

Apr. 12. C.I.Club. Sandfield Park. West Derby.

Apr. 13. Jacaranda Club. Slater Street. Liverpool.

Apr. 14. Reece's. Parker Street. Liverpool. "Freddie Corbett's Dance Band".

Apr. 15. The CAVERN. "The Clayton Squares". "St. Louis' Checks".

Apr. 16. Waterloo. R.U.F.C. Annual Dance. Blundellsands Hotel.

Apr. 17. The CAVERN. "The Riot Squad". "The Hideaways". "Feelgoods" "The Illusions". TOP BILLING.

Apr. 18. Prescot Cables. F.C. Football Ground. Prescot.

Apr. 19. The CAVERN. "The Clayton Squares". "Feelgoods". ← **LAST APPEARANCE OF KEITH BALCOMB** "The Silverstones". "The Clearways".

Apr. 20. Jacaranda Club. Slater Street. Liverpool. First appearance Dave McCarthy. ← **FIRST APPEARANCE OF DAVE McCARTHY**

Apr. 22. N.A.L.G.O. Alder Road, West Derby.

Apr. 24. The CAVERN. TOP BILLING. "Clayton Squares". "Griff Parry 5" "Feelgoods". "Chessmen".

72

CHESTER COLLEGE

The Social Committee

present

the notions

GLADSTONE HALL

SATURDAY, 14TH MARCH, 1964

8 p.m. — 11-45 p.m.

Double 6/6   *Refreshments*

SATURDAY, MARCH 14, 1964

To-morrow GOOD FRIDAY To-morrow
THE CAVERN CLUB presents
BEATERAMA !
EIGHT EXCITING HOURS
3.30 p.m. to 11.30 p.m.
TWELVE TERRIFIC GROUPS
Biggest Show on Merseyside:
1 THE CHANTS
2 THE ROAD RUNNERS
3 THE KIRKBYS
4 THE MASTER SOUNDS
5 THE KUBAS
6 VIC AND THE TT'S
7 THE MARKFOUR
8 THE NOTIONS
9 BILLY BUTLER & TUXEDOS
10 THE HIDEAWAYS
11 THE HARLEMS
12 RUSS AND THE V-TONES
WOW! TWELVE ABSOLUTELY
SENSATIONAL BIG BEAT ACTS!
Don't Miss This Fabulous Show!
7/6 MEMBERS 8/6 VISITORS
Hurry! Hurry! Hurry! To-morrow to
THE CAVERN,
10 MATHEW STREET
(Off North John Street),
LIVERPOOL 2.
THIS SATURDAY — THIS SATURDAY
MIKE COTTON R & B BAND

FRIDAY, MARCH 27, 1964

SOUTHPORT CORPORATION ATTRACTIONS

Floral Hall.—For the Saturday dance a band that is an old favourite will be on the stand, namely Jack Kirkland and his Band, from Stockport. On this occasion the beat group will be The Notions from Liverpool. The comfortable lounge bar will be open until 10·30 p.m.

SATURDAY, APRIL 4, 1964

SATURDAY 4th APRIL 1964

PLAYING TIMES

SUBJECT TO ALTERATION

8·0 — 9·0 pm   JACK KIRKLAND

9·0 — 9·30 pm   THE NOTIONS

9·30 — 10·30 pm   JACK KIRKLAND

10·30 — 11·0 pm   THE NOTIONS

11·0 — 11·45 pm   JACK KIRKLAND

J. G. Robinson
Inspector
4/4/64

FLORAL HALL
SOUTHPORT

Be on stand 5 mins before above times. Fill up P.R.S. form before leaving and return to Stage.

WEDNESDAY, APRIL 15th—
THE RATTLES
THE CLAYTON SQUARES, THE NOTIONS, THE ST. LOUIS CHECKS.

WEDNESDAY, APRIL 15, 1964

SUNDAY, APRIL 19th—
THE CLAYTON SQUARES
THE NOTIONS, THE FEELGOODS, THE SILVERSTONES, THE CLEARWAYS.

SUNDAY, APRIL 19, 1964

AT THE CAVERN
To-night — FRIDAY — To-night
1 THE CLAYTON SQUARES
2 THE NOTIONS
3 THE GRIFF-PARRY 5
4 THE FEELGOODS
5 THE CHESSMEN
Please Be Early To-night—7 p.m. Start

FRIDAY, APRIL 24, 1964

E N G A G E M E N T S.   (CONTINUED).

1964.

Apr. 25. Gilmoss Labour Club.

Apr. 26. N.A.L.G.O. Alder Road, West Derby.

Apr. 27. Lockheeds. Speke. Social Club. "Newtowns". TOP BILLING.

Apr. 28. The CAVERN. RADIO LUXEMBURG RECORDING FOR "SUNDAY NIGHT AT THE CAVERN". "Dennisons". Earl Preston's Realms" "Detonators". Riot Squad".

> **LIVE RECORDING FOR RADIO LUXEMBOURG – BROADCAST DATE WAS MAY 24, 1964 (SEE BELOW)**

Apr. 29. The CAVERN. "Mastersounds". "Clayton Squares"."Easy Beats". "Jaguars".

May. 1. Palace Cinema. Pentre Broughton. Wrexham. ALL STAR VARIETY. Pam Venmore. Percy Hickman. Stan Littlewood. Eric Granville. "The Kobras". TOP BILLING.

May. 2. Y.M.C.A. Duke Street. St. Helens. ""Roadrunners".

May. 3. Strand Ballroom. Winsford. Cheshire. "Tony Allen & the Blue Diamonds".(M/C). TOP BILLING.

May. 4. Jacaranda Club. Slater Street. Liverpool.

May. 6. The CAVERN. "Ian Crawford & the Boomerangs". "Mysteries" "Pilgrims". Recorded tape for SWEDISH RADIO AND INTERVIEWED. Interviewed also by DANISH NEWS AGENCY.

> **LIVE RECORDING FOR SWEDISH RADIO & INTERVIEW BY A DANISH NEWS AGENCY. IT'S ALWAYS POSSIBLE THAT THEY MAY STILL EXIST**

May. 7. Litherland Town Hall. "Lee Castle & the Barons". "Lavelles". "Renicks". "Spidermen".

May. 8. Savoy. Waterloo. "STereos". TOP BILLING.

May. 10. N.A.L.G.O. Alder Road. West Derby.

May. 11. Jacaranda Club. Slater Street. Liverpool.

May. 12. Reece's Ballroom. Liverpool. "Freddie Corbett's Dance Band".

May. 13. The CAVERN. "Kirkbys". "Vic & the T.T.'s". "Renicks".

May. 14. Kirkby Labour Club. (Charity Concert). Mentally Handicapped "Comets"."Crestas".Jimmy Vance. Ken Ryder. Children.

May. 15. C.I.Club. West Derby.

May. 16. Birkdale Palace. Southport."Clayton Squares". "Invaders". TOP BILLING.

May. 17. The CAVERN. "Top Spots". "Dions". "Dene & the Citizens". (M/C)

May. 19. The CAVERN. "Vic & the T.T.'s". "Four Travellers". "Rats".

May. 20. St. Kevins. Kirkby. "Riot Squad". TOP BILLING.

May. 22. The CAVERN. "Escorts". "The Roadrunners"."Easybeats"."Cordes".

May. 23. Victoria Hall. Garston.

May. 24. English Martyrs. Litherland. "Easybeats". TOP BILLING.
Broadcast from RADIO LUXEMBURG - SUNDAY NIGHT AT THE CAVERN

May. 25. Jacaranda Club. Slater Street. Liverpool.

May. 26. The CAVERN. "Kinsleys". "Tabs". "Georgians".

May. 28. Hope Hall. Liverpool. "Elks". TOP BILLING.

May. 29. Plaza Ballroom. St. Helens. "Black Knights". "Citadels". TOP BILLING.

May. 30. Memorial Hall. Northwich. "Hollies". "Some People".

May. 31. N.A.L.G.O. Club. Alder Road. West Derby.

Jun. 1. Jacaranda Club. Slater Street. Liverpool.

Jun. 2. The CAVERN. "Roadrunners". "Herman's Hermits" (M/C). "Poets"

Jun. 3. River Cruise. ROYAL IRIS. (Henderson - Kendall MIlne M/C.) Manchester Jazz Band. TOP BILLING.

Jun. 4. Peppermint Lounge. "Denny Seyton & the "Sabres"."Blackwells".

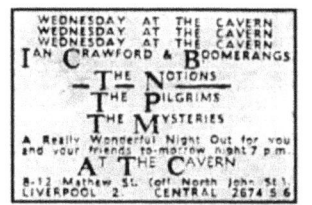

WEDNESDAY, MAY 6, 1964

THURSDAY, MAY 7, 1964

BEAT DANCE
PALACE HOTEL
BIRKDALE — SOUTHPORT

TO-NIGHT (SATURDAY)

Straight from the "CAVERN":

The Notions ★ The Invaders ★ The Kirbys

The Clayton Squares, etc.

Tickets are available at Aldridges. Remember the Night: SATURDAY, MAY 16th

LARGE CAR PARK — FREE

SATURDAY, MAY 16, 1964

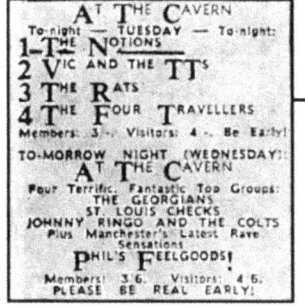

TUESDAY, MAY 19th
THE NOTIONS
VIC & THE T.T.s, THE RATS, THE FOUR TRAVELLERS

TUESDAY, MAY 19, 1964

HOPE HALL — TO-NIGHT
THE NOTIONS, THE ELKS
To-morrow—Friday:
THE CORDES, THE GEORGIANS.
Saturday:
THE PATHFINDERS, NEW PRESSMEN.
Sunday:
THE ROADRUNNERS, DIONS.
Licensed Bar. Minimum Age 18.
Members and Bona Fide Guests ONLY.

THURSDAY, MAY 28, 1964

```
The Notions

        MEMORIAL HALL, NORTHWICH (Saturday, May 30th)

        7.30p.m.  to  8.00p.m.   Records
        8.00p.m.  to  8.30p.m.   Some People
        8.35p.m.  to  9.05p.m.   The Notions
        9.10p.m.  to  9.40p.m.   The Hollies
        9.45p.m.  to 10.15p.m.   Some People
       10.15p.m.  to 10.30p.m.   Records
       10.30p.m.  to 11.00p.m.   Hollies
       11.05p.m.  to 11.45p.m.   The Notions

DRESSING ROOM:  Situated to the right of the stage door entrance.
                Shared with Some People.

EQUIPMENT:  Must be stored in dressing room.

STAGE ARRANGEMENTS:  Check with the electrician and M.C. (Tom McKenzie).

GUESTS:  Not permitted back-stage without permission of the Management.
```

FRANK DELANEY'S SET LIST FOR THE 'NOTIONS', SATURDAY, MAY 30, 1964

TUESDAY, JUNE 2, 1964

MERSEY RIVER BOAT CRUISE
WEDNESDAY JUNE 3rd 1964

**DANCING to a MERSEY BEAT GROUP
and the ALL STAR JAZZ BAND**

★ *FISH & CHIP SALOON - COCKTAIL BAR* ★
*SMOKE ROOM and BARS - BUFFET
REFRESHMENTS AVAILABLE*

Coaches leave Kendals at 6-30 p.m. - return from Liverpool at 11-0 p.m.
ONLY 7/6

WEDNESDAY, JUNE 3, 1964

THE PEPPERMINT LOUNGE
FRASER STREET, LONDON ROAD
TO-NIGHT, THURSDAY, TO-NIGHT
TO-NIGHT, THURSDAY, TO-NIGHT
MERCURY RECORDING ARTISTS
DENNY SEYTON & THE SABRES
PLUS
THE NOTIONS
Don't Miss this Great Show To-night
at the Most Swinging Club in Town.
Licensed Bars.   Free Refreshments.
Admission 5/-   if you want the best
of every world—it must be
THE PEPPERMINT LOUNGE
Tel. North 0753.

THURSDAY, JUNE 4, 1964

ENGAGEMENTS. (CONTINUED).

1964.

Jun. 5. N A L G O . Club. West Derby (Charity Concert). "Boot Hill Billies". "Pretenders". TOP BILLING.

Jun. 6. H.M.S. "Eaglet". Salthouse Dock. Liverpool.

Jun. 7. C.I.Club. Sandfield Park. West Derby.

Jun. 8. Jacaranda Club. Slater Street. Liverpool.

Jun. 9. Reece's Restaurant. Parker Street. Liverpool. "Freddie Corbett' Dance Band".

Jun. 10. The CAVERN. "Escorts". "Vic & the T.T.'s". "Jay & the Juniors".

Jun. 11. Peppermint Lounge. "Earl Royce & the Olympics". "Blackwells". Freddie Starr.

Jun. 12. Savoy. Waterloo. "Four Gents". TOP BILLING.

Jun. 13. Littlewoods Sports Day. Netherton. "Chick Graham & the Coasters". "Mark Peters & the Silhouettes". "Karacters".

Jun. 13. The CAVERN. "Spidermen". "Hideaways". "St. Louis Checks". TOP OF THE BILL.

Jun. 19. Pier Pavilion. Colwyn Bay. "Aristocrats". TOP BILLING.

Jun. 20. Memorial Hall. Northwich. "Rattles". "Fugitives".

Jun. 21. The CAVERN. "Roadrunners". "St. Louis Checks". "Plebs".

Jun. 21. Plaza Ballroom. St. Helens. "Gerry de Ville & City Kings" "Blackwells". TOP BILLING.

Jun. 24. The CAVERN. "Escorts". "Herman's Hermits".

Jun. 25. Peppermint Lounge. "Riot Squad". "Blackwells".

Jun. 26. Drill Hall. Prescot. "Defiants". TOP BILLING.

Jun. 27. Birkdale Palace. Birkdale. Southport. "Calderstones". TOP BILLING.

Jun. 28. C.I.Club. Sandfield Park. West Derby.

Jun. 29. Jacaranda Club. Slater Street. Liverpool.

Jun. 30. KNOWSLEY HALL. LORD DERBY'S COCKTAIL PARTY.

Jul. 1. The CAVERN. "Markfour". "Bobby & the Bachelors". "MerseyFour". TOP BILLING.

Jul. 2. Hope Hall. "Silverstones". TOP BILLING.

Jul. 3. The CAVERN. "Cy Tucker & the Friars". "Vic & the T.T's". "Poets".

Jul. 4. H.M.S. "EAGLET". Earl Scott & the Talismen Dance Band. TOP BILLING.

Jul. 6. Jacaranda Club.

Jul. 7. The CAVERN. "Herman's Hermits". "Dions". "T.T's".

Jul. 8. Gartan Club. Sandon Street. Liverpool. Knights of St. Columbia.

Jul. 9. Carlton Ballroom. ROCHDALE. "Denny Seyton & the Sabres".

Jul. 10. The CAVERN. TOP BILLING. "Savva & the Democrats". "Feelgoods". "Billiy Butler & the Tuxedos".

Jul. 11. Memorial Hall. Northwich. "Lulu & the Luvvers". "Renegades".

Jul. 12. N.A.L.G.O. Alder Road. West Derby.

Jul. 13. Jacaranda Club. Slater Street. Liverpool.

Jul. 14. Reece's Cafe. Liverpool. Freddie Corbett's Dance Band.

Jul. 15. The CAVERN. "Roadrunners". "Clayton Squares". "Marescas".

Jul. 16. St. Bedes. Waterloo.

Jul. 17. The CAVERN. "Kirkbys". "Feelgoods".

Jul. 17. The Plaza Ballroom. St. Helens. "Blackwells". "Kirkbys".

LIVERPOOL N.A.L.G.O. SPORTS AND SOCIAL CLUB
(Machine Room)

Nº 040

Present a

Grand Charity Dance

(In aid of "Seeing Eye Dog" for the Blind)

IN THE CLUBROOMS (Alder Road)
ON FRIDAY JUNE 5th 1964

Dancing to

The Notions — The Politicians — The Pretenders
The Boot Hill-Billys

8 p.m. — Midnight

TICKETS   :   :   5/-

FRIDAY, JUNE 5, 1964

THE CAVERN IS THE ONLY BEAT MUSIC VENUE IN BRITAIN THAT FEATURES FOUR TOP GROUPS AT EVERY EVENING SESSION!

TO-NIGHT AT THE CAVERN

The Year's Biggest R & B Show!
JOHN LEE HOOKER
JOHN MAYALL'S BLUES BREAKERS
THE ROAD RUNNERS
THE CLAYTON SQUARES
THE CORDES
THE HIDEAWAYS
THE ST. LOUIS CHECKS

Please, please be early—7 p.m. start
TO-NIGHT AT THE CAVERN

SATURDAY AFTERNOON AT THE JUNIOR CAVERN CLUB

1 p.m. to 4 p.m. for 13 to 16 year olds
Big 3 Group line-up to-morrow starring
THE ESCORTS!
Please be early.
Members 2/- Visitors 3/-

SATURDAY NIGHT AT THE CAVERN

4 Top Groups—7 p.m. start
1 — THE NOTIONS
2 — THE SPIDERMEN
3 — THE HIDEAWAYS
4 — THE ST. LOUIS CHECKS

This is obviously the Best Show in Town

SATURDAY, JUNE 13, 1964

HOPE HALL — To-night
NOTIONS, SILVERSTONES
Fri.: CORDES, ST. LOUIS CHECKS.
Sat.: THE DOMINOES, THE DIONS.
Sun.: HIDEAWAYS, GERRY DE VILLE.
Licensed Bar. Minimum age 18.
Members and Bona Fide Guests ONLY.

THURSDAY, JULY 2, 1964

S. & S. ELECTRICAL AND WRENS BRANCHES

A

Carnival Dance

on SATURDAY 4th JULY 1964

to EARL SCOTT & HIS TALISMEN

plus — **THE NOTIONS**

2000 hrs. to 2330 hrs.

Bars   Spot Prizes   Tickets 4/-

SATURDAY, JULY 4, 1964

GARTAN CLUB
K. S. C. Squires Council 205
(19a Sandon Street)

Nº 037

"BEAT DANCE"

Featuring from Radio Luxemburg

"The Notions"

IN THE ABOVE CLUBROOMS
ON WEDNESDAY JULY 8th 1964

Commencing 7-30 p.m.   Refreshments available

TICKETS 3/-   :   Tickets Only

WEDNESDAY, JULY 8, 1964

BEATSVILLE
CARLTON
ROC(K)HDALE

Tomorrow Thursday, 2nd July
R'n'B with the
ST. LOUIS CHECKS
7—11 p.m.   2/6

Saturday, 4th July.
FROM LIVERPOOL
THE ROADRUNNERS
7-15—11-45 p.m.   5/-

Sunday, 5th July.
Fontana recording artistes from the Mardi Gras Liverpool.
(Home of the Swinging Blue Jeans)
EARL PRESTON'S REALMS
7-11p.m. Members 2/- Guests 3/-

Thursday, 9th July.
● DOUBLE BEAT ●
DENNY SEYTON AND THE SABRES
AND FROM LIVERPOOL CAVERN
THE NOTIONS

THURSDAY, JULY 9, 1964

E N G A G E M E N T S. (CONTINUED).

1964.

Jul. 18. Ritz Ballroom. RHYL. NorthWales. "Duke Gordon Show Band".
Aug. 12. The CAVERN. "The Mighty Avengers". "Hideaways". TOP BILLING.
Aug. 13. Hope Hall. Liverpool. "Illusions". TOP BILLING
Aug. 14. C.I.Club. Sandfield Park. West Derby.
Aug. 15. Majestic Ballroom. LLANDUDNO.
Aug. 16. Plaza Ballroom. St. Helens. "Secrets". "Pawns". TOP BILLING.
Aug. 17. Longview Labour Club. Huyton. "Approachers". TOP BILLING.
Aug. 19. The CAVERN. ""Phil's Feelgoods" (M/C). "Earl Preston's Real
Aug. 19. Grafton Rooms. Liverpool. FREEDOM FROM HUNGER CHARITY SHOW.
         "Kubas"."Profiles"."St.Louis Checks"."Johnny Ringo & the
         Colts"."Derry Wilkie & the Others"."Pilgrims".
Aug. 21. The CAVERN. "Blackwells"."Denny Seyton & the Sabres".
         "The Mighty Avengers".
Aug. 22. Lion Hotel. Warrington. "Chick Graham & the Coasters"
         "Pathfinders".
Aug. 22. The CAVERN. JUVENILE AFTERNOON SESSION. "Calderstones".
         TOP BILLING.   "Zephers".
Aug. 23. N.A.L.G.O. Alder Road. West Derby.
Aug. 24. Plaza. St. Helens. "THe Centremen". TOP BILLING.
Aug. 25. The CAVERN. "Earl Preston's Realms"."Pilgrims"."Calderstones"
Aug. 27. Hope Hall. "Inbeats". TOP BILLING.
Aug. 28. The CAVERN. "Earl Preston's Realms". "Tokens". "Mr.Smith "
         Some People".
Aug. 29. Northwich Memorial Hall. "Ricky & the Dominant Four".
         "MANFRED MANN" No.1. TOP TWENTY.
Aug. 30. The CAVERN. "Escorts". "Dions".
Aug. 31. Plaza. St. Helens. "HERMAN's Hermits.(No.9 in Charts)
Sept. 2. The CAVERN. "The Mighty Avengers". "The Beat Boys".
Sept. 4. C.I.Club. Sandfield Park. West Derby.
Sept. 5. The CAVERN. JUVENILE AFTERNOON SESSION.
         "Chick Graham & the Coasters". "Traders".
Sept. 5. Northwich Memorial Hall. "Chick Graham & the Coasters"
         "The Night Walkers".
Sept. 6. Hope Hall. Liverpool. "Tabs" TOP BILLING.
Sept. 8. The CAVERN. "Herman's Hermits". "Denny Seyton & the Sabres".
Sept. 10. St. Bedes. Crosby.
Sept. 11. C.I.Club. West Derby Liverpool. "Musketeers". TOP BILLING.
Sept. 12. Mersey View. FRODSHAM. "Chick Graham & the Coasters" "T.T's".
Sept. 13. C.I.Club. West Derby. Liverpool.
Sept. 16. Hope Hall. Liverpool. "T.L. & the Groundhogs". TOP BILLING.
Sept. 18. Rushbury Village Hall. Wall. Much Wenloch. Shropshire.
Sept. 19. The CAVERN. "THE Riot Squad". "Chancellors". "Pilgrims".
         TOP BILLING.
Sept. 20. Plaza Ballroom. St. Helens. "Black Knights". TOP BILLING.
Sept. 21. Longview Labour Club. Huyton.
Sept. 22. The CAVERN. "Kirkbys". "T.T's". "Saints".
Sept. 23. Island Road. GARSTON. Liverpool.

BIG EXCITING SESSIONS

Wednesday 12th August
THE MIGHTY AVENGERS • THE HIDEAWAYS
THE NOTIONS

Wednesday, 19th August
EARL PRESTON'S REALMS • THE NOTIONS
PHIL'S FEELGOODS

To-night — WEDNESDAY — To-night
AT THE CAVERN
EARL PRESTON'S REALMS
THE NOTIONS
PHIL'S FEELGOODS
A Really Terrific Programme!
MEMBERS: 3/6. VISITORS: 4/6.

WEDNESDAY, AUGUST 12 & WEDNESDAY AUGUST 19, 1964

LET'S BEAT HUNGER DANCE

THE PETE BEST FOUR
(DECCA RECORDING ARTISTES)

DERRY WILKIE & THE OTHERS
THE KUBAS • JOHNNY RINGO & THE COLTS
THE PROFILES • THE PILGRIMS
THE NOTIONS • ST. LOUIS CHECKS

GRAFTON ROOMS WEST DERBY ROAD
Wednesday, 19th August
Sponsored by Entertainment Sub-Committee, Liverpool and District "Freedom From Hunger" Campaign.
7-30 — 12-30 : : : : 4/6
LICENCED BAR :: TOMBOLA :: NOVELTIES
Tickets on sale now at A.B.C. Lime Street and Scala Cinemas, Grafton and usual agencies.

WEDNESDAY, AUGUST 19, 1964

To-night FRIDAY To-night
AT THE CAVERN
Big Exciting Night Out!
1 DENNY SEYTON AND THE SABRES
2 THE NOTIONS
3 THE MIGHTY AVENGERS
4 THE BLACKWELLS

To-morrow Afternoon (Saturday) —
JUNIOR CAVERN CLUB
Presents for 13 to 16 year olds:
1 THE NOTIONS
2 THE CALDER STONES
3 THE ZEPHYRS
Members 2/-. Visitors 3/-. That's all.
NEW MEMBERS AND VISITORS ARE ALWAYS MADE WELCOME

FRIDAY, AUGUST 21, 1964
&
SATURDAY, AUGUST 22, 1964

HOPE HALL — To-night
THE NOTIONS THE INBEATS
Fri: THE HIDEAWAYS THE POETS
Saturday:
"LONDON COMES TO LIVERPOOL"
ALEX KORNER NOW RESIDENT HERE
Licensed Bar. Minimum age 18.
Members and Bona Fide Guests ONLY.
Saturday Next. 2.30: JUNIOR SESSION
Membership 1/-. ALEXIS KORNER

THURSDAY, AUGUST 27, 1964

Memorial Hall. NORTHWICH. (Saturday 29th August 1964).

```
7.30 p.m. to  8.00 p.m.    Records.
8.00 p.m. to  8.35 p.m.    The Notions.
8.40 p.m. to  9.10 p.m.    Ricky & the Dominant Four.
9.15 p.m. to  9.45 p.m.    MANFREDD MANN.
9.50 p.m. to 10.20 p.m.    The Notions.
10.20 p.m. to 10.30 p.m.   Records.
10.30 p.m. to 11.00 p.m.   MANFRED MANN.
11.05 p.m. to 11.45 p.m.   Ricky & the Dominant Four.
```

DRESSING ROOM : Situated to the right of the stage door entrance. Shared with Ricky & the Dominant Four.

EQUIPMENT : Must be stored in dressing room.

STAGE ARRANGEMENTS : Check with the electrician and M.C. (Tom McKenzie

GUESTS : Not permitted back stage without permission of the Management.

SATURDAY, AUGUST 29, 1964

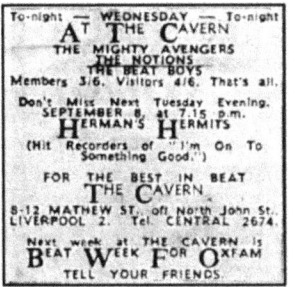

WEDNESDAY, SEPTEMBER 2, 1964

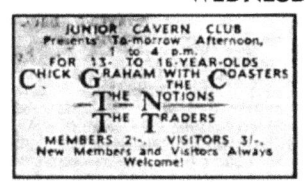

WEDNESDAY, SEPTEMBER 16, 1964

SATURDAY, SEPTEMBER 5, 1964

TUESDAY, SEPTEMBER 22, 1964

ENGAGEMENTS. (CONTINUED).

1964.

Sept.	24.	Childwall Hall County College.
Sept.	25.	The CAVERN. "Clayton Squares". "J.L'S Groundhogs". "Riot Squad".
Sept.	26.	Old Cathinians Football Club Dance. C.I.Club. West Derby.
Sept.	27.	English Martyrs. Litherland. "Roadrunners". "Gibsons".
Sept.	30.	The CAVERN. "Rustiks". "Kirkbys".
Oct.	1.	Hope Hall. "Almost Blues". TOP BILLING.
Oct.	2.	KENDAL TOWN HALL. "Rhythmics". TOP BILLING.
Oct.	3.	Plaza Ballroom. St.Helens. "Riot Squad". TOP BILLING.
Oct.	4.	The CAVERN. "Mark Peters & the Silhouettes". "Hideaways" "Billy Butler & the Tuxedos".
Oct.	5.	Longview Labour Club. "CAVERN NIGHT". "Clayton Squares" "Hideaways".
Oct.	6.	The CAVERN. "Earl Preston's Realms". "Toplins".
Oct.	7.	N.A.L.G.O. Alder Road. West Derby.
Oct.	9.	Prescot Town Football Club Social. Hope Street. Prescot.
Oct.	10.	Mersey View. Frodsham. "DAVE BERRY & THE CRUISERS". "The Pack"
Oct.	11.	Catacomb Club. Southgate, Huddersfield. "Mike Stevens & the Overlanders". TOP BILLING.
Oct.	14.	Gartan Club. Bedford Street, Liverpool.
Oct.	15.	Hope Hall. Hope Street. Liverpool.
Oct.	16.	The CAVERN. "The MIKE COTTON SOUND". "Cordes".
Oct.	17.	The CAVERN. "Feelgoods". "Dions". "Georgians". "Uzz Strangers". TOP BILLING.
Oct.	18.	C.I.Club. Sandfield Park. West Derby. Liverpool.
Oct.	19.	Plaza Ballroom. St. Helens. "Secrets". "Dentons". TOP BILLING.
Oct.	20.	The CAVERN. "Denny Seyton & the Sabres". "Excerts".
Oct.	22.	RADIO CAROLINE STUDIOS. LIVERPOOL. ◄—— **POSSIBLY A RECORDING SESSION - BUT NO FURTHER DETAILS COULD BE FOUND**
Oct.	24.	Stork Hotel. Liverpool. Ray Knight's Wedding. "Markfour" Manager.
Oct.	25.	C.I.Club. Sandfield Park. West Derby.
Oct.	28.	The CAVERN. "Clayton Squares". "Chessmen".
Oct.	29.	Hope Hall. Hope Street. Liverpool. "Approachers". TOP BILLING.
Oct.	30.	Rushbury Village Hall. Wall. Much Wenloch. Shropshire.
Oct.	31.	Majestice Ballroom. Wellington. Salop. "Denny Ryan & the Ravens".
Nov.	1.	The CAVERN. "Clayton Squares". "Playboys". "Dions".
Nov.	5.	Hope Hall. Hope Street. Liverpool. "Centermen". TOP BILLING.
Nov.	6.	The CAVERN. "Clayton Squares". "Roadrunners".
Nov.	7.	Ruthin Town Hall. North Wales.
Nov.	8.	English Martyrs. Litherland. "Roadrunners". "Gibsons".
Nov.	11.	Ministry of Aviation. Civil Service Club. Liverpool.
Nov.	13.	C.I.Club. West Derby. Liverpool. "Detonators". TOP BILLING.
Nov.	14.	Mersey View. Frodsham. "JIMMY NICHOL & THE SHUBDUBS". "Fugitives".

THURSDAY, SEPTEMBER 24, 1964

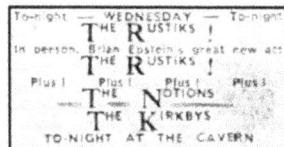

SUNDAY, SEPTEMBER 27, 1964

WEDNESDAY, SEPTEMBER 30, 1964

MONDAY, OCTOBER 5, 1964

TUESDAY, OCTOBER 6, 1964

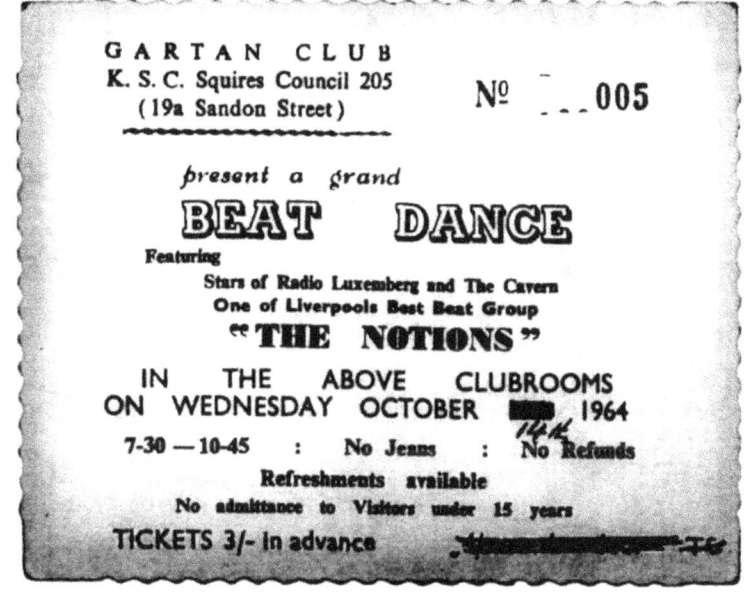

WEDNESDAY, OCTOBER 14, 1964

FRIDAY, OCTOBER 16, 1964

SATURDAY, OCTOBER 17, 1964

THURSDAY, OCTOBER 29, 1964

THURSDAY, NOVEMBER 5, 1964

SUNDAY, NOVEMBER 8, 1964

E N G A G E M E N T S . (CONTINUED).

1964.

Nov. 15. The CAVERN. "Earl Preston's Realms". "St. Louis Cheks"."Senators".

Nov. 17. The CAVERN. "Hideways". "Strolling Bones" (Somerset).
TOP BILLING.

Nov. 18. N.A.L.G.O. Alder Road. West Derby. Liverpool.

Nov. 20. Plaza Ballroom. St.Helens. "Loraine Gray & the Shakeouts"

Nov. 21. Stockport Town Hall. "Mersey Squares". "Barristers". TOP BILLING.

Nov. 22. Hope Hall. Liverpool. "Almost Blues".   TOP BILLING.

Nov. 24. Floral Hall. Southport. "Music Students". "Alibis". TOP BILLING.

Nov. 25. The CAVERN. "Andy & the Chevlons" Glasgow)!'Spidermen"."Klaxons
"Drumbeats".   TOP BILLING.

Nov. 27. C.I.Club. West Derby. Liverpool.

Nov. 28. Chester College. Chester.

Nov. 29. The CAVERN. "MERSEYBEATS". "T.T's". "Excelles". (NOTIONS
BACKING EXCELLES). **LIVE RECORDING FOR RADIO LUXEMBOURG – NOTIONS BACKING THE 'EXCELLES'**

Dec. 2. N.A.L.G.O. West Derby Road. Liverpool.

Dec. 4. West Lancs. Gold Club. "Excelles" (NOTIONS BACKING "EXCELLES")
"Pretenders". **NOTIONS BACK THE 'EXCELLES' AGAIN**

Dec. 5. Memorial Hall. Northwich. "Bo Street Runners". "Stylos".

Dec. 6. N.A.L.G.O. West Derby. Liverpool.

Dec. 9. Cardinal Godfrey's School Dance. C.I.CLUB. "Kubas". "Pikkins"
TOP BILLING.

Dec. 11. The CAVERN. "Escorts". "Cordes"."Spidermen".

Dec. 11. 5th King's Regimental Ball. Townsend Av. Liverpool.

Dec. 12. Mersey View. Frodsham. "The Pagans" (LOndon R.& B.) "Exotics".

Dec. 13. C.I.Club. West Derby. Liverpool.

Dec. 14. Plaza Ballroom. St. Helens. "Chick & the Coasters".

Dec. 16. Gartan Club. Sandon Street. Liverpool. "Hustlers". "Traders".
TOP BILLING.

Dec. 17. Alexander Hall. Crosby. Seafield Convent Dance.
"Mark Peters & the Silhouettes".

Dec. 17. Seaforth House. Inland Revenue Dance.
"Laurie Lee's Dance Band.

Dec. 18. The CAVERN. "Dennisons". "Kruzads". "Abstracts".

Dec. 18. Littlewoods Christmas Dance. Reeces. Parker Street. Liverpool.
"Freddie Corbett's Resident Dance Band".

Dec. 20. English Martyrs. Litherland. "Mr. Lee & Co.". "Earthlings".
"Dions".

Dec. 21. St. Anselm's School Dance. St. Helens.

Dec. 23. Island Road Methodist Youth Club Dance.

Dec. 24. The CAVERN. "Escorts". "Clayton Squares". "Kinsleys".

Dec. 26. The CAVERN. "BOXING NIGHT SHOW" "The Chants". "Roadrunners"
"Hideaways". "Kirkbys". "Cordes"."Pretenders"!'Harlems".

Dec. 26. C.I.Club. Sandfield Park. West Derby. "Riot Squad".

Dec. 27. N.A.L.G.O. Alder Road. West Derby.

Dec. 28. Plaza Ballroom. St. Helens.

Dec. 30. N.A.L.G.O. Alder Road. West Derby.

Dec. 31. The CAVERN.   (85) "Escorts". "Clayton Souares"."Pretenders".
"Earl Preston's Realms"."Hideaways"."Kinsleys"!'Kirkbys".

Dec. 31. C.I.Club. Sandfield Park. West Derby. "Pretenders".

JAZZ & BEAT
SUNDAY AT THE CAVERN, 7 P.M.
EARL PRESTON'S REALMS
THE NOTIONS
ST. LOUIS CHECKS
THE SENATORS

SUNDAY, NOVEMBER 15, 1964

AT THE CAVERN
To-night (Tuesday), at 7.30 p.m.
THE NOTIONS
THE HIDEAWAYS
THE STROLLING BONES
Admission: Members 3/-, Visitors 4/-

TUESDAY, NOVEMBER 17, 1964

JAZZ & BEAT
HOPE HALL, To-night.
THE SECRETS & THE MODES.
Sunday:
THE NOTIONS and ALMOST BLUES
Next Thursday: THE ROADRUNNERS

SUNDAY, NOVEMBER 22, 1964

— FORMBY YOUNG CONSERVATIVES —
present
BIG BEAT NIGHT
featuring
★ THE NOTIONS
★ THE MUSIC STUDENTS
★ THE ALIBIS
At The Floral Hall, Southport
TUESDAY, NOVEMBER 24th
Tickets .... (from Aldridges) 4/-
7-30 — 11-00 p.m.
DON'T MISS IT ! ! ! DON'T MISS IT ! ! !

TUESDAY, NOVEMBER 24, 1964

GO TO THE CAVERN
To-night Saturday, 4 Top Groups with
EARL PRESTON & THE REALMS
To-morrow Night, Sunday, at 7 p.m.
THE MERSEYBEATS
Plus THE NOTIONS and
AMOS BONNY & THE T.T.'s
Plus the sensational new Vocal Act
you saw on "Scene at 6.30" TV
THE EXCELLES
Members: 6/-, Visitors: 7/-. Be early!
THE CAVERN
8-12 Mathew St. (off North John St.)
LIVERPOOL 2.   CENTRAL 2674

SUNDAY, NOVEMBER 29, 1964

THE
WEST LANCASHIRE GOLF CLUB
BLUNDELLSANDS
cordially invite you to a

GRAND COLTS DANCE

FRIDAY 4th. DECEMBER 1964

Featuring on stage direct from the Cavern
THE FABULOUS EXCELLES
THE NOTIONS
THE PRETENDERS

Compere : BOB WOOLER Cavern & Luxembourg Dee-Jay

EVENING DRESS · BUFFET & BAR · DANCING 8 p.m. TO 12-30 a.m.

DOUBLE TICKET   PRICE 35/-

FRIDAY, DECEMBER 4, 1964

CARDINAL GODFREY SCHOOL
BEAT 'N' BLUES
NOTIONS
Plus
KRUZADS
8 - 11pm
Refreshments Available   Wednesday 9th December
AT THE C. I. ROOMS   3/6

WEDNESDAY, DECEMBER 9, 1964

CAVERN CLUB
BIG CHRISTMAS
EVE SESSION
THE ESCORTS
THE CLAYTON SQUARES
THE KIRKBYS
THE NOTIONS
A SHARP START AT 7 p.m.

THURSDAY, DECEMBER 24, 1964

E N G A G E M E N T S. (CONTINUED).

1965.

Jan. 1. C.I.Club. Sandfield Park. West Derby.

Jan. 2. The CAVERN. "Earl Preston's Realms". "Dawnbreakers" - Leeds.
"Expressions". "St. Louis Checks".

Jan. 3. English Martyrs. Litherland. "Carpet Baggers"."Aarons"
TOP BILLING.

Jan. 5. All Hallows Church Hall. Allerton. "Hideaways".

Jan. 6. N.A.L.G.O. Alder Road. Liverpool.

Jan. 8. Sankey Young People's Fellowship Club. Warrington.

Jan. 9. Mersey View. Frodsham. "Marauders". "Coins".

Jan. 10. Plaza Ballroom. St. Helens. "Riot Squad and Rita". TOP BILLING.

Jan. 11. The CAVERN. "Roadrunners".

Jan. 15. Hope Hall. Hope Street. Liverpool. "Almost Blues". TOP BILLING.

Jan. 16. Memorial Hall. Northwich. "Fairies". (London R. & B.)

Jan. 17. The CAVERN. "Earl Preston's Realms". "Feelgoods".

Jan. 17. English Martyrs. Litherland. "Condors". "Shakedowns".TOP BILLING.

Jan. 20. C.I.Club. Sandfield Pk. West Derby. "Rita & the Squad". TOP
BILLING.

Jan. 22. West Lancs. Golf Club. 21st Birthday Party. (Dr. Farmery Smith)

Jan. 23. Birkdale Palace. Southport. (Formby Young Conservatives.)
"Mersey Four". "Motifs". TOP BILLING.

Jan. 24. C.I.Club. West Derby.

Jan. 26. Longview Labour Club. Huyton.

Jan. 27. Liverpool University.(Classics). Wyncote, Mather Avenue.

Jan. 28. Childwall College.

Jan. 29. Plaza Ballroom. St. Helens. "Black Knights". TOP BILLING.

Jan. 30. Mersey View. Frodsham. "FORTUNES".

Jan. 31. Hope Hall. Hope Street. Liverpool. "Smokestacks". TOP BILLING.

Feb. 2. The CAVERN. "Roadrunners"

Feb. 6. Chester College. "Megatones". (Warrington).

Feb. 12. The CAVERN. "Roadrunners". "Johnny Ringo's Colts".

Feb. 12. Officer's Ball. 4th S/Lancs. Regt. T.A. Peninsula Barracks.
Warrington.

Feb. 13. Memorial Hall. Northwich. "Beat merchants" (Southampton)

Feb. 14. English Martyrs. Litherland. "Mr. Lee & Co". "Dions".TOP BILLING.

Feb. 15. Plaza Ballroom. St. Helens. "Amos Bonny & the T.T.'s".

Feb. 17. N.A.L.G.O. Alder Road. West Derby.

Feb. 19. St. Bernadettes Y.C. Withington. Manchester. "St.Louis Checks".
"Pretenders".

Feb. 20. Mersey View. Frodsham. "Keith Powell & the Valots" (London).
"Exotics". (Chester).

Feb. 20. The CAVERN. (ALL NIGHTER). "ALEXIS KORNER". "Roadrunners"
"Hideaways"."Excerts". "St.Louis Checks"."Spidermen".

Feb. 21. C.I. Club. West Derby.

Feb. 24. Cardinal Godfrey's Old Boys Dance. @ C.I.Club."Bumblies"."Pikkins".
TOP BILLING.

Feb. 26. Plaza Ballroom. St. Helens. "Mark Peters & the Silhouettes".

FRIDAY, JANUARY 8, 1965

Y.P.F CHURCH HALL, GREAT SANKEY
Dancing Every Friday Night
JANUARY, 1965 — 7.30 — Admission 2/-

January 1st	KRAKENS
January 8th	NOTIONS (Liverpool)
January 16th (Saturday)	JIMMY AND THE JOKERS
January 22nd	TRAKKERS
January 29th	TEMPLARS and THE HI-CATS (Liverpool)

Only The Very Best In Beat — Friday Night is Y.P.F. Night (p1918w)

FRIDAY, JANUARY 15, 1965

JAZZ & BEAT
FLAMINGO CLUB, Chester. — See Restaurant and Cabaret column
HOPE HALL To-night
THE NOTIONS & ALMOST BLUES
Sat. CONDORS & PRETENDERS
Sun. MEMPHIS COMBO, THE BUMBLIES

SUNDAY, JANUARY 17, 1965

ENGLISH MARTYRS, LITHERLAND.
SUNDAY: THE NOTIONS,
THE CONDORS,
THE SHAKEDOWNS.
7.30 to 11 p.m.

WEDNESDAY, JANUARY 27, 1965

L,POOL UNIVERSITY GUILD OF UNDERGRADUATES

A GRAND DANCE
(PRESENTED BY THE CLASSICAL SOCIETY)

will be held

IN WYNCOTE PAVILION (Mather Avenue)
ON WEDNESDAY JANUARY 27th 1965

Dancing to 'THE NOTIONS'

7-30 p.m. — 11 p.m.   ::   Licensed Bar

TICKETS 3/-   ●   Non Member

SUNDAY, JANUARY 31, 1965

HOPE HALL TO-NIGHT
THE CROUPIERS.
The Music Students.
Sunday THE NOTIONS,
The SMOKESTACKS.
Licensed Bar.
Members and Bone Fide Guests ONLY.

THURSDAY, JANUARY 28, 1965

Nº 140

Liverpool Education Committee
CHILDWALL HALL STUDENTS UNION

Thursday, 28th January 1965
7-30 p.m. — 10-30 p.m.

Grand Dance
with
The Notions

Refreshments on sale
No admission after 9-30.   TICKETS 3/-

FRIDAY, FEBRUARY 12, 1965

SPEND A STOMPIN' WEEKEND AT THE

CAVERN
8-12 MATHEW ST.,
(off North John Street)
LIVERPOOL

Friday, 12th February
Roadrunners
Notions
JOHNNY RINGO'S
COLTS

Saturday, 13th February
Earl Preston's
Realms
Clayton Squares
The Dions

Sunday, 14th February
The Hideaways
Hipster Image
Expressions

SATURDAY, FEBRUARY 20, 1965

Mersey View Ballroom, Frodsham
Telephone 3108
Saturday, February 20th—By Popular Demand, Return visit of
KEITH POWELL AND THE VALETS plus THE NOTIONS AND EXOTICS
Admission 6/6
Saturday, March 6th—THE PRETTY THINGS. Tickets 8/6 on sale now at Music Shop Runcorn and Widnes, Kents' Shoe Shop, Runcorn.
Coaches Arpley Bus Station

WEDNESDAY, FEBRUARY 24, 1965

CARDINAL GODFREY OLD BOYS SOCIETY

Grand Dance

Dancing to the

NOTIONS   **PIKKINS**
BUMBLIES

on

Wednesday 24th February 1965
from 7-30 p.m. to 11 p.m.
at
the C.I. SANDFIELD PARK

Refreshments Available   Tickets 4/-

E N G A G E M E N T S - (CONTINUED).

1965

Feb.	27.	THE CAVERN. "Hideaways". "Spidermen". "Michael Allen Group".
Feb.	27.	Waterloo Rugby Football Club. Blundellsands Pavilion.
Feb.	28.	Hope Hall. Hope Street. Liverpool. "Defiants". TOP BILLING.
Mar.	3.	St. Helens Co-Operative Rec. & Social Club.
Mar.	4.	Blair Hall. Walton. Liverpool. (Inland Revenue).
Mar.	5.	Lowther Gardens Pavilion. Lytham. St/Annes. "Bruce & the Spiders".
Mar.	6.	Winter Gardens. Waterloo. "Jensons". "Harpos". "Black Dynamites" TOP BILLING.
Mar.	6.	C.I.Club. Sandfield Park. West Derby. "Travelors". TOP BILLING.
Mar.	7.	St. Elizabeth's. Hornby Boulevarde. Litherland. "Mersey Gonks". TOP BILLING.
Mar.	9.	Cavern Studios. Recording Session. ◄
Mar.	10.	N.A.L.G.O. Alder Road. West Derby.
Mar.	11.	Childwall College. Childwall. Liverpool.
Mar.	12.	Sankey Young People's Fellowship Club. Warrington.
Mar.	13.	Plaza Ballroom. St. Helens. TOP BILLING.
Mar.	14.	THE CAVERN. ALL NIGHTER. "Clayton Squares". "Earl Preston's Realms". "Black Knights". "Factotums". "Kris Ryan" & the Questions" "Hideaways". "Roadrunners". "St. Louis Checks".
Mar.	14.	Hope Hall. Hope Street. Liverpool. "Modes". TOP BILLING.
Mar.	19.	Casino Ballroom. Leigh. "John Prior & his Orchestra".
Mar.	20.	Birkenhead Youth Club. Carlton Road. Birkenhead.
Mar.	21.	C.I.Club. Sandfield Park. West Derby. "Almost Blues". TOP BILLING.
Mar.	22.	Parr Hall. Warrington. "THE WHO".
Mar.	23.	THE CAVERN. "Earl Preston's Realms". "Rooters".
Mar.	24.	N.A.L.G.O. Alder Road. West Derby.
Mar.	26.	C.I.Club. Sandfield Park. West Derby.
Mar.	27.	Memorial Hall. Northwich. "Rhythm & Blues Inc". "Lancastrians" (M/C).
Mar.	28.	Plaza Ballroom. St. Helens. "Gerry de Ville & the City Kings" TOP BILLING.
Apl.	1.	Peppermint Lounge. Fraser Street. Liverpool. "Four Dimensions".
Apl.	2.	Masonic Hall. Southport. (21st Birthday). "Douglas de Belle Quartet"
Apl.	3.	Hope Hall. Hope Street. Liverpool.
Apl.	4.	N.A.L.G.O. Alder Road. West Derby.
Apl.	5.	Litherland Town Hall. "Roadrunners". "Music Students" TOP BILLING.
Apl.	9.	Sankey Young People's Fellowship Club. Warrington.
Apl.	10.	THE CAVERN. "Terry Hines Sextet". "Almost Blues". "St. Louis Checks".
Apl.	10.	Birkdale Palace Hotel. "Secrets". TOP BILLING.
Apl.	11.	C.I.Club. Sandfield Park. West Derby.
Apl.	12.	Plaza St. Helens. "Detours". TOP BILLING.
Apl.	14.	Gartan Club. Sandon Street. Liverpool. "Rita & the Squad". TOP BILLING
Apl.	15.	Peppermint Lounge. Fraser Street. Liverpool. "Earl Royce & the Olympics".
Apl.	16.	THE CAVERN. EIGHT HOUR SESSION. "Chris Ryan & Questions"."Roadrunners". "Hideaways"."Earl Preston's Realms". "Richmond Group". "Runaways".
Apl.	17.	Memorial Hall. Northwich. "Lulu & the Luvvers".
Apl.	18.	Maggie May Club. Seel Street. Liverpool. "Modes". TOP BILLING.
Apl.	19.	Locarno Ballroom. DERBY. "Tiffany's Dimensions". "Mansfields".
Apl.	21.	Brimstage Hall. Bebington. Cheshire.
Apl.	23.	Plaza Ballroom. St. Helens. "Lavells". TOP BILLING.
Apl.	24.	THE CAVERN. "Peasants" (LONDON). "Hideaways". "T.T's with Amos & Carl".
Apl.	24.	Henderson's Stores. Annual Staff Dance.

> **DAVE DELANEY STILL HAS AN ACETATE FROM THIS SESSION THAT INCLUDES "GO ON HOME GIRL" FEATURING JOE SHORT AND "MEMORIES ARE MADE OF THIS" BY THE ENTIRE GROUP**

THURSDAY MARCH 11, 1965

No. 136

Liverpool Education Committee
CHILDWALL HALL STUDENTS UNION
Thursday 11th March 1965
7-30 p.m. - 10-30 p.m.

Grand Dance

Come Dance with
The Notions

Refreshments on sale
No admission after 9-30.   TICKETS 3/-

SUNDAY MARCH 14, 1965

AT THE CAVERN
TO-NIGHT   SATURDAY   TO-NIGHT
FABULOUS ALL NIGHTER
PART I. 7.30 p.m. to 11.15 p.m.
THE CLAYTON SQUARES
EARL PRESTON'S REALMS
THE BLACK KNIGHTS
FACTOTUMS
MEMBERS 5/-   VISITORS 6/-
PART II. 11.45 p.m. to 6 a.m.
KRIS RYAN & QUESTIONS
EARL PRESTON'S REALMS
ROADRUNNERS
HIDEAWAYS
ST. LOUIS CHECKS
NOTIONS
MEMBERS 5/6   VISITORS 7/6.
TO-MORROW ——— TO-MORROW
THE SHEFFIELDS
MASTER MINDS
BLUES ANGELS
SHAKESPEARES
ANNETTE & THE RIVERSDALES
MEMBERS 5/-   VISITORS 6/-
Don't Forget Our Lunchtime Sessions
Every Lunchtime, 12 noon to 2.15 p.m.
MEMBERS 1/-   VISITORS 1/6
THIS MONDAY LUNCHTIME
EARL PRESTON'S REALMS
Always the Best in Bargain Best.
AT THE CAVERN

FRIDAY, MARCH 19, 1965

THE CASINO

LUXURY BALLROOM   Tel. Leigh 73244
For those who prefer the best

SATURDAY, 13th MARCH
BRIARCROFT O.A.P. DANCE
8 p.m.—Midnight. Fully Licensed Bars. Admission 5/-

MONDAY, TUESDAY, AND THURSDAY
CASINO BINGO CLUB
STARTS 8 p.m.   DOORS OPEN 7 p.m.
SNACK BAR   ADMISSION 2/-
IT'S MORE THAN BINGO — IT'S A NIGHT OUT

FRIDAY, 19th MARCH
J. W. ROBERTS LTD. DANCE
Presenting THE NOTIONS
8 p.m.—1 a.m. Fully Licensed Bars. Tickets 7/6

SATURDAY, 20th MARCH
Guide Dogs for the Blind Society Dance
8 p.m.—Midnight. Fully Licensed Bars. Admission 5/-

THE CASINO IS AVAILABLE FOR PRIVATE FUNCTIONS
WITH YOUR RESIDENT HOST, JOHNNY PRIOR, AND
THE CASINO BALLROOM ORCHESTRA

SATURDAY, MARCH 20, 1965

CHRIST CHURCH & ST. MICHAELS

THE NOTIONS
(THE CAVERN'S CHOICE)

will play at
THE YOUTH CENTRE, CARLTON ROAD
on
SATURDAY, MARCH 20th, at 8-0 p.m.

Tickets 4/-   To be paid at the door

MONDAY MARCH 22, 1965

Y.O.R. CLUBS OF STARS
Parr Hall
WARRINGTON
Mon., 22nd March
TOP 20 HIT STARS
THE WHO
THE NOTIONS
Tues., 23rd March
Stamford Hall
ALTRINCHAM
LONG JOHN BALDRY
And The
HOOCHIE COOCHIE MEN
Tickets for Drifters and Kinks
on sale at above dances
Monday, 29th March
THE DRIFTERS
Monday, 5th April
THE KINKS

MONDAY, APRIL 5, 1965

L. G. C. presents,
A GRAND CHARITY DANCE.
FEATURING THE

ROADRUNNERS.

NOTIONS.

MUSIC STUDENTS.

RAVEONS

at LITHERLAND TOWN HALL
on MONDAY 5th APRIL
Commencing at 7-30pm - 11-pm

TICKETS 3/-
ADMISSION at Door 3/- Before 8-30p.m. 3/6 After 8-30p.m.

E N G A G E M E N T S - (CONTINUED).

1965.

Apl.	25.	C.I.Club. Sandfield Park. West Derby.
Apl.	26.	Litherland Town Hall. "Ranchers". "Defenders". "Jensons" TOP BILLING.
Apl.	27.	Peppermint Lounge. Fraser Street. Liverpool. "Kirkbys".
Apl.	28.	St. Helens Co-Operative Social Club. Washway Lane. St. Helens.
Apl.	30.	Parr Hall. Warrington. "Rita & the Squad". "Hi-Lites". "Trappers" TOP BILLING.
May.	1.	Plaza Ballroom. St. Helens. "Abstracts". TOP BILLING.
May.	2.	St. Michael's Youth Club. Widnes.
May.	3.	Strand Ballroom. Winsford.
May.	7.	C.I.Club. Sandfield Park. West Derby. "Pikkins" TOP BILLING.
May.	7.	St. Edward's College. Sandfield Park. West Derby. "Pikkins". TOP BILLING.
May.	8.	Mersey View. Frodsham. "Johnny Kidd & the Pirates". "The Pack".
May.	9.	N.A.L.G.O. Alder Road. West Derby.
May.	10.	Plaza Ballroom, St. Helens. "T.T's with Amos & Karl". "Deans" TOP BILLING.
May.	12.	Gartan Club. Sandon Street. Liverpool.
May.	14.	THE CAVERN. "EARL ROYCE & THE OLYMPICS". "Hideaways".
May.	15.	Hope Hall. Hope Street. Liverpool. "Newtowns". TOP BILLING.
May.	16.	St. Elizabeth's. Litherland. "Corsairs". TOP BILLING.
May.	19.	N.A.L.G.O. Alder Road. West Derby.
May.	20.	Childwall College. Childwall.
May.	21.	Plaza Ballroom. St. Helens. "Pretenders". "T.T.'s". TOP BILLING.
May.	22.	Birkdale Palace Hotel. Southport. "Secrets"."Scorpions". TOP BILLING.
May.	23.	English Martyrs. Litherland. "Easybeats". TOP BILLING.
May.	24.	Parr Hall. Warrington. "PRETTY THINGS".
May.	26.	N.A.L.G.O. West Derby.
May.	28.	Parr Hall. Warrington. "Eric Pepp & his Show Band".
May.	29.	Casino Ballroom. Leigh. Lancs. "John Prior & his Band". "Scripts".
Jun.	4.	Sankey Young People's Fellowship Club. Sankey. Warrington.
Jun.	5.	Plaza Ballroom. St. Helens. "Centermen". "Denims". TOP BILLING.
Jun.	6.	St. Michael's Youth Club. Widnes.
Jun.	7.	Litherland Gala. (Afternoon). "Ranchers". "Exits". TOP BILLING.
Jun.	7.	THE CAVERN. WHIT-SUN EIGHT HOUR SPECTACULAR. "Clayton Squares". "Earl Preston's Realms". ""Johnny Gus Set". "St.Louis Checks". "Terry Hines Sextet". "Michael Allen Group"."Richmonds". "Maraccas".
Jun.	9.	Civil Service Club. (Ministry of Aviation Football Club. Dance.)
Jun.	11.	C.I.Club. West Derby.
Jun.	16.	N.A.L.G.O. West Derby.
Jun.	17.	Peppermint Lounge. "LITTLE FRANKIE & THE COUNTRY GENTLEMEN"
Jun.	19.	Mersey View. Frodsham. "THE INCROWD". "THE FENMEN".
Jun.	24.	Peppermint Lounge. "Earl Royce & the Olympics".
Jun.	25.	THE CAVERN. 100th PERFORMANCE. "Hideaways". "Richmonds". ← **100th CAVERN APPERANCE BY THE NOTIONS**
Jun.	26.	Memorial Hall. Northwich. "JOHNNY KIDD & THE PIRATES".
Jun.	27.	Strand Theatre Club & Ballroom. Winsford. Cheshire.
Jun.	30.	Gartan Club. Liverpool.
Jul.	2.	Maggie May. Liverpool.
Jul.	3.	Cardinal Allen School Dance. Honeysgreen Lane. West Derby. "St.Louis Checks". TOP BILLING.
Jul.	4.	St. Michael's. Widnes.
Jul.	7.	C.I.Club. Notre Dame School Dance. "Detonators". TOP BILLING.
Jul.	8.	Civil Service Club. Liverpool.

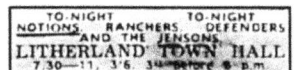

MONDAY, APRIL 26, 1965

THE PEPPERMINT LOUNGE
(FRASER STREET, LIVERPOOL)
TO-MORROW (TUESDAY)
THE KIRKBYS
THE NOTIONS
REMEMBER ADMISSION BEFORE
8.30 P.M. IS ONLY 2/-
MAKE YOUR NIGHT OUT TOMORROW
THE PEPPERMINT LOUNGE

TUESDAY, APRIL 27, 1965

FRIDAY, APRIL 30, 1965

Mersey View Ballroom, Frodsham
Telephone 3108
SATURDAY, May 8th—
JOHNNY KIDD AND THE PIRATES
Plus THE NOTIONS and THE PACK
Make this a date and don't be late! — Admission 7/6
Coaches Arpley Bus Station

SATURDAY, MAY 8, 1965

GARTAN CLUB
K.S.C (Squires Council 205)
19a Sandon Street   No. 087

WE INVITE YOU TO DANCE TO MUSIC SUPPLIED
BY OUR RESIDENT GROUP

"THE NOTIONS"

IN THE ABOVE CLUBROOMS
ON WEDNESDAY MAY 12th 1965
BRING YOUR FRIENDS THEY'LL LIKE IT

Come Early :: No Jeans :: Refreshments available

TICKETS 4/- : — : 7-30—10-45 p.m

WEDNESDAY, MAY 12, 1965

PARR HALL — Y.O.R. CLUB — WARRINGTON
TELEVISED NIGHT IS MONDAY, MAY 24th, 7.45 to 10.45
Return of The Wild Boys — Second only to The Rolling Stones
The Pretty Things
On Stage 8.45 to 10 p.m. World-Wide TV will film this Dance. So don't miss it !
Plus Runcorn's Stars, THE NOTIONS
Get your Tickets early at Dawson's, 7/6, or pay at door 8/6
SEE YOURSELF ON TV WITH THE PRETTY THINGS
Monday, May 31st: THE HOLLIES. Monday, June 14th: YARDBIRDS (w

MONDAY, MAY 24, 1965

C.S.C.A. MINISTRY OF AVIATION LIVERPOOL H.Q.

Midsummer Dance

on THURSDAY, JULY 8th 1965.

Dancing 8-00 p.m. to 11-45 p.m.

WITH "THE NOTIONS"

THE MERSEYSIDE CIVIL SERVICE CLUB
(LOWER CASTLE STREET)

Tickets 4/- Each.   ::   Bar Extension until 11-30

AT THE CAVERN
TO-NIGHT FRIDAY TO-NIGHT
THE HIDEAWAYS
THE NOTIONS
THE RICHMOND
THE CALDERSTONES
Make a note of these special attractions
who are coming to The Cavern shortly
MONDAY, JULY 12.
INNEZ AND
CHARLIE FOXX
AND VERY VERY SOON
JACKIE DE SHANNON

FRIDAY, JUNE 25, 1965
100th APPEARANCE
AT THE CAVERN

THURSDAY, JULY 8, 1965

ENGAGEMENTS - (CONTINUED).

1965.

Jul. 9.	C.I.Club. West Derby.
Jul. 10.	Mersey View. Frodsham. "SHAKEOUTS". "Missing Links".
Jul. 11.	C.I.Club. West Derby.
Jul. 14.	Bull's Head. Trentham. Staffordshire.
Jul. 16.	Peppermint Lounge. "Aztecs". "Cossacks" (Somerset). TOP BILLING.
Jul. 17.	Cambridge Hall. Lord Street. Southport. "Hideaways". "Secrets".
Jul. 24.	Memorial Hall. Northwich. "ANIMALS". "Pack of Cards".
Jul. 28.	N.A.L.G.O. West Derby.
July. 30.	C.I.Club. West Derby.
July. 31.	Peppermint Lounge. Liverpool. "Easybeats". "Citybeats". "Flower Pot Men".
Aug. 1.	Plaza Ballroom. St. Helens. "Mr. Lee & Co." TOP BILLING.
Aug. 4.	Co-Operative Social Club. St. Helens. TOP BILLING.
Aug. 6.	Parr Hall. Warrington. "Prowlers". "Rod Simon Combo". TOP BILLING.
Aug. 7.	Co-Operative Hall. Warrington. "Bluesett". "Missing Links". TOP BILLING.
Aug. 8.	St. Elizabeths. Litherland. "Corsairs". TOP BILLING.
Aug. 11.	N.A.L.G.O. West Derby.
Aug. 12.	Locarno Ballroom. DERBY.
Aug. 13.	West Lancs. Golf Club. (John Hagen's 21st Birthday).
Aug. 14.	Memorial Hall. Northwich. "MEASLES".
Aug. 15.	English Martyrs. Litherland. "Roadrunners".
Aug. 18.	Gartan Club. Liverpool.
Aug. 20.	C.I.Club. West Derby.
Aug. 21.	Plaza Ballroom. St. Helens. "Mr. Lee & Co". TOP BILLING.
Aug. 22.	Bank Park. Warrington. "POP IN THE PARK" SUNDAY OPEN AIR SHOW. "Eric Pep and his Music".
Aug. 27.	Sankey Y.P.F.C. Warrington.
Aug. 28.	Lewis's Hall. Litherland.
Aug. 29.	Plaza Ballroom. St. Helens. "Lavells". TOP BILLING.
Aug. 30.	Plaza Ballroom. St. Helens. (Bank Holiday). "Abstracts". TOP BILLING.
Sep. 2.	Spider's Web Club. R.A.F. Haydock.
Sep. 3.	Prescot Town Social Club. "Aarons". TOP BILLING.
Sep. 4.	La Scala Ballroom. Runcorn. "Blues & Root". "Blues Four".
Sep. 4.	Lion Hotel Ballroom. Warrington. "Blues & Root". "Pilgrims".
Sep. 5.	St. Anne's Social Club. Marmaduke St. Liverpool. (JOE LEAVES GROUP) ← **LAST APPEARANCE OF JOE SHORT**
Sep. 8.	N.A.L.G.O. West Derby. FIRST APPEARANCE OF KEVIN SHORT. ← **FIRST APPEARANCE OF KEVIN SHORT**
Sep. 10.	Peppermint Lounge. "Hillsiders". TOP BILLING.
Sep. 11.	Co-Operative Hall. Warrington. "Trakkers". "B-Jays". TOP BILLING.
Sep. 12.	St. Mary's Old Boys. Moor Lane. Crosby.
Sep. 13.	Left Bank Club. Birkenhead.
Sep. 15.	Plaza Ballroom. St. Helens. "Aarons". TOP BILLING.
Sep. 17.	Co-Operative Social Club. St.Helens.
Sep. 18.	Memorial Hall. Northwich. "WALKER BROTHERS", "Quotations","Scorpions".
Sep. 19.	C.I.Club. West Derby. "Motifs". TOP BILLING.
Sep. 22.	N.A.L.G.O. West Derby.
Sep. 23.	Peppermint Lounge. Liverpool. "Dave the Rave" - Discotheque. TOP BILLING.
Sep. 24.	C.I.Club. West Derby.
Sep. 25.	Plaza Ballroom. St. Helens. "Johnny Ringo's Colts". TOP BILLING.
Sep. 26.	Strand Theatre Club. Winsford. Cheshire.
Sep. 29.	Gartan Club. Liverpool.

MERSEY VIEW BALLROOM, FRODSHAM
Telephone 3108
SATURDAY, JULY 10th
The Shakeouts
THE NOTIONS and THE MISSING LINKS
Admission 6/6 — Coaches Arpley Bus Station

SATURDAY, JULY 10, 1965

BIG RAVE
Cambridge Hall
TO-NIGHT
Featuring the:
HIDEAWAYS
THE NOTIONS
THE SECRETS
8 — 11-45 p.m.   Admission 5/-

SATURDAY, JULY 17, 1965

THE PEPPERMINT LOUNGE,
FRASER STREET, LONDON ROAD.
To-night (Friday)
THE DETOURS.
THE SOUL-SEEKERS.
To-morrow (Saturday):
THE NOTIONS
THE CITY BEATS
THE FLOWER POT MEN
Sunday:
EARL PRESTONS REALMS
THE CONNOISSEURS

SATURDAY JULY 31, 1965

BANK PARK
OPEN AIR DANCING
SATURDAY, AUGUST 21st, 1965, 7.30 p.m. to 10 p.m.
THE KEN PHILLIPS SOUND with THE RONDEX GROUP
Specially laid Dance Floor
Admission 2/6
"POP IN BANK PARK"
SUNDAY, AUGUST 22nd, 1965, 3.00 p.m. to 5.00 p.m.
ERIC PEP AND HIS MUSIC
Featuring THE NOTIONS
Admission: Adults 1/-, Children 6d.

SUNDAY, AUGUST 22, 1965

LION HOTEL
BRIDGE STREET, WARRINGTON
ANOTHER FAB SATURDAY NIGHT—
THE BLUES AND ROOTS
Plus THE PILGRIMS Plus Plus THE NOTIONS
Dancing 7.30 to 11.30 — LICENSED BAR — Admission 6/-
EVERY THURSDAY—
THE CROMWELL JAZZ CLUB
THURSDAY, September 9th, 1965—
From London
SPENCER'S WASH BOARD KINGS
LATE BAR EXTENSION

SATURDAY, SEPTEMBER 4, 1965

PRESCOT TOWN SOCIAL CLUB,
HOPE STREET, PRESCOT.
To-night To-night To-night
NOTIONS plus AARONS.
To-morrow: PATHFINDERS
plus MERSEY GONKS.

FRIDAY, SEPTEMBER 3, 1965

THE PEPPERMINT LOUNGE
FRASER STREET, LIVERPOOL.
To-night, Friday:
THE NOTIONS
THE HILLSIDERS
Saturday:
THE ROADRUNNERS
THE POWER-HOUSE-SIX
THE DEFENDERS
Sunday:
You saw them on R.S.G.
Now see them in Person
THE MASTERMINDS
THE ABSTRACTS
Licensed Bars—Free Refreshments

FRIDAY, SEPTEMBER 10, 1965

Nº 030   GARTAN CLUB
K.S.C (Squires Council 205)
19a Sandon Street

Features

OUR RESIDENT GROUP
' THE NOTIONS '
IN THEIR LAST APPEARANCE HERE TILL CHRISTMAS
IN THE ABOVE CLUBROOMS
ON WEDNESDAY SEPTEMBER 29th 1965

Music from 7-30 p.m.

Come Early   —   Bring Your Friends

TICKETS 4/-   ::   Refreshments available

WEDNESDAY, SEPTEMBER 29, 1965

1965 E N G A G E M E N T S. (CONTINUED).

Sep.	30.	U.S.A.C. (United Sulphuric Acid Co. Social Club. Widnes).
Oct.	1.	C.I.Club. West Derby.
Oct.	2.	Lion Hotel Ballroom. Warrington. "Ian & the Zodiacs". "Easybeats"."Trakkers".
Oct.	2.	La Scala Ballroom. Runcorn. "Stix". "Pilgrims"."B-Jays". TOP BILLING.
Oct.	2.	Plaza Ballroom. St. Helens. "Abstracts". TOP BILLING.
Oct.	6.	N.A.L.G.O. West Derby.
Oct.	8.	Peppermint Lounge. Fraser St. Liverpool. "Tiffany's Thoughts".
Oct.	9.	Memorial Hall. Northwich. "SILKIE". "Scorpions".
Oct.	10.	Royal Hotel. Crewe. TOP BILLING.
Oct.	13.	Assoc.Christian Society. Catholic Chaplaincy. Brownlow Hill. Liverpool.
Oct.	15.	C.I.Club. West Derby.
Oct.	16.	Y.M.C.A. St. Helens. "Almost Blues". TOP BILLING.
Oct.	16.	CAVERN. ALLNIGHTER. "MERSEYBEATS". "Earl Royce & Olympics"."Hideaways". "Masterminds". "Gideon's Few" (M/C)."Denems". "Freddie Starr & Delmonts". "Du-Fay".
Oct.	17.	St. Michael's Y.C. Columba Hall. Frederick St. Widnes.
Oct.	20.	N.A.L.G.O. West Derby.
Oct.	21.	Ashton Palais Ballroom. Ashton - under - Lyne. Manchester.
Oct.	22.	Plaza Ballroom. St. Helens.
Oct.	23.	TOW BAR INN. Egremont. Cumberland.) Special Week-end Booking.
Oct.	24.	TOW BAR INN. Egremont. Cumberland.) "The Phlok". TOP BILLING.
Oct.	27.	N.A.L.G.O. West Derby.
Oct.	29.	CAVERN. "Big Three". "Tributes".
Oct.	30.	Mersey View. Frodsham. "Inmates". TOP BILLING.
Oct.	31.	St. Elizabeths. Litherland. "Profits". TOP BILLING.
Nov.	5.	Peppermint Lounge. "Mark Peter's Method". TOP BILLING.
Nov.	6.	Memorial Hall. Northwich. "P.J. PROBY & THE PROBY ORCHESTRA". "Pack of Cards".
Nov.	7.	English Martyrs. Litherland. "Hideaways". "St. John's Precinct".
Nov.	11.	Civil Service Club. Liverpool.
Nov.	12.	C.I.Club. West Derby.
Nov.	13.	Prescot Town Social Club. "Corsairs". TOP BILLING.
Nov.	13.	Lion Hotel Ballroom. Warrington. "Easybeats". "Steve Day's Drifters". "Monos".
Nov.	14.	C.I.Club. West Derby.
Nov.	17.	St. Luke's Hall. "The Jive Hive". "Bentios". TOP BILLING.
Nov.	18.	Peppermint Lounge. "Easybeats". TOP BILLING.
Nov.	19.	Formby Round Table. Victoria Hall. Formby. "Nick Kearsley & his Orchestra".
Nov.	20.	B.I.C.C. Hall. Helsby. Frodsham. "Easybeats". JOINT TOP BILLING.
Nov.	22.	Royal Hotel. Crewe. TOP BILLING.
Nov.	24.	N.A.L.G.O. West Derby.
Nov.	25.	Spider's Web Club. R.A.F. Haydock. St. Helens.
Nov.	26.	Plaza Ballroom. St. Helens. "Motifs". TOP BILLING.
Nov.	27.	Lion Hotel Ballroom. Warrington. "Hickory Stix". "Black Abbotts".
Nov.	28.	St. Elizabeth's. Litherland. "The Mersey Gonks". TOP BILLING.
Dec.	1.	College of Technology. Manchester University.
Dec.	2.	Peppermint Lounge. Liverpool. "Easybeats". TOP BILLING.
Dec.	3.	Officer's Ball. 5th Liverpool King's Regt. T.A. Liverpool. "Bobby Nick & his Music". TOP BILLING.
Dec.	4.	Memorial Hall. Northwich. "HOLLIES". "Pacifics".

**SATURDAY
OCTOBER 16, 1965**

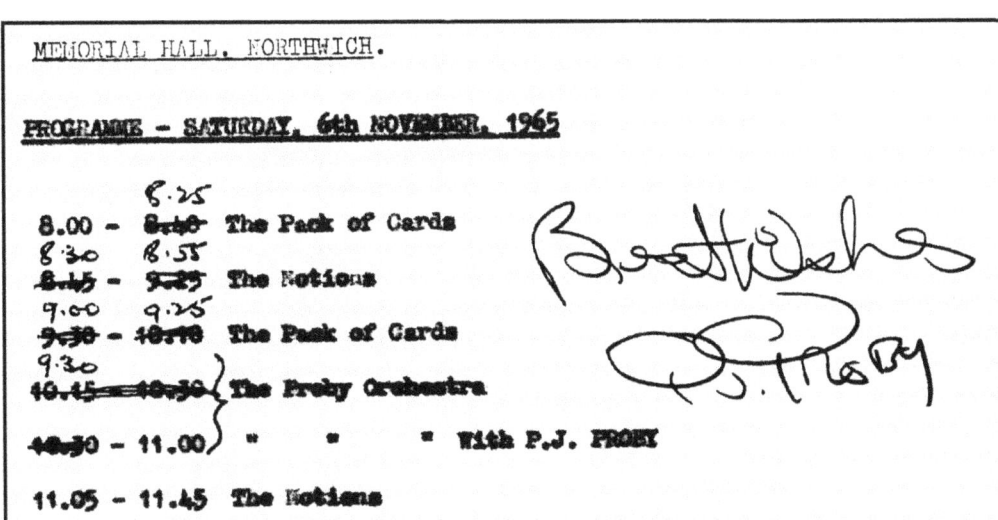

**FRANK DELANEY'S SET LIST FOR SATURDAY, NOVEMBER 6, 1965
THE 'NOTIONS' SUPPORTING P.J. PROBY & HIS ORCHESTRA**

ENGLISH MARTYRS. LITHERLAND.
Sunday: THE HIDEAWAYS
The Notions
ST. JOHN'S PRECINCTS

SUNDAY, NOVEMBER 7, 1965

MINISTRY OF AVIATION & DEFENCE
RECREATIONAL SOCIETY.

Football Club Dance

on THURSDAY, NOVEMBER 11th 1965.

Dancing 8-00 p.m. to 11-45 p.m.
WITH "THE NOTIONS"
THE MERSEYSIDE CIVIL SERVICE CLUB
(LOWER CASTLE STREET)

Tickets 4/- Each. :: Bar Extension until 11-30

THURSDAY, NOVEMBER 11, 1965

ST. LUKE'S HALL
CROSBY
TO-NIGHT   TO-NIGHT.
Only Two Shillings Before 8 p.m.
THE NOTIONS
THE BENTLES
THE MERCEDES
Closed For One Night Only.
SATURDAY, NOVEMBER 20

WEDNESDAY, NOVEMBER 17, 1965

THE PEPPERMINT LOUNGE
FRASER STREET LIVERPOOL
TO-NIGHT   THURSDAY   TO-NIGHT
THE NOTIONS
PLUS
THE EASYBEATS
The Finest Supper In Town Is On
Display All Night. All Inclusive In Your
Admission of 5/-
TO-MORROW   FITZ AND STARTZ

THURSDAY, NOVEMBER 18, 1965

FRIDAY, NOVEMBER 19, 1965

E N G A G E M E N T S. (CONTINUED).

1965.

Dec. 5. C.I.Club. West Derby.
Dec. 7. Community Centre. Speke. "Bentics".   TOP BILLING.
Dec. 9. Downbeat Club. Liverpool.   "Mark Peters' Method". JOINT TOP BILLING.
Dec. 10. C.I.Club. West Derby.
Dec. 11. Mersey View. Frodsham. "Optimists Incorporated". "Blues Four".   TOP BILLING.
Dec. 12. N.A.L.G.O. West Derby. Liverpool.
Dec. 15. Gartan Club. "Pikkins".   TOP BILLING.
Dec. 16. St. Peters & St. Pauls. (Seafield Convent). "Mersey Gonks". "Precincts".
Dec. 16. Peppermint Lounge. "Tiffany's Thoughts".   TOP BILLING.
Dec. 17. C.I.Club. West Derby.   JOINT TOP BILLING.
Dec. 18. Co-Operative Hall. Warrington. "Five Nites". "Colours". TOP BILLING.
Dec. 19. English Martyrs. Litherland. "Mersey Gonks". "Aztecs". TOP BILLING.
Dec. 20. Metal Box Social Club. Aintree. "Modes". "Fables".   TOP BILLING.
Dec. 21. Countess of Derby School. Xmas Dance. Netherton.
Dec. 22. Cardinal Godfrey School Xmas Dance. C.I.Club. "Pikkins". TOP BILLING.
Dec. 24. Strand Theatre Club & Ballroom. Winsford.   TOP BILLING.
Dec. 27. Peppermint Lounge. "Corvettes" (Glasgow). "Rory Storm & the Hurricanes".
Dec. 27. St. Annes. Edgehill. Social Club.
Dec. 29. St. Mary's Parish Hall. Woolton. "Vikki & the Moonlighters". TOP BILLING.
Dec. 30. Peppermint Lounge. "Denny Seyton Group".
Dec. 31. Student's Union. Liverpool University. "Easybeats". "Tiffany's Thoughts".
Dec. 31. C.I.Club. West Derby. "Detonators". TOP BILLING.   TOP BILLING.

1966.

Jan. 1. Memorial Hall. Northwich. "KINKS". "Pack of Cards".
Jan. 2. C.I.Club. West Derby.
Jan. 3. Quaintways. Chester. "Deacons". "Hall City Jazzmen". TOP BILLING.
Jan. 5. Alexander Hall. Heswell.
Jan. 7. Mardi Gras. Liverpool. "Cy Tucker's Friars".
Jan. 8. Hills Ballroom. OLDHAM. "Merv's Bardots".   TOP BILLING.
Jan. 9. Plaza Ballroom. St. Helens. "Rita & the Vogue".   TOP BILLING.
Jan. 13. Peppermint Lounge.   "The Tabs". JOINT TOP BILLING.
Jan. 14. West Lancashire Golf Club. (Private Party).
Jan. 15. Prescot Town Social Club. "Expressions". TOP BILLING.
Jan. 15. Lion Hotel Ballroom. Warrington. "Dennisons"."MIKE COTTON SOUND".
Jan. 16. N.A.L.G.O. West Derby. Liverpool.
Jan. 17. Mardi Gras. Liverpool. "ESCORTS".   TOP BILLING.
Jan. 20. Spider's Web Club. R.A.F. Haydock.
Jan. 21. Student's Union. Elizabeth Gaskell College. MANCHESTER. "Country Gentlemen".
Jan. 27. U.S.A.C. Tanhouse Lane. Widnes.
Jan. 28. C.F.Mott Teachers Training College. Prescot.
Jan. 29. Memorial Hall. Northwich. "DRIFTERS". "Trendsetters Ltd". "Dene Wayne" and the Exiles".
Jan. 30. C.I.Club. West Derby.
Feb. 1. Mr. Smith's Club. Hanley. S.O.T.
Feb. 4. Hulme Hall Port Sunlight. Land & Marine Contractors Dance. "Orchestra of N.D.O. & B.B.C."
Feb. 5. Grange Valley Youth Club. Haydock.
Feb. 6. Plaza Ballroom. St. Helens. "Detours".   TOP BILLING.
Feb. 8. Peppermint Lounge. "Discotheque". "She & Her". "Rita & Sheleen" "Lorna & Peter".
Feb. 11. C.I.Club. West Derby.

WEDNESDAY, DECEMBER 15, 1965

GARTAN CLUB
K.S.C. Squires (Council 205)
19a Sandon Street

N⁰ 012

Present a Grand

CHRISTMAS DANCE

IN THE ABOVE CLUBROOMS
ON WEDNESDAY DECEMBER 15th 1965

FEATURING THE GARTAN CLUBS TOP GROUPS
'THE NOTIONS' plus 'THE PIKKINS'

:: 7 p.m. — 11 p.m. ::

DONT MISS THIS ALL STAR DANCE

TICKETS :: 5/-

THURSDAY, DECEMBER 16, 1965

SEAFIELD SIXTH FORM

DANCE

will be held in
SS. PETER & PAULS HALL
on
THURSDAY, DECEMBER 16th, 1965
7-30 p.m. — 11-0 p.m.

★ THE NOTIONS and THE MERSEY GONKS ★

TICKETS 4/6   Refreshments Included

PROGRAMME – SATURDAY, 1st JANUARY, 1966

8.00 – 8.40   The Notions
8.45 – 9.30   The Pack of Cards
9.35 – 10.15 The Notions
10.20 – 11.00 THE KINKS
11.05 – 11.45 The Notions

FRANK DELANEY'S SET LIST FOR THE 'NOTIONS'
SATURDAY, JANUARY 1, 1966 SUPPORTING THE 'KINKS'
SATURDAY, JANUARY 29, 1966 SUPPORTING THE 'DRIFTERS'

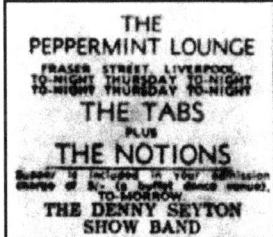

THURSDAY JANUARY 13, 1966

SATURDAY JANUARY 15, 1966

MONDAY JANUARY 17, 1966

PROGRAMME – SATURDAY, 29th JANUARY

7.45 – 8.15   The Notions
8.20 – 8.55   The Exiles
9.00 – 9.40   Trendsetters Ltd.
9.45 – 10.15 The Notions
10.20 – 11.00 THE DRIFTERS
11.05 – 11.45 The Notions

Copies to:-
Mr. S. Wakefield
Mr. V. Connolly
Mr. P. Scott
The Drifters
The Notions
The Exiles

E N G A G E M E N T S.   (CONTINUED).

1966.

Feb.	12.	Y.M.C.A. Duke St. St. Helens. "Big 3". "Johnny Ringo's Colts". TOP BILLING.
Feb.	12.	Peppermint Lounge. "Countdowns". "Dions". TOP BILLING.
Feb.	13.	English Martyrs. Litherland. "Secrets". "Mersey Gonks". TOP BILLING.
Feb.	15.	21 Club. Croxteth. Young Conservatives Dance.
Feb.	17.	Hendersons Stores Charity Dinner Dance & Cabaret.
		CABARET ARTISTES - Ray Barton (Accordian). Al Rogers (Comedian)
		Clwyd & Blodwyn Pierce -(Singers)
		Tommy Smith Quintet.
Feb.	18.	Plaza Ballroom. St. Helens. "Coins". TOP BILLING.
Feb.	19.	Mardi Gras. "Stereos". TOP BILLING.
Feb.	20.	St. Elizabeth's. Litherland. "Mersey Gonks". TOP BILLING.
Feb.	22.	St. Theresa's. Norris Green. Liverpool.
Feb.	24.	Downbeat Club. Liverpool. "Almost Blues".
Feb.	25.	Greening Recreation Club. Warrington. "Styles". TOP BILLING.
Feb.	26.	**Memorial Hall. Northwich.** "MINDBENDERS". "Pacifics".
Feb.	27.	76 Club. Burton on Trent.
Mar.	3.	Rice Lane Labour Club. (St.Francis de Sales F.C.).
Mar.	4.	Peppermint Lounge. "Defenders". TOP BILLING.
Mar.	5.	Co-Operative Hall. Warrington. "Styles". "Denins". TOP BILLING.
Mar.	6.	Strand Theatre Club. Winsford. "Farrier's Blues". TOP BILLING.
Mar.	11.	Kabel Club. Prescot. "Gerry de Ville & the City Kings". TOP BILLING.
Mar.	11.	Peppermint Lounge. "Mark Peter's Method".
Mar.	12.	Students Union. Liverpool University. "Big 3". TOP BILLING.
Mar.	13.	**English Martyrs. Litherland.** "Mersey Gonks". TOP BILLING.
Mar.	17.	N.A.L.G.O. West Derby. "Halers". "Tenor C's". TOP BILLING.
Mar.	17.	Peppermint Lounge. Liverpool. "Amigos" (Ireland). "Seftons".
Mar.	18.	Queen's Ballroom. Cleveleys. BLACKPOOL. "Heebie Jeebies" (Bolton).
		"The Moonie Gang" (Blackpool. TOP BILLING.
Mar.	19.	Palmerston Tennis Club. Mossley Hill Institute."Corsairs". TOP BILLING.
Mar.	20.	Clayton Lodge Hotel. NEWCASTLE. Staffs. "Reflections". (Stoke).TOP BILLING.
Mar.	23.	Students Union. Liverpool University. "VICTOR BROX BLUES TRAIN".
Mar.	24.	Blue Candle Club. Warrington.
Mar.	25.	Mardi Gras. Liverpool. "Cordes". TOP BILLING.
Mar.	26.	**Memorial Hall. Northwich.** "SMALL FACES". "Elite".
Mar.	27.	C.I.Club. West Derby.
Mar.	31.	Peppermint Lounge. "The Whole Scene". TOP BILLING.
Apl.	1.	Kelvinator Club. Bromborough. "Hignett Quartet". TOP BILLING.
Apl.	2.	Mardi Gras. Liverpool. "Cordes". TOP BILLING.
Apl.	3.	Plaza Ballroom. St. Helens. "Herb Set". TOP BILLING.
Apl.	4.	South Shore Tennis Club. BLACKPOOL.
Apl.	5.	SHOW DANCE - "A NIGHT FOR MIKE" - Memorial Tribute to MIKE MILLWARD
	Grafton	Late member of the FOURMOST. Charity Show in aid of
	Rooms.	Cancer Research. A host of Stars including "FOURMOST"
	Liverpool.	"BILLY J.KRAMER & THE DAKOTAS", "SILKIE", "REMO 4",
		"Escorts", "Dennisons", "NOTIONS", "Warriors" etc.,etc.,
Apl.	6.	Stafford Moreton Youth Club. Maghull.
Apl.	7.	Casino Club. BLACKPOOL. "Moonie's Gang". TOP BILLING.
Apl.	8.	Mardi Gras. Liverpool. "Dimensions". TOP BILLING.
Apl.	9.	Mersey View. Frodsham. "TONY JACKSON & THE VIBRATIONS".
Apl.	10.	**English Martyrs. Litherland.** "Pitiful". TOP BILLING.
Apl.	11.	**Memorial Hall. Northwich.** "LEAGUE OF GENTLEMEN".

CAVERN CLOSES FEBRUARY 28, 1966

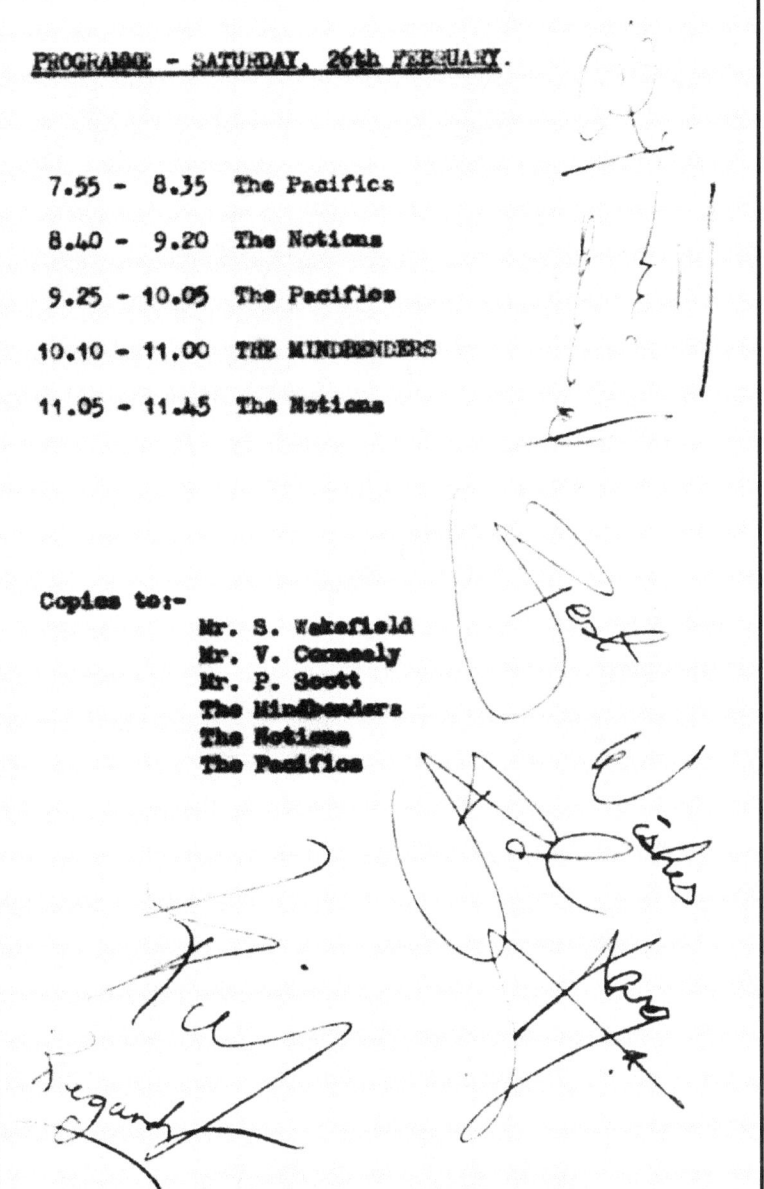

FRANK DELANEY'S SET LIST FOR THE 'NOTIONS'
SATURDAY, FEBRUARY 26, 1966
SUPPORTING THE 'MINDBENDERS'

```
PROGRAMME - SATURDAY, 26th FEBRUARY.

7.55 -  8.35   The Pacifics
8.40 -  9.20   The Notions
9.25 - 10.05   The Pacifics
10.10 - 11.00  THE MINDBENDERS
11.05 - 11.45  The Notions

Copies to:-
    Mr. S. Wakefield
    Mr. V. Connealy
    Mr. P. Scott
    The Mindbenders
    The Notions
    The Pacifics
```

FRANK DELANEY'S SET LIST FOR THE 'NOTIONS'
MONDAY, APRIL 11, 1966
SUPPORTING THE 'LEAGUE OF GENTLEMAN'

```
PROGRAMME - EASTER MONDAY      MEMORIAL HALL.
                                NORTHWICH.

7.50 -  8.25   The Notions
8.30 -  9.15   The League of Gentlemen
9.20 -  9.55   The Notions
10.00 - 11.00  The League of Gentlemen
11.05 - 11.45  The Notions
```

TUESDAY
APRIL 5, 1966

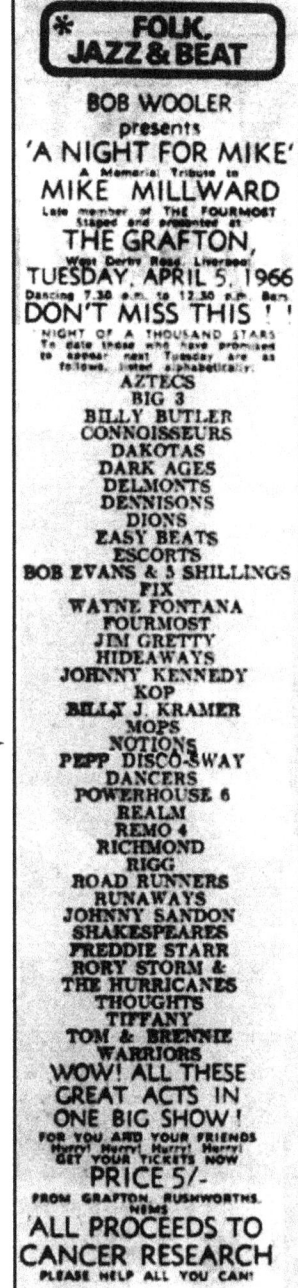

FOLK, JAZZ & BEAT

BOB WOOLER presents
'A NIGHT FOR MIKE'
A Memorial Tribute to
MIKE MILLWARD
Late member of THE FOURMOST
Staged and presented at
THE GRAFTON,
West Derby Road, Liverpool
TUESDAY, APRIL 5, 1966
Dancing 7.30 p.m. to 12.30 a.m. 8am
DON'T MISS THIS !!!
NIGHT OF A THOUSAND STARS
To date those who have promised to appear next Tuesday are as follows, listed alphabetically:

AZTECS
BIG 3
BILLY BUTLER
CONNOISSEURS
DAKOTAS
DARK AGES
DELMONTS
DENNISONS
DIONS
EASY BEATS
ESCORTS
BOB EVANS & 5 SHILLINGS
FIX
WAYNE FONTANA
FOURMOST
JIM GRETTY
HIDEAWAYS
JOHNNY KENNEDY
KOP
BILLY J. KRAMER
MOPS
NOTIONS
PEPP DISCO-SWAY DANCERS
POWERHOUSE 6
REALM
REMO 4
RICHMOND
RIGG
ROAD RUNNERS
RUNAWAYS
JOHNNY SANDON
SHAKESPEARES
FREDDIE STARR
RORY STORM & THE HURRICANES
THOUGHTS
TIFFANY
TOM & BRENNIE
WARRIORS

WOW! ALL THESE GREAT ACTS IN ONE BIG SHOW!
FOR YOU AND YOUR FRIENDS
Hurry! Hurry! Hurry! Hurry!
GET YOUR TICKETS NOW
PRICE 5/-
FROM GRAFTON, RUSHWORTHS, NEMS
ALL PROCEEDS TO CANCER RESEARCH
PLEASE HELP ALL YOU CAN!

ENGAGEMENTS. (CONTINUED).

1966.

Apl.	15.	Peppermint Lounge. "ALMOST BLUES". Joint TOP BILLING.
Apl.	16.	Prescot Town Social Club. (Kabel Club). "Detonators". TOP BILLING.
Apl.	16.	Lion Hotel Ballroom. Warrington.
Apl.	17.	C.I.Club. West Derby.
Apl.	21.	MARQUEE CLUB. LONDON. Practice for Recording with POLYDOR.
Apl.	22.	ADVISION STUDIOS. LONDON. Recording Session with POLYDOR.
Apl.	23.	Memorial Hall. Northwich. "MANFRED MANN". "Scorpions".
Apl.	24.	Mr. Smiths. Strand Theatre Club. Winsford.
Apl.	25.	Downbeat Club. Liverpool.(Wallasey A.F.C. Dance)."Cy Tucker's Friars".
Apl.	29.	St. Sebastian's Youth Club. West Derby.
Apl.	30.	Mardi Gras Club. Liverpool."The Victors". TOP BILLING.
May.	1.	St. Elizabeths. Litherland. "The Pitiful". TOP BILLING.
May.	6.	Peppermint Lounge. Liverpool. "The Detonators". TOP BILLING.
May.	7.	Mersey View. Frodsham. "Petals" (M/c). JOINT TOP BILLING.
May.	8.	N.A.L.G.O. West Derby.
May.	9.	South Shore Tennis Club. BLACKPOOL.
May.	10.	Mardi Gras. Liverpool. "Cy Tucker's Friars".
May.	12.	Casino Club. BOLTON. "Surf Side Six". TOP BILLING.
May.	13.	St. Edward's College. West Derby. "Detonators". TOP BILLING.
May.	14.	Haydock (Grange Valley) Youth Club.
May.	15.	Mardi Gras. Liverpool. "Hillsiders".
May.	19.	Peppermint Lounge. Liverpool. "Aztecs". TOP BILLING.
May.	21.	Kabel Club. Prescot. "Centurmen". TOP BILLING.
May.	21.	Lion Hotel Ballroom. Bridge Street. Warrington. "MIKE COTTON SOUND". "The Fix".
May.	22.	76 Club. Burton on Trent.
May.	24.	Royal Iris River Cruise.
May.	26.	Mardi Gras. Liverpool. "Cordes". TOP BILLING.
May.	27.	C.I.Club. West Derby.
May.	28.	Faculty of Technology. Manchester. "MARK LEEMAN FIVE".
May.	29.	Mr. Smiths. Strand. Winsford.
May.	30.	Litherland Gala. Open Air. "Efforts". TOP BILLING.
May.	30.	Kabel Club. Prescot.
June.	1.	St. Elizabeths. Litherland.
June.	3.	Mardi Gras. Liverpool. "Fix". JOINT TOP BILLING.
June.	4.	Co-Operative Hall. Warrington. "Times". "Optimists Incorporated". TOP BILLING.
June.	5.	English Martyrs. Litherland. "Profits". TOP BILLING.
June.	6.	South Shore Tennis Club. BLACKPOOL.
June.	7.	Mardi Gras Club. Liverpool. "Cordes". TOP BILLING.
June.	10.	C.I.Club. West Derby.
June.	11.	Marine Hall. Fleetwood. "Creeping Vines" (Preston). TOP BILLING.
June.	12.	Blue Ball Hotel. Risley. Derby.
June.	13.	Mr. Smith's Club. Winsford.
June.	15.	Downbeat Club. Liverpool. "Cy Tucker's Friars".
June.	17.	Roscoe Hall. Greenbank. Liverpool. Liverpool University. Students Union. "Mojos". "Bobby Nick & Orchestra". "Rod Hamer Band".
June.	18.	Palmerston Tennis Club. Rose Lane. Liverpool. "Fix".
June.	18.	Lion Hotel Ballroom. Warrington. "The HERD" London.

[Side note, April 22]: POLYDOR RECORDING SESSION - LONDON SONGS RECORDED WERE "THE LAST TIME I'LL BE TAKING YOU HOME" SUNG BY FRED LLOYD (POLYDOR A&R MAN) WITH THE 'NOTIONS' BACKING HIM - PLUS "ANOTHER TIME" AND "CAN YOU SEE A WAY" BY THE 'NOTIONS', BOTH OF THE 'NOTIONS' SONGS WERE RE-RELEASED (2012-2013) ON 'MERSEYSIDE RECORDS' CD'S

[Side note, May 26]: LAST APPEARANCE OF DAVE McCARTHY

PEPPERMINT
LOUNGE
Fraser Street, Liverpool
TO-NIGHT FRIDAY TO-NIGHT
The Return of the Fabulous
ALMOST BLUES
NOTIONS
Saturday — Saturday — Saturday
CORSAIRS
STEVE DAY'S
KINSMEN
DENIMS
Sunday — Sunday — Sunday
CALDERSTONES
AZTECS
Plus — Plus — Plus
Every Night the Lovely
Pepp-o-Teque Dancers
Come along early —
Everybody's going to the Pepp.
Supper included in admission price.

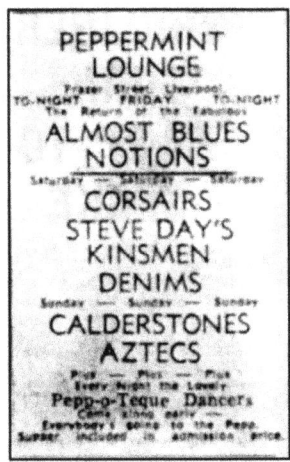

FRIDAY
APRIL 15, 1966

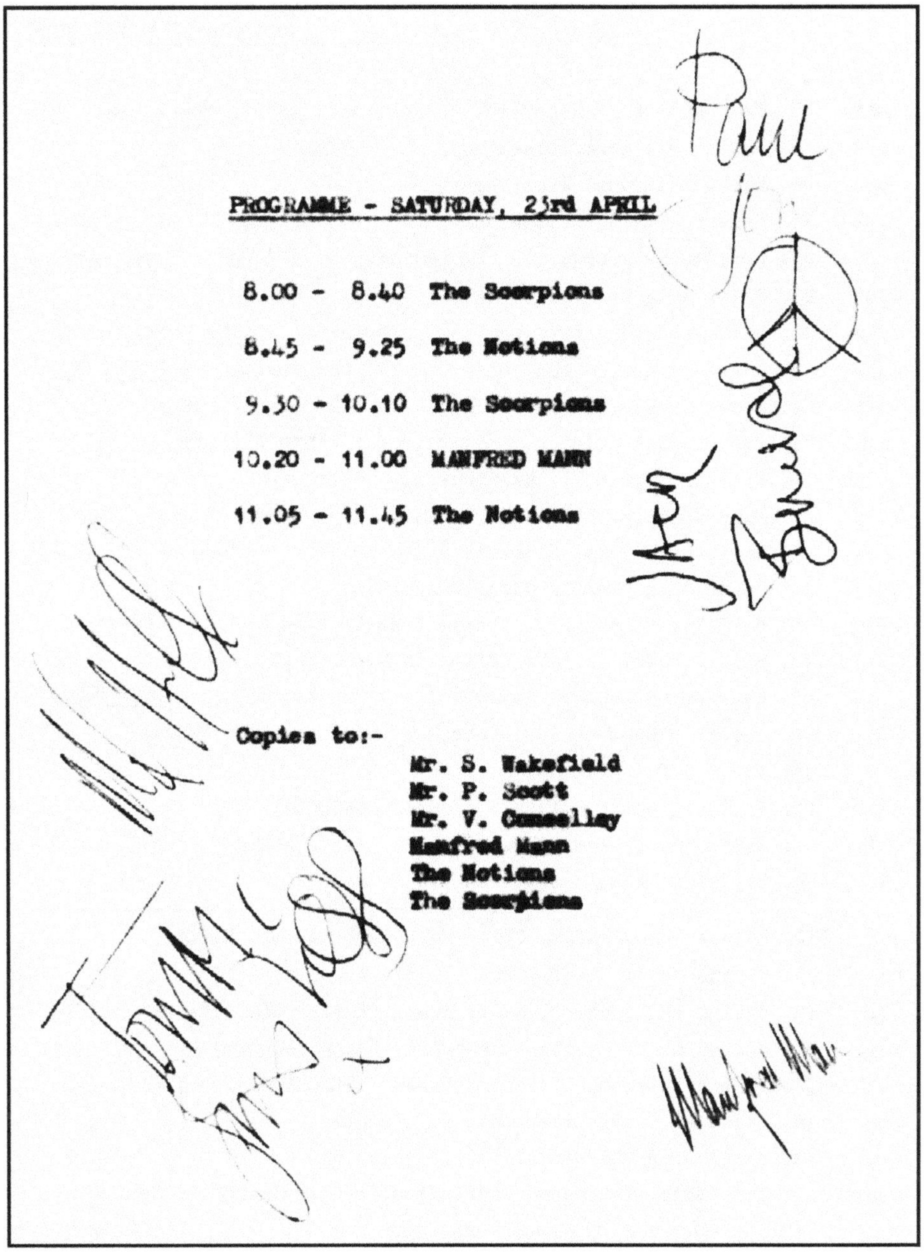

PROGRAMME - SATURDAY, 23rd APRIL

8.00 - 8.40 The Scorpions

8.45 - 9.25 The Notions

9.30 - 10.10 The Scorpions

10.20 - 11.00 MANFRED MANN

11.05 - 11.45 The Notions

Copies to:-

Mr. S. Wakefield
Mr. P. Scott
Mr. V. Connelley
Manfred Mann
The Notions
The Scorpions

FRANK DELANEY'S SET LIST FOR THE 'NOTIONS'
SATURDAY, APRIL 23, 1966
SUPPORTING 'MANFRED MANN'

WALLASEY A.F.C.

DANCE

at the
DOWNBEAT CLUB
VICTORIA STREET
on
MONDAY, 25th APRIL, 1966
(MEMBERS ONLY)
Featuring...
CY TUCKER'S FRIARS & THE NOTIONS

Ticket 5/-.
(No admission under 18)

Bar Extension
till 11-30

MONDAY, APRIL 25, 1966

Palmerston Hard Court
Tennis Club

№ ...085

PRESENT

"THE FIX"
AND
"THE NOTIONS"

AT MOSSLEY HILL INSTITUTE
ON SATURDAY JUNE 18th 1966

7-30 till 11 p.m. :: No Pass-outs

ADMISSION :-: 5/-

SATURDAY, JUNE 18, 1966

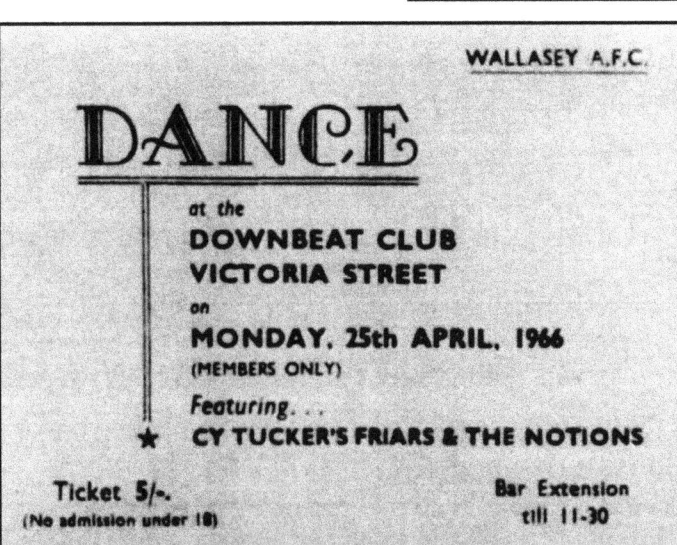

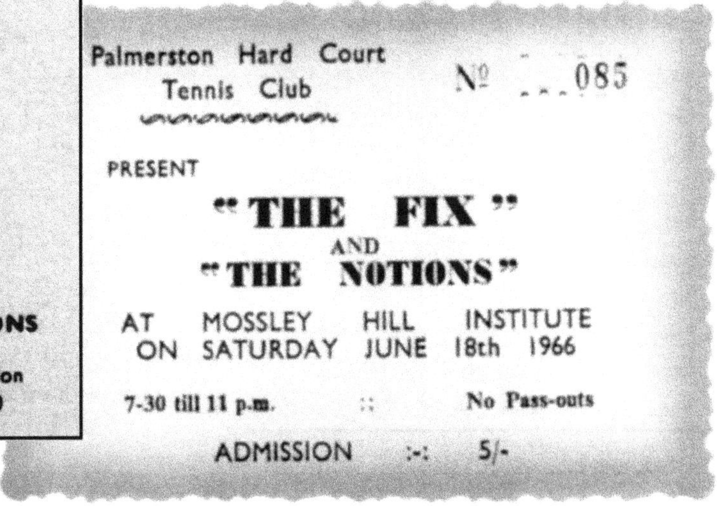

E N G A G E M E N N T S . (CONTINUED)

1966.

June. 19. Mr. Smith's. Manchester. "Demokrats". (M/C). "Konchords".(M/C). TOP BILLING.
June. 20. Casino Ballroom. Blackpool.   "KIRKBYS".
June. 24. St. Sebastians. West Derby.
June. 25. Memorial Hall. Northwich.   "Crying Shames". "St. Franklyn".
June. 26. Peppermint Lounge.   "Bobby Grey Soul Band".   TOP BILLING.
June. 28. Royal Iris Cruise. Methodist Union.   "Kinsmen" (Folk). TOP BILLING.
June. 29. Downbeat Club. Liverpool.   "Fix".   TOP BILLING.
June. 30. Casino Club. BOLTON.   "Zonics". (Chorley).   TOP BILLING.
July. 1. Kabel Club. Prescot. "Gerry de Ville & City Kings". TOP BILLING.
July. 1. Peppermint Lounge.   "Steve Day's Kinsmen". TOP BILLING.
July. 2. Co.Operative Hall. Warrington.   "Herb Set". "Pack of Cards". TOP BILLING.
July. 2. Lion Hotel Ballroom. Warrington.   "Power House Six". "Dave Bowie & the Buzz".
July. 3. English Martyrs. Litherland.   "Halers". "Heatwave". TOP BILLING.
July. 4. South Shore Tennis Club. BLACKPOOL.
July. 5. Catholic Chaplaincy. (Notre Dame College Dance). Liverpool.
July. 7. Spider's Web. R.A.F. OFficer's Club. Haydock.
July. 8. Peppermint Lounge. Liverpool.   "Toplins".   TOP BILLING.
July. 9. Formby Flower Show. "Country Rhythm Boys". "Timon". TOP BILLING.
July. 10. N.A.L.G.O. West Derby.
July. 11. Victoria Hotel. Central Pier. BLACKPOOL.
July. 13. Mardi Gras. Liverpool.   "Hillsiders". "Twig".
July. 15. C.I.Club. West Derby.

CAVERN REOPENS SATURDAY, JULY 23, 1966

Aug. 12. Talbot Conservative Club. Melbourne St. BLACKPOOL.
Aug. 13. Marine Hall. FLEETWOOD.   "Blackpool's Ramblers".   TOP BILLING.
Aug. 14. Casino Ballroom. Pleasure Beach. BLACKPOOL. "Top Katz".(Blackpool). TOP BILLING.
Aug. 15. Casino Club. Marton. BLACKPOOL. "John Evans Band". TOP BILLING.
Aug. 16. Casino Ballroom. Pleasure Beach. BLACKPOOL. "Johnny Breeze & the Atlantics". TOP BILLING.
Aug. 18. Downbeat Club. Liverpool.   "ESCORTS".
Aug. 19. Mardi Gras. Liverpool.   "Fix".   JOINT TOP BILLING.
Aug. 20. Lion Hotel Ballroom. Warrington. "M.I.5 Group". "Some Other Guys".
Aug. 21. N.A.L.G.O. West Derby. Liverpool.
Aug. 22. Mr. Smith's Club. Winsford.
Aug. 23. Beachcomber (Mirabel Club). Liverpool. "Detours".   TOP BILLING.
Aug. 25. Casino Club. Bolton.   "Senators". (Blackpool).   TOP BILLING.
Aug. 26. Peppermint Lounge. Liverpool.
Aug. 27. Memorial Hall. Northwich. "TROGGS". "Smith's People".
Aug. 28. English Martyrs. Litherland.
Aug. 29. Kabel Club. Prescot.
Sep. 2. Mardi Gras.,Liverpool.   "Detours".   TOP BILLING.
Sep. 3. Talbot Road Conservative Club. BLACKPOOL.
Sep. 4. Wally's Disc Club. PRESTON.
Sep. 8. Casino Club. BOLTON.   "Howie Casey & the Seniors". TOP BILLING.
Sep. 9. C.I.Club. West Derby.
Sep. 10. Mardi Gras. Liverpool. "Jason Eddie & Centermen". TOP BILLING.
Sep. 11. Peppermint Lounge. Liverpool.   "UNDERTAKERS".
Sep. 12. Mr. Smith's Club. WINSFORD.

ST. SEBASTIANS YOUTH CLUB

Present a

MID-SUMMER DANCE

with

" THE NOTIONS "

IN THE CLUBROOMS (Lockerby Road)
on FRIDAY JUNE 24th 1966

★ Dancing from 8 p.m. till 10-45 p.m. ★

— NO ADMISSION AFTER 9-30 p.m. —

TICKETS 3/6   ::   Refreshments

FRIDAY, JUNE 24, 1966

THE METHODIST CHURCH
LIVERPOOL DISTRICT YOUTH COUNCIL

Evening Cruise

with the "*NOTIONS*"
(well known Liverpool group)

TUESDAY, 28th JUNE, 1966

ON

M.V. "ROYAL IRIS II"

Embark Liverpool Landing Stage 7-15 p.m. prompt
Return approximately 10-15 p.m.

TICKETS 4/6 each   Light Refreshments obtainable

TUESDAY, JUNE 28, 1966

Notre Dame High School, Woolton Hall   F. VI.

presents...

THE NOTIONS

ON TUESDAY, JULY 5th, 1966

at the

LIVERPOOL UNIVERSITY CATHOLIC CHAPLAINCY

7-30 — 11 p.m.   Tickets 3/6
Refreshments

TUESDAY, JULY 5, 1966

Talbot Conservative Club
MILBOURNE ST. Affiliated

TONIGHT

Direct from Liverpool —

THE NOTIONS

SATURDAY —

JOHNNY BREEZE and the ATLANTICS

FRIDAY AUGUST 12, 1966

* FOLK, JAZZ & BEAT

Strictly Members Only.
Visitors Not Admitted.

THE DOWNBEAT CLUB
77 Victoria Street.

JUST BACK FROM SWITZERLAND!
GREAT RETURN APPEARANCE!

Tonight:

THE ESCORTS
also
THE NOTIONS

TUESDAY AUGUST 23, 1966

TUESDAY AUGUST 23, 1966

MEMORIAL HALL.	NORTHWICH.	Saturday 27th August 1966.
7.50 – 8.20	NOTIONS.	
8.30 – 9.10	SMITHS PEOPLE.	
9.15 – 9.45	TROGGS..	
9.50 – 10.25	NOTIONS.	
10.30 – 11.00	TROGGS.	
11.10 – 11.40	NOTIONS.	

FRANK DELANEY'S SET LIST FOR THE 'NOTIONS' SATURDAY, AUGUST 27, 1966 - SUPPORTING THE 'TROGGS'

E N G A G E M E N T S. (CONTINUED).

1966.

Sept. 16. Kabel Club. PRESCOT.
Sept. 17. Y.M.C.A. St. Helens. "Softons". TOP BILLING.
Sept. 18. Mardi Gras Club. Liverpool. "HILLSIDERS".
Sept. 19. Casino Club. BOLTON. "Shyms". (Wigan). TOP BILLING.
Sept. 23. Peppermint Lounge. Liverpool. "Crescendos".(CANADA). TOP BILLING.
Sept. 24. Teacher's Training College. Padgate. Warrington. "Pebbles". TOP BILLING.
Sept. 25. Casino Ballroom. Pleasure Beach. BLACKPOOL. "Top Katz". TOP BILLING.
Sept. 26. Casino Club. Marton. BLACKPOOL. "Senators". TOP BILLING.
Sept. 30. Casino Club. Westhoughton. "Rocking Vicars". "Cortinas".
Oct. 1. Talbot Road Conservative Club. BLACKPOOL.
Oct. 2. Carlton Club. WARRINGTON. "Embers West". "Escorts".
Oct. 3. Quaintways. CHESTER. "Sands" (London)."Prowlers"."Wall City Jazzmen".
Oct. 5. Christ College. Woolton. "Runaways". TOP BILLING.
Oct. 7. Mardi Gras Club. Liverpool. "Cy Tucker & the Friars". TOP BILLING.
Oct. 8. Haydock Youth Club.
Oct. 9. Casino Ballroom. Pleasure Beach. BLACKPOOL. "Johnny Breeze & the
Oct. 10. South Shore Tennis Club. BLACKPOOL. ATLANTICS". TOP BILLING.
Oct. 12. Faculty of Technology. University of MANCHESTER.
Oct. 14. C.I.Club. West Derby.
Oct. 15. Mardi Gras Club. Liverpool. "Cy Tucker & the Friars". TOP BILLING.
Oct. 16. Peppermint Lounge. Liverpool. "Mistake". TOP BILLING.
Oct. 21. Teacher's Training College. Maryland St. Liverpool. "Mistake". TOP BILLING.
Oct. 22. Lion Hotel Ballroom. Warrington. "MAJORITY" (London). "Fix - with Steve
Oct. 23. English Martyrs. Litherland. "Tomorrow's People". TOP BILLING. Aldo".
Oct. 25. Mardi Gras Club. Liverpool. "Escorts".
Oct. 26. Mirabel - Beachcomber Club. Seel St. Liverpool. "Concords". TOP BILLING
Oct. 28. Downbeat Club. Liverpool. "Rory Storm & the Hurricanes". TOP BILLING.
Oct. 29. Students Union. Liverpool University. "TEMPERANCE SEVEN".
Oct. 30. N.A.L.G.O. West Derby. Liverpool.
Oct. 31. Casino Club. Marton. BLACKPOOL. "Johnny Breeze & the Atlantics". TOP
Nov. 4. Mardi Gras Club. Liverpool. "Calderstones". TOP BILLING. BILLING.
Nov. 5. Conservative Club. BARROW.
Nov. 7. Mr. Smith's Club. Winsford.
Nov. 8. Beachcomber Club. Liverpool. "Jason Eddie & the Centermen". TOP BILLING.
Nov. 12. Lion Hotel Ballroom. Warrington. "Soulseekers" (LONDON). "Beechwoods".
Nov. 13. Mardi Gras Club. Liverpool. "Dresdens". TOP BILLING.
Nov. 16. Salisbury & McNair Hall. Liverpool University. "Prowlers". TOP BILLING.
Nov. 18. Casino Club. WESTHOUGHTON. "The Spiders" (Blackpool). TOP BILLING.
Nov. 19. Mardi Gras Club. Liverpool. "Dresdens". TOP BILLING.
Nov. 20. N.A.L.G.O. West Derby. Liverpool.
Nov. 21. South Shore Tennis Club. BLACKPOOL.
Nov. 24. Peppermint Lounge. Liverpool. "Vogue". TOP BILLING.
Nov. 25. Downbeat Club. Liverpool. "Mistake". TOP BILLING.
Nov. 26. Student's Union. Liverpool University. "SOUNDS INCORPORATED" (Brian
Nov. 27. C.I.Club. West Derby. Liverpool.   Epstein).
Nov. 29. Beachcomber Club. Seel. Liverpool. "Pikkins". TOP BILLING.

SATURDAY, SEPTEMBER 17, 1966

MONDAY, SEPTEMBER 19, 1966

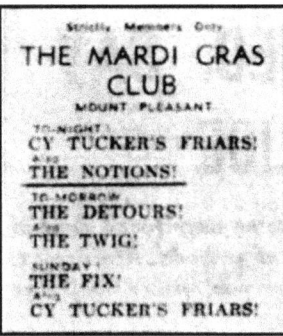

FRIDAY, OCTOBER 7, 1966

SUNDAY, OCTOBER 16, 1966

SUNDAY, OCTOBER 23, 1966

FRIDAY, OCTOBER 28, 1966

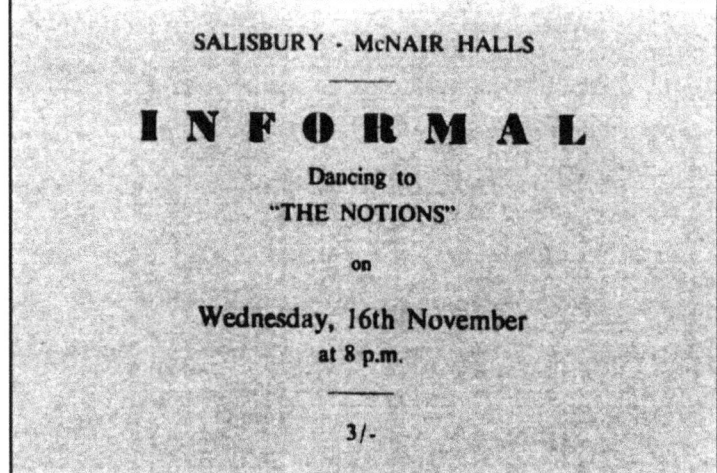

WEDNESDAY, NOVEMBER 16, 1966

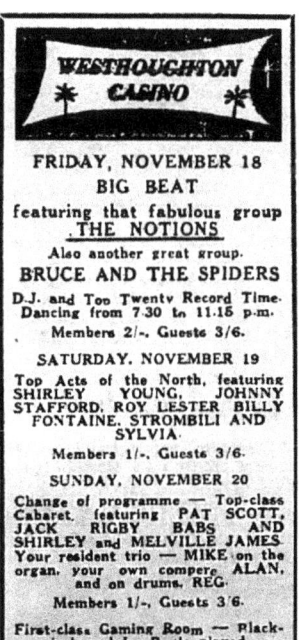

FRIDAY, NOVEMBER 18, 1966

THURSDAY, NOVEMBER 24, 1966

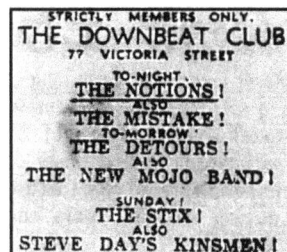

FRIDAY, NOVEMBER 25, 1966

TUESDAY, NOVEMBER 29, 1966

E N G A G E M E N T S . (CONTINUED).

1966.

Dec. 3. Lion Hotel Ballroom. WARRINGTON. "Maze". "Vampires".
Dec. 4. Mardi Gras Club. Liverpool. "Cordes". TOP BILLING.
Dec. 5. Casino Club. BOLTON. "Symptons". (Wigan). TOP BILLING.
Dec. 7. Peppermint Lounge. Liverpool. "Seftons". "Protems". TOP BILLING.
Dec. 8. Elder Dempster Lines. Kingston House. Liverpool. "Art & Sound". TOP BILLING.
Dec. 9. Casino Club. Westhoughton. "Shymms". (Wigan) TOP BILLING.
Dec. 10. Mardi Gras Club. Liverpool. "Connoisseurs". TOP BILLING.
Dec. 11. Inland Revenue Xmas Dance. Mons Hotel. Bootle. "Laurie Lee Quintet".
Dec. 12. Mr. Smith's Club. WINSFORD. TOP BILLING.
Dec. 13. Casino Club. BLACKPOOL. "Johnny Breeze & Atlantics" (BLACKPOOL). TOP BILLING.
Dec. 14. Cardinal Godfrey School Dance. C.I.Club. "Pikkins". TOP BILLING.
Dec. 15. Metal Box Co. Staff Dance. Aintree. "Fix".
Dec. 17. St. George's Hall. Liverpool. "Ronnie Aldrich & the Squadronaires" B.B.C. Dance Orchestra.
Dec. 18. Casino Club. Haweside Lane. BLACKPOOL. "Spiders". TOP BILLING.
Dec. 19. South Shore Tennis Club. BLACKPOOL.
Dec. 22. Peppermint Lounge. Liverpool.
Dec. 24. Downbeat Club. Liverpool. "Detours". "Steve Day's Kinsmen". TOP BILLING.
Dec. 24. Mardi Gras Club. Liverpool. "HILLSIDERS". "Detours".
Dec. 29. South Shore Tennis Club. BLACKPOOL.
Dec. 30. C.I.Club. West Derby. Liverpool.
Dec. 31. South Shore Tennis Club. New Year Party.

1967.

Jan. 1. Casino Club. Hawes Side Lane. BLACKPOOL. "Spiders". TOP BILLING.
Jan. 6. Lt. Worrall. (5th Kings) 21st Party. Linnet Lane. Liverpool.
Jan. 7. Talbot Conservative Club. Melbourne St. BLACKPOOL.
Jan. 8. Mardi Gras Club. Liverpool. "Connoisseurs". TOP BILLING.
Jan. 13. Carlton Club. WARRINGTON. "Silhouettes". TOP BILLING.
Jan. 14. Mardi Gras Club. Liverpool. "Them Calderstones". TOP BILLING.
Jan. 15. Casino Club. Hawes Side Lane. BLACKPOOL. "The New Slant". TOP BILLING.
Jan. 20. Salisbury & McNair. Liverpool University. Hall of Residence.
        "TONY RIVERS & THE CASTAWAYS". "Chris.Lamb & the Universals".
Jan. 21. Kabel Club. PRESCOT. "Tiffany's Showband".
Jan. 21. Christ College. Woolton Road. Liverpool. "Phoenix Sound". TOP BILLING.
Jan. 22. Mardi Gras Club. Liverpool. "Connoisseurs". TOP BILLING.
Jan. 27. Downbeat Club. Liverpool. "Detours". TOP BILLING.
Jan. 28. Talbot Conservative Club. BLACKPOOL.
Jan. 29. Mardi Gras Club. Liverpool. "Calderstones". TOP BILLING.
Jan. 31. Mardi Gras Club. Liverpool. "Runaways". TOP BILLING.
Feb. 4. Memorial Hall. NORTHWICH. "Guy Darrell". "Gnomes of Zurich".(London).
Feb. 5. The CAVERN. "Hari Kari".(Manchester). "Prowlers".
Feb. 10. Floral Hall. Southport. N.A.L.G.O. Annual Ball. "Ted Peters Orchestra".
Feb. 11. Y.M.C.A. North Street. ST. HELENS. "Johnny Breeze & Atlantics". TOP BILLING.
Feb. 12. Casino Club. BLACKPOOL. "New Slant". TOP BILLING.
Feb. 17. Carlton Club. WARRINGTON. "Sons & Daughters" (M/C). TOP BILLING.
Feb. 18. Mardi Gras Club. Liverpool. "Connoisseurs". TOP BILLING.
Feb. 19. Mardi Gras Club. Liverpool. "Runaways". TOP BILLING.
Feb. 24. Students Union. Liverpool University. "ALAN PRICE SET". "Obsession".

THURSDAY, DECEMBER 8, 1966

RIVER HOUSE

CHRISTMAS DANCE

to be held at

Kingston House, James Street, Liverpool

On THURSDAY, 8th DECEMBER, 1966

Dancing from 8 p.m. till 11 p.m. to

"The New Art and Sound" and "The Notions"

TICKETS 4/- EACH. BAR EXTENSION

FRIDAY, DECEMBER 9, 1966

WESTHOUGHTON CASINO

BIG BEAT ALL WEEK-END
FRIDAY, DECEMBER 9
Return visit from Liverpool of that great group
THE NOTIONS
Also THE SHYMS
Members 2/-. Guests 3/6.
SATURDAY, DECEMBER 10
The fantastic
ELECTONES
Also The BLUES BY FIVE
SUNDAY, 11th.
The fabulous
INCAS
Plus GIDEONS WAY
D.J. and Top Twenty Record Time.
Dancing each evening from 7.30 to 11.15 p.m.
Members 2/-. Guests 3/6.
Your resident trio — BARRY on the Organ; your own compere ALAN, and on Drums, REG.
First-class Gaming Room, Blackjack and La Boule played.
FORTHCOMING ATTRACTIONS
Westhoughton Casino Club — December 16, for one night only —
America's Star of Rock 'n' Roll
The One and Only —
LITTLE RICHARD
(He's the Greatest)
Also Supporting Groups
Members 5/-. Guests 7.6

SATURDAY, DECEMBER 10, 1966

Strictly Members Only
THE MARDI GRAS CLUB
MOUNT PLEASANT.
TO-NIGHT!
THE PROWLERS!
ALSO
THE MISTAKE!
TO-MORROW!
THE NOTIONS!
ALSO
THE CONNOISSEURS!
SUNDAY!
CY TUCKER'S FRIARS!
ALSO
THE DRESDENS!

THURSDAY, DECEMBER 15, 1966

THE METAL BOX CO.,
Park Lane, Aintree.
THE FIX!
THE NOTIONS
THURSDAY, DECEMBER 15.
at 7.30 p.m.
Price 4/-. Buses 30, 93, 92, 20, 61, 500 and 57a.

SATURDAY, DECEMBER 17, 1966

KRAFT No 1397

FACTORY CHRISTMAS BUFFET DANCE

ST. GEORGE'S HALL, LIVERPOOL.

dancing to RONNIE ALDRICH and his SQUADRONAIRS

also THE THREE NOTIONS

SATURDAY, 17th DECEMBER 1966. 7-30 p.m. — 11-45 p.m.
NO ADMITTANCE AFTER 9-45 p.m.   LICENCED BAR (Extended Licence)
:: ADMIT ONE — TICKET NOT TRANSFERABLE ::

THURSDAY, DECEMBER 22, 1966

PEPPERMINT LOUNGE
FRASER STREET, LIVERPOOL
TO-NIGHT (THURSDAY) TO-NIGHT
NOTIONS
NOTIONS
ADMISSION BEFORE 8.30 ONLY 3/6
Strictly Members Only.

SATURDAY, DECEMBER 24, 1966

STRICTLY MEMBERS ONLY
THE DOWNBEAT CLUB
77 VICTORIA STREET.
TO-NIGHT
THE ESCORTS!
ALSO
THE B.R.I.C.!
TO-MORROW
THE NOTIONS!
ALSO
STEVE DAY'S KINSMEN!
AND
THE DETOURS!
OPEN MONDAY
BOXING DAY.

SUNDAY, JANUARY 8, 1967

Strictly Members Only
THE MARDI GRAS CLUB
Mount Pleasant
TO-NIGHT!
THE BEECHWOODS!
also
THE DETOURS!
TO-MORROW!
CY TUCKER'S FRIARS!
also
THE TWIG!
SUNDAY!
THE NOTIONS!
also
THE CONNOISSEURS!

SATURDAY, JANUARY 14, 1967

STRICTLY MEMBERS ONLY
THE MARDI GRAS CLUB
MOUNT PLEASANT
To-night!
THE FIX!
also
THE CONNOISSEURS!
To-morrow!
THE NOTIONS!
also
THEM CALDERSTONES!
Sunday!
CY TUCKER'S FRIARS!
also
THE DETOURS!

SATURDAY, JANUARY 21, 1967

CHRIST COLLEGE VOLLEY BALL

Present

The Notions

and

The Phoenix Sound

on Saturday, 21st January, 1967
at 7.30 p.m.

Tickets .. 4/-   Licensed Bar

ENGAGEMENTS. (CONTINUED).

1967.

Feb.	25.	Kabel Club. PRESCOT. "B-Jays". TOP BILLING.
Feb.	25.	Lion Hotel Ballroom. WARRINGTON. "The Gods".(London)."Executives"(B'pool).
Feb.	26.	Casino Club. Marton. BLACKPOOL. "Spiders". TOP BILLING.
Mar.	3.	Rathbone Hall of Residence. Liverpool University. FORMAL DANCE. "Seftons". "Savoy Jazzmen". "Jazz Depression" (Jug Band). TOP BILLING.
Mar.	4.	Memorial Hall. NORTHWICH. "The CREATION". (LONDON).
Mar.	5.	Mardi Gras Club. Liverpool. "The Fix" with Steve Aldo.
Mar.	10.	Starlight Room. Kingsway Club. SOUTHPORT. "Silhouettes" TOP BILLING.
Mar.	11.	Mardi Gras Club. Liverpool. "Cordes". TOP BILLING.
Mar.	12.	Downbeat Club. Liverpool. "Colts". TOP BILLING.
Mar.	17.	Mardi Gras Club. Liverpool. "Expressions". TOP BILLING.
Mar.	18.	Warrington Co.Op. Hall. WARRINGTON. "Denims". "23rd Image". TOP BILLING.
Mar.	19.	Maghull Y.C. "Tyme & Motion". TOP BILLING.
Mar.	20.	South Shore Tennis Club. BLACKPOOL.
Mar.	23.	Gillmoss Labour Club. Liverpool. CHARITY SHOW IN AID OF LIVERPOOL SPINAL BIFADA ASSOCIATION. SPONSORED BY RADIO CAROLINE.
Mar.	24.	(Good Friday). Talbot Conservative Club. BLACKPOOL.
Mar.	25.	Lion Hotel Ballroom. Warrington. "Bobby Hurst & the Big Taste". (NOTTS).
Mar.	26.	Mardi Gras Club. Liverpool. "Escorts".
Mar.	27.	Easter Casino Club. Marton. BLACKPOOL. "Beechwoods". TOP BILLING.
Mar.	31.	Downbeat Club. Liverpool. "Detours". TOP BILLING.
Apl.	1.	Mardi Gras Club. Liverpool. "Connoisseurs". TOP BILLING.
Apl.	2.	Mr. Smith's Club. WINSFORD.
Apl.	7.	Talbot Conservative Club. BLACKPOOL.
Apl.	8.	Gillmoss Labour Club.
Apl.	9.	Mardi Gras Club. Liverpool. "Tremas". TOP BILLING.
Apl.	14.	Carlton Club. Warrington. "Factotums".
Apl.	15.	Royal Oak Hotel. CHORLEY. 21st Birthday Party. Miss Angela Williams.Wigan.
Apl.	16.	Maghull Youth Club. "Konda Group". TOP BILLING.
Apl.	21.	Inland Revenue (Cricket Section) Dance. Mons Hotel. Bootle. TOP BILLING. "Pikkins". "Laurie Lee's Dance Orchestra".
Apl.	22.	Ocean Room. Blackpool Tower. BLACKPOOL. "Mike Hurst & the Trekkers" JOINT TOP BILLING. (PRESTON.)
Apl.	23.	Mardi Gras Club. Liverpool. "Cordes". TOP BILLING.
Apl.	28.	Talbot ConservativeClub. BLACKPOOL.
Apl.	29.	Kabel Club. PRESCOT. "Admins". TOP BILLING.
Apl.	29.	LION Hotel Ballroom. Bridge Street. WARRINGTON. "VARIATIONS".(Exeter).
Apl.	30.	Downbeat Club. Liverpool. "Beechwoods". JOINT TOP BILLING.
May.	5.	Mardi Gras Club. Liverpool. "Runaways". TOP BILLING.
May.	6.	Faculty of Technology. MANCHESTER. "MANFRED MANN".
May.	6.	Maghull Youth Club. MAGHULL. "Konda Group". TOP BILLING.
May.	12.	Starlight Club. Kingsway. SOUTHPORT. "Connoisseurs". "Munchkins". TOP BILLING.
May.	13.	Mardi Gras Club. Liverpool. "Concordes". TOP BILLING.
May.	17.	GRANADA T.V. Studios. MANCHESTER. "FIRST TIMERS" AUDITION. by JOHN HAMP.
May.	21.	Maghull Youth Club. MAGHULL. "Detonators". TOP BILLING.
May.	26.	Downbeat Club. Liverpool. "Beechwoods". TOP BILLING.
May.	27.	Co-Operative Hall. Warrington. "B-Jays". "Jinx Soul Band". TOP BILLING.
May.	28.	Mardi Gras Club. Liverpool. "Connoisseurs". TOP BILLING.
May.	29.	South Shore Tennis Club. BLACKPOOL.

AUDITION FOR GRANADA TV SHOW "FIRST TIMERS" THE 'NOTIONS' SANG 'VOICE YOUR CHOICE'

SATURDAY
FEBRUARY 25, 1967

```
                                    25. FEB. 1967.
           LION HOTEL BALLROOM. WARRINGTON.

7.30 – 8.15.   Executives (Blackpool).
8.15 – 9.00    The Gods.  (London).
9.00 – 9.40    Executives.
9.40 – 10.20   The Gods.
10.25 – 11.30  The NOTIONS.
```

FRANK DELANEY'S SET LIST FOR THE 'NOTIONS'
SATURDAY, FEBRUARY 25, 1967

STRICTLY MEMBERS ONLY
THE MARDI GRAS CLUB
MOUNT PLEASANT
TO-NIGHT!
THE CONNOISSEURS!
ALSO
THE CORDES!
TO-MORROW!
THE RUNAWAYS!
ALSO
THE DRESDENS!
SUNDAY!
THE FIX!
ALSO
THE NOTIONS!

SUNDAY
MARCH 5, 1967

STRICTLY MEMBERS ONLY
THE MARDI GRAS CLUB
MOUNT PLEASANT
TO-NIGHT!
THE BEECHWOODS!
also
THE CONNOISSEURS!
TO-MORROW!
THE NOTIONS!
also
THE CORDES!
SUNDAY!
THE RUNAWAYS!
also
THEM CALDERSTONES!

SATURDAY
MARCH 11, 1967

Strictly Members Only.
THE MARDI GRAS CLUB
Mount Pleasant
To-night!
THE CALDERSTONES!
also
CHAPTER SIX
To-morrow!
THE ESCORTS!
also
THE NOTIONS!

SUNDAY
MARCH 26, 1967

Strictly Members Only!
THE MARDI GRAS CLUB,
MOUNT PLEASANT.
To-night:
THE DETOURS!
also
CHAPTER SIX!
To-morrow:
THE CONNOISSEURS!
also
THE CALDERSTONES!
Sunday:
THE NOTIONS!
also
THE TREMAS!

SUNDAY
APRIL 9, 1967

STRICTLY MEMBERS ONLY
THE MARDI GRAS CLUB
MOUNT PLEASANT
TO-NIGHT!   TO-NIGHT!
       THE FIX!
          also
       THE TWIG!
TO-MORROW!   TO-MORROW!
THE DETOURS!
also
THE PRINCIPALS!
SUNDAY!   SUNDAY!
       THE NOTION!
          also
       THE CORDES!

SUNDAY
APRIL 23, 1967

STRICTLY MEMBERS ONLY.
THE DOWNBEAT CLUB
77 VICTORIA ST. CENTRAL 2396
TO-NIGHT!
THE CONCORDES!
ALSO
FRED'S LOT!
TO-MORROW!
THE EXPRESSIONS!
ALSO
THE STIX!
SUNDAY!
THE BEECHWOODS!
ALSO
THE NOTIONS!

SUNDAY
APRIL 30, 1967

STRICTLY MEMBERS ONLY
THE MARDI GRAS CLUB
MOUNT PLEASANT
TO-NIGHT!
THE NOTIONS!
ALSO
THE RUNAWAYS!
TO-MORROW!
THE DETOURS!
ALSO
THE CORDES!
SUNDAY!
THE FIX!
ALSO
THE CONNOISSEURS!

FRIDAY
MAY 5, 1967

THE MARDI GRAS CLUB
Mount Pleasant
To-night!
THE DIMPLES!
also
THE BEECHWOODS
To-morrow!
THE NOTIONS!
also
THE CONCORDES!
Sunday!
THE RUNAWAYS!
also
THE CORDES!

SATURDAY
MAY 13, 1967

STRICTLY MEMBERS ONLY
THE DOWNBEAT CLUB
77 VICTORIA STREET. CEN. 2396
TO-NIGHT
THE NOTIONS!
also
THE BEECHWOODS!
TO-MORROW!
FRED'S LOT!
also
THE PROTEMS!
SUNDAY
THE ESCORTS!
also
BOSSOUNDSENSATION!
BOOKER T. &
THE DRIFTERS!

FRIDAY
MAY 26, 1967

THE KABELS
PRESCOT TOWN SOCIAL CENTRE
HOPE STREET, PRESCOT
To-night
THE PRO-TEMS
To-morrow
THE NOTIONS
THE BJAYS
No person under 18 admitted

ENGAGEMENTS. (CONTINUED).

1967.

June.	2.	Mardi Gras Club. Liverpool. "Expressions". TOP BILLING.
June.	3.	Fylde Rugby Club. LYTHAM. ST.ANNES.
June.	4.	Downbeat Club. Liverpool. "Seftons". TOP BILLING.
June.	10.	Kabel Club. Prescot. "Munchkins". TOP BILLING.
June.	10.	Lion Hotel Ballroom. WARRINGTON. "Robert Hurst & Big Taste". (NOTTS). "Motifs" (BURY).
June.	11.	Mardi Gras Club. Liverpool. "Connoisseurs". TOP BILLING.
June.	16.	Mardi Gras Club. Liverpool. "Detours". TOP BILLING.
June.	17.	Memorial Hall. NORTHWICH.
July.	15.	Lion Hotel. Warrington. "Montannas" (Wolverhampton). Connoisseurs.
July.	15.	Kabel Club. Prescot. "Gray Soul Band". TOP BILLING.
July.	16.	Downbeat Club. Liverpool. "Stir". TOP BILLING.
July.	17.	Casino Club. Blackpool.
July.	21.	Downbeat Club. Liverpool. "Concords". TOP BILLING.

SATURDAY
JUNE 10, 1967

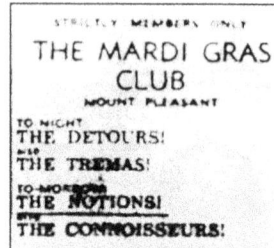
SUNDAY
JUNE 11, 1967

FRIDAY
JUNE 16, 1967

'OTHER' GROUPS AND ENTERTAINERS THAT THE 'NOTIONS' APPEARED WITH

GROUPS WITH WHOM THE "NOTIONS" HAVE APPEARED.

A.
Abstracts. (1)
Astrals.
Aristocrats. (HUDDERSFIELD)
Abstracts. (2)
Approachers.
Almost Blues.
Aarons.
Andy & Chevlons (GLASGOW).
Amos Bonny & T.T.s.
Alibis.
Alexis Korner. (DECCA)
Aztecs.
ANIMALS.
Amigos.
Atlantics (Johnny Breeze). BLACKPOOL.
Art & Sound.
Aldrich, Ronnie & Squadronaires. (B.B.C.)
Admins.

B.
Black Knights.
Blue Diamonds & Tony Allen (M/c).
Bobby & Halers.
Blackwells.
Bobby & Batchelors.
Billy Butler & Tuxedos.
Black Abbots. (CHESTER).
Black Velvets.
BARRON KNIGHTS.
BIG THREE.
Barney Beats.
Bruce Harris & Cavaliers.
Boot Hill Billies.
Beat Boys (WIGAN).
Barristers.
Bluesett.
Blues & Root. (BIRMINGHAM).
Blues Four.
BO STREET RUNNERS. (LONDON).
BEAT MERCHANTS. (SOUTHAMPTON).
B - Jays.
Bumblies.
Bruce & the Spiders. (BLACKPOOL).
Black Dynamites.
Big Three. (2).
Blue Diamond Combo.
Blues Gospel Unit.
Bentics.
Bobby Nick's Orchestra.
Backdor Men. (MANCHESTER).
Breakers. (MANCHESTER).
Beechwoods.
BILLY J. KRAMER & DAKOTAS.
Bobby Grey Soul Band.
BIG TASTE, Bobby Hurst. (NOTTINGHAM).

"C".
CHICK GRAHAM & COASTERS.
Chris & Aristocrats.
Coins.
Cordes.
Cordells.
Crescendos. (CANADA)
Cortinas. (BOLTON)
Concords.
CRESTERS. (SHEFFIELD)
Casuals.
Centermen.
Cy Tucker's Friars.
CLAYTON SQUARES.
Classics. (ST. HELENS)
City Slickers.
Citadels.
Clansmen.
Chessmen.
Cracksmen.
Commancheros.
Condors.
Conchords. (MANCHESTER)
Corsairs.
Chancellors.
CHANTS.
Cossacks. (SOMERSET).
Caveners.
Challengers.
Citybeats.
Clearways.
Calderstones.
Comets.
Crestas.
Country Gentlemen. (MANCHESTER)
Carpetbaggers.
Chequers.
Christine & Wranglers.
Chariots.
Connoisseurs.
Countdowns.
Colours.
Corvettes. (GLASGOW)
Creeping Vines. (PRESTON)
Country Rhythm Boys.
Castaways. & Tony Rivers.
Creation. (LONDON).

"D".

DENNY SEYTON & THE SABRES.
Denny Curtis & Renegades.
Del Remos.
Dominators.
Detonators.
Dimensions.
Dr. Feelgoods. (MANCHESTER).
DERRY WILKIE & THE OTHERS.
Derry Wilkie & the Pressmen.
Delmonts.
DENNISONS.
Denems.
Denims.
Defiants.
Dean Stacey & Detonators.
Danny Havoc & Secrets.
Dions.
DAVE BERRY & CRUISERS.
Duke Gordon Showband.
DENNY SEYTON SHOWBAND.
Dentons.
Denny Ryan & Ravens.
Drumbeats.
Dawnbreakers. (LEEDS)
Douglas de Belle Quartet. (SOUTHPORT)
Detours.
Defenders.
Deans.
Du-Fays.
Dark Ages.
Demokrats. (MANCHESTER)
Deek Rivers & Big Sound. (MANCHESTER)
Del Raymond & Estelles.
Dee - Jays.
Dene & Citizens. (MANCHESTER)
Dusty Road Ramblers.
Deacons. (CHESTER)
DRIFTERS. (U.S.A.)
Dene Wayne & Exiles. (CREWE)
Dave Bowie & the Buzz. (LONDON)
Dresdens.
DARRELL, GUY. (C.B.S. Records).

"E".

EXECUTIVES.
Expressions.
Easybeats.
Excelles.
ESCORTS.
EARL PRESTON'S T.T.'s (MERSEYBEAT L/P)
EARL PRESTON'S REALMS.
Exotics. (CREWE)
Excerts.
EARL ROYCE & OLYMPICS.
Elks.
Exits.
Earl Scott & Talismen.
Earthlings.
Eric Pepp Showband. (WARRINGTON)
Elite. (NORTHWICH)
Evans (Bob) & Five Shillings.
Evan (John) R. & B. Band.
Embers West. (LONDON).

"F".

FORTUNES.
Feelgoods.
FOURMOST.
FIVE EMBERS.
Freddie Corbett's Dance Band.
FREDDIE STARR & MIDNIGHTERS.
Falcons.
FAIRIES. (LONDON)
Flintstones.
Futurists.
Five Shillings.
FOUR PENNIES. (BLACKBURN)
Freddie Starr & Delmonts.
FENMAN.
Four Travellers.
Four Gents.
Fugitives. (CHESTER)
Forgers.
Fables.
Factotums. (MANCHESTER)
Flower Pot Men.
Four Dimensions.
Four Just Men.
Five Nites. (WARRINGTON)
Farrier's Blues. (MANCHESTER)
Fix with Eddie Cave.
Fix with Steve Aldo.

"G"

Georgians.
Greenbeats. (IRELAND)
Group One.
Griff Parry Five.
Gibsons.
Gideon's Few. (MANCHESTER)
Gerry de Ville & City Kings.
Galaxies.
Gretty (Jim).
Gnomes of Zurich. (London).
GODS. (LONDON).
Gray Soul Band.

"H".

HOLLIES.
Hickory Stix (STOKE)
HERMAN'S HERMITS.
Hi-Five.
HILLSIDERS.
Huntsmen.
Hustlers.
HARLEMS.
Harpos.
Hideaways.
Hi-Lites.
Hispanos.
Heebie Jeebies. (BLACKPOOL)
Hignett Quartet. (CHESTER)
Hari-Kari. (MANCHESTER).

"I".
IN CROWD.
Inmates.
Incas.
IAN & THE ZODIACS.
Illusions.
Invaders.
Inbeats.
IAN CRAWFORD & BOOMERANGS. (MANCHESTER)

"J"
Johnny Gus Set.
JOHNNY KIDD & THE PIRATES.
John Prior Orchestra.
JIMMY NICHOL & THE SHUBDUBS. (LONDON)
Johnny Ringo's Colts.
Jensons.
Jay & the Juniors.
JEANNIE & THE BIG GUYS.
J.J. & the Hi-Lites.
Jaguars.
Jackie Gleason & Topspots.
Johnny Marlowe & Whipcords.
Jazz Depression. (Jug Band).
Jinx Soul Band.

"K".
KIRKBYS.
Kinsleys.
Kirklands Dance Band.
KUBAS.
KEITH POWELL & VALOTS. (BIRMINGHAM)
Klaxons.
Karacters.
Kruzads.
KINGSIZE TAYLOR & THE DOMINOES.
Kobras.
KARL DENVER TRIO.
Kris Ryan & Questions.
KINKS.
Kop.
Konchords. (MANCHESTER)
Kinsmen. (Folk)
Kenda Group.

"L".
Lee Eddy Five.
LEE CASTLE & THE BARONS.
Laurie Lee Orchestra.
Liver Birds.
Lee Eddy & the Chevrons.
LULU & THE LUVVERS.
Lenny & the Teammates.
Lavelles.
LORAINE GREY & THE SHAKEOUTS.
LANCASTRIANS.
LITTLE FRANKIE & COUNTRY GENTLEMEN.
League of Gentlemen (LONDON)
Laurie Lee Quintet.

"M".
MERSEYBEATS.
Mr. Smith & Sum People.
MILLIE & THE EMBERS. (LONDON)
Mysteries.
Memphis Three.
MIKE COTTON SOUND. (LONDON)
Mafia.
Markfour.
Mark Peter's Method.
MARK PETER'S SILHOUETTES.
Mastersounds.
MASTERMINDS.
Mersey Blue Beats.
MOJOS.
Manchester Jazz Band.
Mersey Four.
Marescas.
MIGHTY AVENGERS. (BIRMINGHAM)
Musketeers.
MANFRED MANN.
Mike Stevens & the Overlanders.
Mersey Squares.
Music Students.
Michael Allen Group.
Mr. Lee & Co.
MARAUDERS. (STOKE)
Motifs.
Modes.
Megatones. (WARRINGTON.)
Mersey Gonks.
Maraccas.
Missing Links.
MEAZLES. (MANCHESTER)
Monos.
Mike Taylor & Marion Stockley.
Merv's Bardots. (MANCHESTER)
MINDBENDERS. (MANCHESTER)
Moonie Gang. (BLACKPOOL)
Mistake.
MARK LEEMAN FIVE. (LONDON)
Mop.
M.I.5. Group (LONDON)
MAJORITY. (LONDON)
MAZE. (LONDON).
Munchkins.
Motifs. (BURY).
Montannas. (Wolverhampton).

"N".
NOCTURNS.
Newtowns.
Nomads.
Nightwalkers.
NORTHERN DANCE ORCHESTRA & B.B.C. ORCHESTRA.
New Slant. (BLACKPOOL).

"O".
Optimists Incorporated.
Obsession.

"P".
Pawns.
POWELL & THE 5 DIMENSIONS. (LONDON)
Panthers.
PATHFINDERS.
Pilgrims.
Pretenders.
Prophets.
Profits.
Poets.
Plebs. (LONDON)
Phil's Feelgoods. (MANCHESTER)
Profiles.
Pack.
Pack of Cards. (CREWE)
Playboys. (MANCHESTER)
Pikkins.
Pagans. (LONDON)
Phil Ryan & the Crestas.
Prowlers.
PRETTY THINGS. (LONDON)
Phlok. (CUMBERLAND)
PEASANTS. (LONDON)
P.J. PROBY. (U.S.A.)
PETE BEST FOUR.
Psychos.
Pat and the Stormers.
Pacifics. (CREWE)
Precinots. (SOUTHPORT)
POWERHOUSE SIX. (MANCHESTER)
Pitiful.
Petals. (MANCHESTER)
Pobbles. (BOLTON)
Phoenix Sound.
Peters, Les Orchestra.
PRICE, ALAN, SET. (LONDON).

"Q".
Quotations. (LONDON)

"R".
RUSTIKS. (DEVON) (BRIAN EPSTEIN)
Rod Simon Combo.
Rhythmics. (KENDAL)
Rooters.
Ricky & Dominant Four.
RANCHERS.
R. & B. INC.
REMO FOUR. (BRIAN EPSTEIN)
RORY STORM & THE HURRICANES.
RATTLES. (GERMAN No. I.)
Ricky Gleason & the Topspots.
ROADRUNNERS.
Red River Jazzmen.
Riot Squad.
Rita & the Squad.
Rainmakers. (MANCHESTER)
Richmond Group.
Rita & the Vogue.
Russ and the V. Tones.
Runaways.
Renicks.
Rats.
Renegades.
Roaring Storms. (BLACKBURN)
Reflections. (STOKE)
Realm.
Rigg.
Rod Hamer Dance Band.
Ramblers. (BLACKPOOL)
ROCKING VICARS.

"S".
SEARCHERS.
Some People. (CHESTER)
Spidermen.
Secrets.
SCREAMING LORD SUCH & THE SAVAGES.
Shondells.
SONNY WEBB & THE CASCADES.
St. Louis Checks.
Silverstones.
Stereos.
Savva & the Democrats.
Saints.
SOULSEEKERS. (LONDON)
Senators. (MANCHESTER)
Senators. (BLACKPOOL)
Senators.
Strolling Bones. (SOMERSET)
Stylos. (MANCHESTER)
Scorpions. (CREWE)
Script. (WIDNES)
Stix. (RUNCORN)
SILKIE. (LONDON). (BRIAN EPSTEIN)
Saxons.
SHAKEOUTS. (SHEFFIELD)
Shakedowns.
Smokestacks.
St.John's Precinots.
Steve Day's Drifters.
Strollers with Johnny Doran.
Steve Allen & the Flyovers.
Styles. (WARRINGTON)
Seftons.
SMALL FACES. (LONDON)
Surf Side Six. (BLACKBURN)
St. Franklin.
Steve Day's Kinsmen.
Smith's People. (WINSFORD)
Some Other Guys. (MANCHESTER)
Seniors with Howie Casey (BOLTON)
Shymms. (WIGAN)
SANDS. (LONDON)
Spiders (BLACKPOOL)
SOUNDS INCORPORATED. (LONDON)(BRIAN EPSTEIN)
Symptons. (Wigan).
Silhouettes.
Sons & Daughters. (MANCHESTER).
Savoy Jazzmen.

"T".
TEMPERANCE SEVEN.
Top spots.
Terry Hines Sextet.
Tributes. (1)
Triumphs.
Tom Hughes Orchestra.
TOPLINS. (Rael Brook)
Tabs.
Trakkers.
T.T.'s
Terry Gore Jazzmen.
Tokens.
Traders.
T.L. Groundhogs.
Travelors.
T.T.'s with Amos & Carl.
TIFFANY'S DIMENSIONS.
TIFFANY'S THOUGHTS.
Trappers.
Talismen.
Tributes. (2).
Thunderbirds with Mike Byrne.
Trendsetters Limited.
Tommy Smith's Quintet.
Tenor C's.
Tom & Brennie.
TONY JACKSON & THE VIBRATIONS.
Times. (WARRINGTON)
Timon. (Folk Singer)
TROGGS.
Tomorrow's People.
Twenty Third Image.(WARRINGTON).
Tyme & Motion.
Tremas.
Trekkers (With Mike Hurst).PRESTON.

"U".
UNDERTAKERS.
Uzz Strangers.
Universals & Chris Lamb. (LONDON)

"V".
Varasounds.
Vic & the Spidermen.
Vic & the T.T.'s
Vigilantes. (MANCHESTER)
Vikki & the Moonlighters.
VICTOR BROXX TRAIN.
Victors.
Vogue.
Vampires.
VARIATIONS. (EXETER).

"W".
WHO. (LONDON)
WALKER BROTHERS. (U.S.A)
Wall City Jazzmen (CHESTER)
Whole Scene.
Warriors. (MANCHESTER)

"Y".
YARDBIRDS. (LONDON)

"Z".
Zenith Six. (LONDON)
Zephors.

A LIST OF VENUES THAT THE 'NOTIONS' PERFORMED AT

V E N U E S .

A.
Alexandra Hall. Crosby, Ballroom.
All Saints. Allerton.
Arts & Crafts College.
Alexandra Hall, Lower Room. Crosby.
Alexandra Hall. Heswall. Ches.

B.
Blair Hall. Walton.
Birkenhead Youth Club.
Birkdale, Palace Hotel.
Bemrose, State Cafe. L'pool.
Blue Angel. L'pool.
Blundells ands Hotel. Crosby.
Brimstage Hall. Heswall.
Bull's Head Hotel. Trentham.
Bank Park. Warrington.
Blue Ball. Liverpool.
Bootle Labour Club. Knowsley Road.
Blue Candle Club. Warrington.
Blue Ball Hotel. Risley. DERBY.

C.
Cavern.
C.I.Club. West Derby.
Cardinal Allen School. C.I.Club.
Chester College.
Childwall College.
Congregational Hall. Crosby.
Catacomb Club. Huddersfield.
Crane Hall. Liverpool.
Casino Ballroom. Leigh.
Civil Service Club. L'pool.
Co-Operative Hall. Warrington.
Co-Operative Social Club. St. Helens.
Carlton Ballroom. Rochdale.
Christ Church. Waterloo.
Cardinal Godfrey's O.B. C.I.Club.
Cavern Studios.
Cambridge Hall. Southport.
Catholic Chaplaincy. Brownlow Hill. L'pool.
Columba Hall. Widnes.
Community Centre. Speke.
Countess of Derby School. Netherton.
Clayton Lodge Hotel. Newcastle.
Casino Club. Blackpool.
Casino Club. Bolton.
College of Technology. Manchester.
Casino Ballroom. Pleasure Beach. Blackpool.
Conservative Club. BARROW.
Casino Club. Westhoughton.
Carlton Club. Warrington.
Christ College. Woolton. Liverpool.

D.
Derby Cinema. Burscough.
Durning Road Conservative Club.
Dunlop Social Club. Garston.
Downbeat Club. Liverpool.

E.
Empress Ballroom. Wigan.
English Martyrs. Litherland.
Eaglet. H.M.S. (R.N. Training Ship).
English Electric Social Club.
Elizabeth Gaskell College. Manchester.

F.
Floral Hall. Southport.
Forefield Lane Hall. Crosby.
Freshfield Ice Rink. Formby.
Faculty of Technology. Manchester.
Formby Flower Show.

G.
Gartan Club. L'pool.
Grafton Rooms. L'pool.
Gilmoss Labour Club.
Grange Valley Youth Club Hall. Haydock.
Greening Recreation Club. Warrington.

H.
Hope Hall. L'pool.
Hambleton Hall. Clubmoor.
Henderson's Stores. L'pool.
Hill's Ballroom. Oldham.
Hulme Hall. Port Sunlight.

I.
Inland Revenue. Seaforth.
Iron Door. L'pool.
Island Road Methodist Hall. Garston.

J.
Jacob's Social Club. Aintree.
Jacaranda Club. L'pool.

VENUES.

K.
Kendal Town Hall.
Kirkby Labour Club.
Klic Klic Club. Southport.
Knowsley Hall. LORD DERBY'S RESIDENCE.
Kabel Club. Prescot.
Kelvinator Club. Bromborough.
Kingston House. Liverpool.

L.
Lion Hotel. Warrington.
La Scala Ballroom. Runcorn.
Left Bank Club. Birkenhead.
Locarno Ballroom. Derby.
Lewis's Hall. Litherland.
L'pool King's Regt. T.A. 5th Kings.
Lockheed's Social Club. Speke.
Littlewood's Social Club. State Cafe.
Littlewoods Sports Club. Reece's Cafe.
Littlewoods Sports Club. Netherton.
Litherland Town Hall.
Litherland Labour Club.
Litherland British Legion.
Litherland Gala. Open Air.
Longview Labour Club.
Lowther Gardens Pavilion. Lytham St.Annes.
Lowlands. West Derby.
Lowlands. West Derby. Top Club.
Linnet Lane. (Private).

M.
Majestic Ballroom. Llandudno.
Majestic Ballroom. Birkenhead.
Maggie May Club. L'pool.
Merseyside Artists Association.
Majestic Ballroom. Wellington. Salop.
Maghull Institute.
Maghull Youth Club.
Marine Hall. Fleetwood.
Masonic Hall. Southport.
M.A.N.W.F.B. West Derby.
Memorial Hall. Northwich.
Merchant Taylor's Girls' School. Crosby.
Mersey View Ballroom. Frodsham.
Metal Box Club. Aintree.
Mardi Gras. Liverpool.
Mott Training College. Prescot.
Mr. Smith's Club. Hanley. S.O.T.
Mr. Smiths. Manchester.
Mr. Smiths. Winsford.
Mons Hotel Ballroom. Bootle.
Mossley Hill Institute.

N.
Nashville Tennessee Club. L'pool.
N.A.L.G.O. West Derby.
Norman's Cafe. Waterloo.
Norwest Social Club. Netherton.

O.
Our Lady, Queen of Peace, Social Club.
Our Lady, Queen of Peace, Youth Club.
Old Cathinian's. C.J.Club.
Ocean Room. Tower Ballroom. BLACKPOOL.

P.
Plaza Ballroom. St. Helens.
Palace Theatre. Pentre Broughton. Wrexham.
Peppermint Lounge. L'pool.
Philharmonic Hall. L'pool.
Palace Ballroom. Wigan.
Palais Ballroom. Ashton under Lyne.
Prescot Drill Hall.
Prescot Town F.C. Social Club.
Parr Hall. Warrington.
Pier Pavilion. Colwyn Bay. Nth.Wales.

Q.
Quaintways Ballroom. Chester.
Queen's Ballroom. Cleveleys. Blackpool.

R.
Ritz Ballroom. Rhyl. Nth.Wales.
Reece's Ballroom. 2nd Floor. L'pool.
Reece's Ballroom. 3rd Floor. L'pool.
Royal Iris. M.V. Cruise Boat.
Rushden Hall. Much Wenlock. Salop.
Rediffusion. (Blundellsands Hotel).
Ramp. Low Hill. L'pool.
Royal Hotel. Crewe.
Rice Lane Labour Club. Liverpool.
Roscoe Hall. Liverpool University.
Rathbone Hall. Liverpool University.
Royal Oak Hotel. CHORLEY.

VENUES.

S.
St. Edward's College. Sandfield Park.
St. Anne's Social Club. Kensington.
St. Faith's Hall. Crosby.
St. Helen's Youth Club. Crosby.
St. Thomas of Canterbury Hall. Waterloo.
St. Bernadette's Hall. Manchester.
St. Peter & St. Paul Youth Club. Waterloo.
St. Mary's Old Boys. Moor Lane. Crosby.
St. Edward's O.B. C.I.Club.
St. Elizabeth's Youth Club. Litherland.
St. Edmond's Youth Club. Waterloo.
St. George's Hall. Liverpool.
St. Katharine's College. Allerton.
St. Anselm's School. St. Helens.
St. Bede's School. Crosby.
St. Gerrard's Youth Club. Boundary St. L'pool.
St. Michael's Youth Club. Widnes.
St. Mary's Social Club. Kirkby.
St. Mary's Youth Club. Kirkby.
St. Kevin's Youth Club. Kirkby.
St. John's Hall. Bootle.
St. Nicholas' Youth Club. Blundellsands.
St. Luke's Hall. Crosby. ("Jive Hive").
Spider's Web Club. R.A.F. Haydock. St. Helens
Stockport Town Hall.
Sankey Y.P.F.Club.
Sankey Conservative Social Club.
South Lancs Regt. T.A. 4th. Warrington.
Seafield Convent. Waterloo.
Seafield House. Seaforth. L'pool.
Stork Hotel. L'pool.
Spastic School. West Derby.
Southport Technical School.
Strand Theatre Club & Ballroom. Winsford.
Savoy Hall. Waterloo.
St. William of York Youth Club. Thornton.
St. Mary's Parish Hall. Woolton.
Students Union. Liverpool University.
St. Theresa's Youth Club. Norris Green.
Seventy Six (76) Club. Burton on Trent.
South Shore Tennis Club. Blackpool.
St. Sebastian's Youth Club. West Derby.
Salisbury & McNair Hall. Liverpool University.

T.
Tudor Rooms. West Derby.
Temple Bar Restaurant. L'pool.
Temple Bar Ballroom. L'pool.
Tow Barr Inn. Egremont. Cumberland.
Twenty One Club. Croxteth.
Talbot Conservative Club. Blackpool.
Teacher's Training College. Padgate.
Teacher's Training College. Maryland St. Liverpool.

U.
U.S.A.C. Tanhouse Lane. Widnes.

V.
Vaughan's. West Derby.
Victorial Hall. Garston.
Victoria Hall. Formby.
Victoria Hotel. Blackpool.

W.
West Lancs. Golf Club.
Waterloo R.U.F.C. Pavilion. Blundellsands.
Wyncote. Allerton. L'pool University.
Winter Gardens. Waterloo.
Walker's Social Club. Warrington.
Wall's Disc Club. PRESTON.

Y.
Y.M.C.A. St. Helens.

A PHOTO ALBUM OF
THE 'PHANTOMS'
&
THE 'NOTIONS'
(IN CRONOLOGICAL ORDER)

THE 'PHANTOMS' FIRST LINE UP
OCTOBER 7, 1962 - MARCH 28, 1963

DAVE DELANEY
DAVE ARMSTRONG
PETE LITTLE
DAVE POWELL

L to R: Dave Armstrong, Pete Little, Dave Powell & Dave Delaney

L to R: Dave Powell, Pete Little, Dave Armstrong & Dave Delaney

L to R: Dave Powell, Dave Armstrong, Pete Little & Dave Delaney
The 'Phantoms' at the Congregational Hall, Crosby
November 1, 1962
(Their fourth ever live apperance)

L to R: Dave Powell, Dave Armstrong, Dave Delaney & Pete Little

L to R: Dave Powell, Dave Delaney & Pete Little   **L to R: Dave Armstrong, Dave Delaney & Pete Little**

All three photographs above taken at St. Nicholas Youth Club Dance - December 14, 1962

**Photo taken at the Delaney's home
sometime in 1962
L to R: Pete Little, Dave Delaney & Dave Powell**

THE 'PHANTOMS' SECOND LINE UP
MARCH 29, 1963 - APRIL 18, 1963

DAVE DELANEY
DAVE ARNSTRONG
DAVE POWELL

L to R: Dave Powell, Dave Armstrong & Dave Delaney
(Venue & date unknown - possibly April 15, 1963 St. Peter & St. Paul dance)

THE 'PHANTOMS' THIRD LINE UP
APRIL 19, 1963 - SEPTEMBER 24, 1963

DAVE DELANEY
DAVE ARMSTRONG
KEITH BALCOMB

L to R: Dave Delaney, Dave Armstrong & Keith Balcomb (Undated)

L to R: Keith Balcomb, Dave Delaney & Dave Armstrong - May 1963

L to R: Keith Balcomb, Dave Armstrong & Dave Delaney
(Undated)

L to R: Keith Balcomb, Dave Armstrong & Dave Delaney
(Undated)

L to R: Keith Balcomb, Dave Armstrong & Dave Delaney
R.C.M.P. Mess, Seaforth Barracks, August 17, 1963

L to R: Keith Balcomb, Dave Armstrong & Dave Delaney

L to R: Keith Balcomb, Dave Armstrong & Dave Delaney
Both photos dated September 21, 1963 - Lewis's Hall, Beach Road, Litherland

---

THE 'NOTIONS' FIRST LINE UP
SEPTEMBER 25, 1963 - APRIL 19, 1964

DAVE DELANEY
DAVE ARMSTRONG
KEITH BALCOMB
JOE SHORT

THE 'PHANTOMS' OFFICALLY BECAME
THE 'NOTIONS' EFFECTIVE OCTOBER 1, 1963
THEREFORE, THIS PUBLICITY PHOTO, WHICH
INCLUDES JOE SHORT WAS OBVIOUSLY TAKEN
TO CONINCIDE WITH THE NAME CHANGE

L to R: Dave Armstrong, Dave Delaney, Keith Balcomb & Joe Short

L to R: Keith Balcomb, Dave Armstrong, Joe Short & Dave Delaney (Undated)

**L to R: Keith Balcomb, Joe Short, Dave Armstrong & Dave Delaney
The 'Notions' at the Cavern, February 1, 1964**

**A very significant day in the history of the Cavern as this was the first ever
Saturday afternoon 'Juvenile Club' session which went on to become a regular Cavern event.
The photographs on the following two pages were all taken at that first session.**

Dave Delaney, February 1, 1964

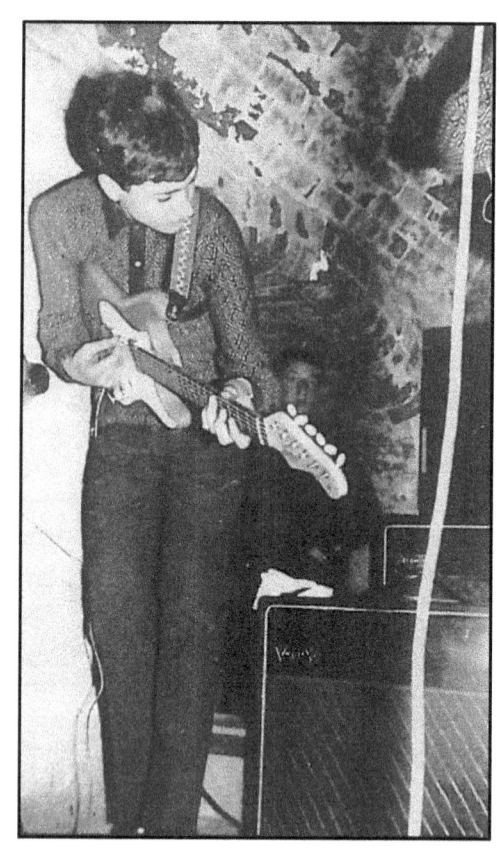

Keith Balcomb, February 1, 1964

**Dave Armstrong
February 1, 1964**

L to R;
Keith Balcomb
Joe Short
Dave Armstrong
Dave Delaney

February 1, 1964

A SELECTION OF PUBLICITY PHOTOGRAPHS TAKEN AT LIVERPOOL'S DOCK AREA (UNDATED)

L to R: Keith Balcomb, Joe Short, Dave Armstrong & Dave Delaney

L to R: Keith Balcomb, Joe Short, Dave Armstrong & Dave Delaney

L to R: Joe Short, Dave Armstrong, Keith Balcomb & Dave Delaney

L to R: Dave Delaney, Keith Balcomb, Joe Short & Dave Armstrong

L to R: Keith Balcomb, Dave Armstrong, Dave Delaney & Joe Short

THE 'NOTIONS' SECOND LINE UP
APRIL 20, 1964 - SEPTEMBER 5, 1965

DAVE DELANEY
DAVE ARMSTRONG
JOE SHORT
DAVE McCARTHY

L to R: Joe Short, Dave McCarthy (Bob Wooler) & Dave Delaney

Another significant piece of Cavern history, the date is April 28, 1964 and the 'Notions' are recording 'Sunday Night at the Cavern' for Radio Luxembourg the recording was broadcast on May 24, 1964.

Dave McCarthy & Joe Short at the Radio Luxembourg recording session

Dave McCarthy (Bob Wooler) & Dave Delaney
All photographs on this page taken at the Radio Luxembourg recording session - April 28, 1964.

Dave Delaney   **Dave Armstrong**

L to R: Dave McCarthy, Joe Short & Dave Delaney
All photographs on this page taken at the Radio Luxembourg recording session - April 28, 1964

Dave McCarthy

Dave Delaney

A SELECTION OF PUBLICITY PHOTOGRAPHS

**L to R:
Dave McCarthy
Dave Delaney
Dave Armstrong
Joe Short**

**L to R:
Dave McCarthy
Joe Short
Dave Armstrong
Dave Delaney**

**L to R:
Dave McCarthy
Dave Delaney
Dave Armstrong
Joe Short**

L to R:
Dave McCarthy
Dave Delaney
Dave Armstrong
Joe Short

L to R:
Dave Delaney
Dave McCarthy
Joe Short
Dave Armstrong

L to R: Dave McCarthy, Dave Armstrong, Joe Short & Dave Delaney

L to R:
Dave McCarthy
Dave Delaney
Dave Armstrong
Joe Short

A SELECTION OF PHOTOGRAPHS OF THE 'NOTIONS' AT THE CAVERN

THOSE INTERESTED IN INSTRUMENTS OF THE ERA WILL NOTICE THAT DAVE McCARTHY IS PLAYING A 1963 HOFNER 'PRESIDENT' IN THESE PHOTOGRAPHS - A CHANGE FROM HIS PREVIOUS HOFNER MODEL 164 COLORAMA THAT HAD BEEN MODIFIED WITH A FENDER STRATOCASTER STYLE BODY.

Dave Delaney

L to R
Dave McCarthy
Joe Short
Dave Delaney

L to R
Dave McCarthy
Joe Short
Dave Delaney

Dave Delaney

L to R
Dave McCarthy
Joe Short
Dave Armstrong
Dave Delaney

L to R
Dave McCarthy
Joe Short
Dave Delaney

Dave Armstrong

L to R
Dave McCarthy
Joe Short
Dave Armstrong
Dave Delaney

Dave Armstrong

L to R
Dave McCarthy
&
Joe Short

Dave McCarthy
&
Joe Short

L to R
Dave McCarthy
Joe Short
Dave Delaney

L to R
Dave McCarthy
Joe Short
Dave Delaney

Dave Armstrong

L to R
Dave McCarthy
Joe Short
Dave Delaney

L to R
Dave McCarthy
Joe Short
Dave Armstrong
Dave Delaney

Dave Armstrong

L to R
Dave McCarthy
Joe Short
Dave Delaney

L to R
Dave McCarthy
Joe Short
Dave Armstrong
Dave Delaney

L to R
Dave McCarthy
Joe Short
Dave Armstrong
Dave Delaney

Dave Delaney & Joe Short

Dave Delaney

Dave McCarthy

Dave Armstrong

Dave McCarthy, Joe Short & Dave Delaney

LITHERLAND GALA - WHIT MONDAY JUNE 7, 1965 - DAVE McCARTHY NOW PLAYING A GIBSON 'ES 335'

L to R: Joe Short, Dave McCarthy & Dave Delaney

THE POSED PUBLICITY PHOTOGRAPHS ON THIS PAGE WERE TAKEN JUST PRIOR TO JOE SHORT HANDING OVER THE POSITION OF BASS GUITAR TO HIS BROTHER KEVIN. INTERESTINGLY THERE IS ALSO ANOTHER OBVIOUS CHANGE OF INSTRUMENTS AS JOE IS HOLDING A GIBSON BASS AND DAVE McCARTHY A HAGSTROM JUMBO ACOUSTIC

Joe Short

L to R: Joe Short, Dave McCarthy, Dave Armstrong & Dave Delaney

Joe Short hands over his bass guitar and his position in the 'Notions' to his brother Kevin

THE 'NOTIONS' THIRD LINE UP
SEPTEMBER 6, 1965 - MAY 26, 1966

DAVE DELANEY
DAVE ARMSTRONG
DAVE McCARTHY
KEVIN SHORT

Dave McCarthy

Dave Armstrong

September 1966

Dave Delaney

Kevin Short

IT WAS NOT POSSIBLE TO ACCURATELY IDENTIFY THE VENUE OR THE DATE OF THE FOLLOWING PHOTOS.
HOWEVER, BASED ON THE EQUIPMENT, THE ATTIRE AND THE FACT THAT DAVE McCARTHY IS IN THE LINE UP
THEY WERE TAKEN SOMETIME BETWEEN EARLY MARCH AND MAY 26, 1966

L to R: Kevin Short, Dave McCarthy, Dave Armstrong & Dave Delaney

L to R: Kevin Short, Dave McCarthy, Dave Armstrong & Dave Delaney

Dave Armstrong

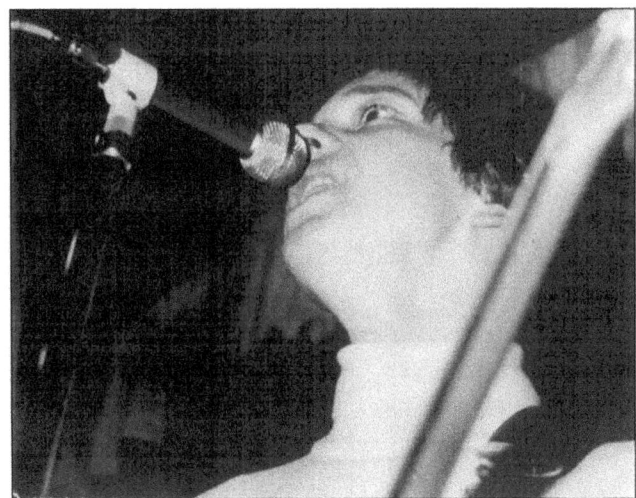
Dave Delaney

DAVE McCARTHY LEAVES THE 'NOTIONS' AFTER THEIR MAY 26, 1966 APPEARANCE AT THE MARDI GRAS CLUB (LIVERPOOL) TO JOIN THE LONDON BASED GROUP 'THE LEAGUE OF GENTLEMAN' THE 'NOTIONS' CONTINUE ON AS A TRIO.

THE 'NOTIONS' FINAL LINE UP
MAY 27, 1966 - JULY 21, 1967

DAVE DELANEY
DAVE ARMSTRONG
KEVIN SHORT

L to R: Kevin Short, Dave Armstrong & Dave Delaney

L to R: Dave Armstrong, Dave Delaney & Kevin Short

LITHERLAND GALA - WHIT MONDAY - MAY 30, 1966

L to R: Dave Armstrong, Dave Delaney & Kevin Short

L to R: Kevin Short & Dave Armstrong

L to R: Both Images - Kevin Short, Dave Armstrong (Obscured) & Dave Delaney

---

CO-OPERATIVE HALL - WARRINGTON - JUNE 4, 1966

Dave Delaney

Dave Armstrong

L to R: Kevin Short, Dave Delaney & Dave Armstrong

L to R: Kevin Short, Dave Armstrong & Dave Delaney

**ROSCOE HALL
LIVERPOOL UNIVERSITY
JUNE 17, 1966**

L to R:
Kevin Short
Dave Armstrong
Dave Delaney

L to R:
Kevin Short
Dave Armstrong
Dave Delaney

L to R: Kevin Short, Dave Delaney & Dave Armstrong

'ROYAL IRIS' - RIVER CRUISE - JUNE 28, 1966

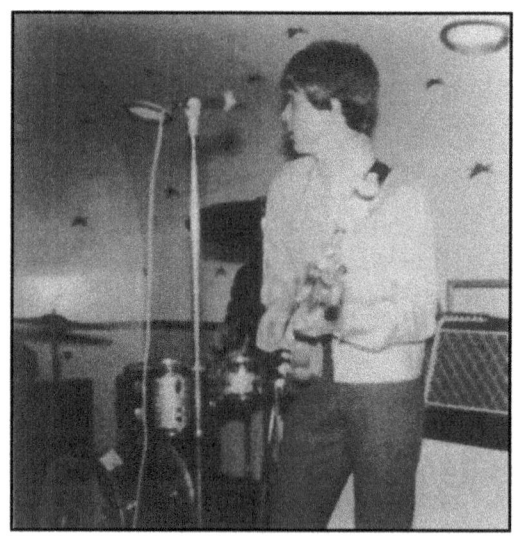

Dave Delaney

Dave Armstrong

Kevin Short

L to R: Dave Armstrong, Kevin Short & Dave Delaney

CASINO CLUB - BLACKPOOL - AUGUST 15, 1966

L to R: Dave Armstrong, Kevin Short & Dave Delaney

L to R: Dave Delaney & Kevin Short

LION HOTEL - WARRINGTON - FEBRUARY 25, 1967

L to R: Dave Armstrong & Dave Delaney

L to R: Kevin Short & Dave Delaney

L to R: Kevin Short, Dave Armstrong & Dave Delaney

Kevin Short

MARDI GRAS CLUB - LIVERPOOL - DATE UNKNOWN BUT SOMETIME BETWEEN MARCH AND JUNE 1967

Dave Delaney

Kevin Short

Both Images - Dave Armstrong

Both Images - Kevin Short

Both Images - L to R: Dave Armstrong & Dave Delaney

A SELECTION OF POSTERS AND HANDBILLS FEATURING THE 'NOTIONS' (IN CRONOLOGICAL ORDER)

MEMORIAL HALL
NORTHWICH

LEWIS BUCKLEY ENTERTAINMENTS, LTD.
PRESENT

SAT. NOV. 9   7/6 Pay at Door

PARLOPHONE HIT RECORDERS OF "SEARCHIN'"—THE

HOLLIES

PYE "DON'T LIE TO ME" RECORDERS

JEANNIE AND THE BIG GUYS

THE NOTIONS

* * * * * * * * * * * * *

SAT. NOV. 16   7/6 Pay at Door

THE SENSATIONAL

TONY MEEHAN
COMBO

DENNY CURTIS AND THE RENEGADES
CRUISERS with KARL TERRY

DANCING 7.45 to 11.45 p.m.
USUAL LATE TRANSPORT

Arthurs, Woodchester, Stroud

MEMORIAL HALL
NORTHWICH

LEWIS BUCKLEY ENTERTAINMENTS, LTD.
PRESENT

SAT. DEC. 28   7/6 Pay at Door

SCREAMIN'

LORD SUTCH
AND THE SAVAGES

VIC AND THE SPIDERMEN
THE BROKERS

* * * * * * * * * * *

SATURDAY, 4TH JANUARY—NO DANCE
(HALL USED FOR PANTOMIME)

* * * * * * * * * * *

SAT. JAN. 11   7/6 Pay at Door

HIT RECORDERS OF "STILL"—THE

KARL DENVER
TRIO

BRUCE HARRIS AND THE CAVALIERS
THE NOTIONS

**DANCING 7.45 TO 11.45 P.M.
USUAL LATE TRANSPORT**

S & S Electrical & Wrens Branches

DANCE
WITH THE "NOTIONS"
On Board

H.M.S EAGLET
SALTHOUSE DOCK

TO BE HELD ON

SAT. FEB. 8TH

Tickets 5/-

2 Licensed Bars

Printed by Woodland Press, 150 Rawson Road, Seaforth

MEMORIAL HALL
NORTHWICH

LEWIS BUCKLEY ENTERTAINMENTS LTD.
PRESENT

SAT. FEB. 15   7/6 Pay at Door

FABULOUS DECCA RECORDING STARS

PETER JAY
AND THE
JAYWALKERS

BRUCE HARRIS AND THE CAVALIERS
TONY AND THE SILVERTONES

★ ★ ★ ★ ★ ★ ★ ★ ★ ★ ★

SAT. FEB. 22   7/6 Pay at Door

Hit Recorders of "IT'S LOVE THAT REALLY COUNTS" and "I THINK OF YOU"

THE
MERSEYBEATS
THE NOTIONS
THE HI-FIVE

DANCING 7.45 to 11.45 p.m.
USUAL LATE TRANSPORT

Arthurs, Woodchester, Stroud

PALACE CINEMA

PENTRE BROUGHTON. Tel. BRYMBO 433.

★ ALL STAR VARIETY SHOW ★

ON THE STAGE
6-15   Two Separate Houses   8-45

FRIDAY, MAY 1st, 1964

The Fabulous Resident Group direct from the 'Cavern', Liverpool

"THE NOTIONS"

PAM VENMORE (Personality in Song)
from Blackpool and Leeds Palace of Varieties

PERCY HICKMAN on the ELECTRONIC ORGAN

STAN LITTLEWOOD, WIZARD ON THE DRUMS

and from the Goon Show, the Original Goon

Eric Granville Comedian/Ventriloquist
Star of B.B.C. T.V. and Radio Fame

and Finally from Liverpool

The Kobras Rhythm Group
of Cavern, Iron Door and Peppermint Lounge Fame

First House Prices — Adults 5/-.   Children 2/6
Second House Prices — Front & Circle 6/6. Stalls 5/-

Seats can be booked direct from the Cinema or from Crane's, Wrexham — Book Yours Now

MEMORIAL HALL
NORTHWICH

LEWIS BUCKLEY ENTERTAINMENTS LTD.
PRESENT

SAT. MAY 23   8/6 Pay at Door

"EVERYTHING'S AL' RIGHT"—THE

MOJOS

FOUR DIMENSIONS
SAVVA AND THE DEMOCRATS

★ ★ ★ ★ ★ ★ ★ ★ ★ ★

SAT. MAY 30   10/- Pay at Door

"JUST ONE LOOK"—THE

HOLLIES

THE NOTIONS
SOME PEOPLE

DANCING 7.45 to 11.45 p.m.
USUAL LATE TRANSPORT

Arthus, Woodchester, Stroud

SPORTS DAY

13th JUNE 1964 Opening at 3 p.m.

The Mersey Sound
from 4.45 p.m. to 6.15 p.m.

Twist and Shout
with a galaxy of Well Known Groups

including the Sensational boy Singer

CHICK GRAHAM
and the Coasters

Supported by

- The Notions
- Mark Peters and the Silhouettes
- The Karacters
- and many others ? ?

Enter the Twist and Shake Competition

L.P. Record Vouchers as Prizes

It is cheaper to buy your ticket before the day (See main poster)

MEMORIAL HALL
NORTHWICH

LEWIS BUCKLEY ENTERTAINMENTS LTD.
PRESENT

SAT. JUNE 20   7/6 Pay at Door

GERMANY'S BEATLES—THE

RATTLES

THE NOTIONS
FUGITIVES

★ ★ ★ ★ ★ ★ ★ ★ ★ ★ ★

SAT. JUNE 27   10/- Pay at Door

SWINGING BLUE JEANS

DENNY CURTIS AND THE RENEGADES
THE GONKS

DANCING 7.45 to 11.45 p.m.
USUAL LATE TRANSPORT

ARTHURS, WOODCHESTER, STROUD

MEMORIAL HALL
NORTHWICH

LEWIS BUCKLEY ENTERTAINMENTS LTD.
PRESENT

SAT. JULY 4   8/6 Pay at Door

NO. 1 HIT RECORDERS OF "JULIET"

FOUR PENNIES

BRUCE HARRIS AND THE CAVALIERS
THE MEGATONES

★ ★ ★ ★ ★ ★ ★ ★ ★ ★ ★

SAT. JULY 11   7/6 Pay at Door

TOP TEN HIT RECORDER OF "SHOUT"

LULU
AND THE LUVVERS
THE NOTIONS
THE RENEGADES

DANCING 7.45 to 11.45 p.m.
USUAL LATE TRANSPORT

ARTHURS, WOODCHESTER, STROUD

Saturday, 18th July
THE NOTIONS
Admission 6/6 : Dancing 8—11.45 : Late Transport

No admittance with or without ticket or pass-out after 10.30 p.m.

WEDNESDAY, 15th JULY
DUKE GORDON'S RITZONAUTS
Admission 4/- Dancing 8—11.30

FRIDAY, 17th JULY
Beat Nite Out
with
THE SAPHIRES
Admission 4/- Dancing 8—11.30

No admission after 10.30 p.m.

Duke Gordon's Ritzonauts

RITZ BALLROOM
RHYL, NORTH WALES

MEMORIAL HALL
NORTHWICH

LEWIS BUCKLEY ENTERTAINMENTS LTD.
PRESENT

SAT. AUG. 29   **8/6 Pay at Door**

THE DO WAH DIDDY BOYS

MANFRED MANN

BRITAIN'S TOP R & B GROUP

RICKY AND THE DOMINANT FOUR

★ ★ ★ ★ ★ ★ ★ ★ ★ ★

SAT. SEPT. 5   **6/6 Pay at Door**

Decca's Fabulous Liverpool Disc Star "I KNOW" "A LITTLE YOU"

CHICK GRAHAM
AND THE COASTERS

THE NOTIONS
THE NIGHT WALKERS

DANCING 7.45 to 11.45 p.m.
USUAL LATE TRANSPORT

ARTHURS, WOODCHESTER, STROUD

Rushbury Village Hall

A

DANCE

WILL BE HELD AT THE ABOVE HALL,

ON FRIDAY, SEPT. 18th

From 9-45 p.m. to 1-30 a.m.

Featuring the 'Cavern's' Choice for 1964

THE NOTIONS

ADMISSION 5/-

The Stretton Press, Church Stretton

WALL UNDER HEYWOOD
CHURCH STRETTON, SHROPSHIRE

MEMORIAL HALL
NORTHWICH

LEWIS BUCKLEY ENTERTAINMENTS LTD.
PRESENT

SAT. DEC. 5 **7/6 Pay at Door**

DECCA R & B STARS

BO STREET RUNNERS

LIBERTY RECORDERS "HEAD OVER HEELS"

STYLOS

THE CAVERN'S FAVOURITES

NOTIONS

★ ★ ★ ★ ★ ★ ★ ★ ★ ★

SAT. DEC. 12 **7/6 Pay at Door**

THE FABULOUS

ORIGINAL CHECKMATES

BRITAIN'S NO. 1 FOLK GROUP
FONTANA RECORDERS "DIRTY OLD TOWN"

SPINNERS

JOHNNY RINGO and the COLTS

DANCING 7.45 to 11.45 p.m.
USUAL LATE TRANSPORT

ARTHURS, WOODCHESTER, STROUD

MEMORIAL HALL
NORTHWICH

LEWIS BUCKLEY ENTERTAINMENTS LTD.
PRESENT

SAT. JAN. 16   6/6 Pay at Door

DECCA R and B STARS
THE WILD, WILD

FAIRIES

THE CAVERN'S FAVOURITES

NOTIONS

★ ★ ★ ★ ★ ★ ★ ★ ★ ★

SAT. JAN. 23   6/6 Pay at Door

MERSEYSIDE'S NEW STAR GROUP
FONTANA "LOUIE, LOUIE"

RHYTHM & BLUES INCORPORATED

COLUMBIA "I GOTTA WOMAN" FROM
GERRY and PACEMAKERS FILM "FERRY ACROSS THE MERSEY"

BLACK KNIGHTS

**DANCING 7.45 to 11.45 p.m.
USUAL LATE TRANSPORT**

MEMORIAL HALL
NORTHWICH

LEWIS BUCKLEY ENTERTAINMENTS LTD.
PRESENT

SAT. FEB. 13   **7/6 Pay at Door**

Columbia Recorders of "PRETTY FACE" and "SO FINE"

THE SENSATIONAL

BEAT MERCHANTS
NOTIONS

★ ★ ★ ★ ★ ★ ★ ★ ★ ★

SAT. FEB. 20   **7/6 Pay at Door**

DYNAMIC R & B STARS

LONG JOHN BALDRY
AND THE
HOOCHIE COOCHIE MEN
MEGATONES

DANCING 7.45 to 11.45 p.m.

USUAL LATE TRANSPORT

ARTHURS, WOODCHESTER, STROUD

MEMORIAL HALL
NORTHWICH
Licensee and Manager: J. L. GWILI LEWIS

LEWIS BUCKLEY ENTERTAINMENTS LTD.
PRESENT

SAT. MAR. 27   7/6 Pay at Door

Featuring the Pick of the Top Twenty Hit Tunes
Fontana's Fabulous Recorders "LOUIE, LOUIE"

RHYTHM AND BLUES INCORPORATED

Pye Recorders "WE'LL SING IN THE SUNSHINE"
and "LET'S LOCK THE DOOR"

LANCASTRIANS
NOTIONS

DANCING 7.45 to 11.45 p.m.
USUAL LATE TRANSPORT

ARTHURS, WOODCHESTER, STROUD

LIVERPOOL UNIVERSITY STUDENTS UNION

SAT. 26th NOV.

SOUNDS INCORPORATED

THE NOTIONS

TICKETS 4'6

FROM THE TICKET OFFICE IN THE UNION

TWO BARS / COFFEE
7.30 - 11.30

DOWNBEAT CLUB
77 Victoria St.
COMMENCING 7·30

WED · 12 · JULY
THE ADMINS
BOSSOUNDSENSATION
SUE LABEL * BOOKER T

THUR · 13 · JULY
THE SEFTONS
THE DETOURS

FRI · 14 · JULY
THE FIX
BOSSOUNDSENSATION
JOE TEX * EARL VAN DYKE

SAT · 15 · JULY
THE PRO-TEMS
Georgies Germs

SUN · 16 · JULY
THE NOTIONS
THE STIX

EPILOGUE
What happened to the 'Notions' after the group disbanded in 1967

The individual group members tell the stories of their personal lives, from the group's finale to the present day.

It is not surprising to find that, in each case, music remained some part of their lives, either as a spasmodic involvement or a chosen career path.

As anyone who has been involved in making music from an early age will tell you, once it gets into your blood, it's there for good!

The 1963-64 line up of the 'NOTIONS' at the Pheasant pub in Hightown, October 29, 2011
L to R Keith Balcomb, Dave Armstrong, Joe Short & Dave Delaney

LIFE AFTER THE 'NOTIONS' – KEITH BALCOMB

Like most ex-band members of that time, I just went back to doing my normal day job as an auto detailer at Huyton Volkswagen and, over the period I worked there, I also honed my skills as a paint and body man. The manager of that dealership was Victor Anton who (years later) I would discover had some obscure association with the Cavern and also the Beatles. During my time at the Volkswagen dealership, I availed myself of the opportunity to purchase some of the better 'trade ins' for my own use which culminated in the acquisition of an almost new 1967 Ford Cortina GT. Not long after that purchase, Victor, my mentor, took me aside and told me to stop wasting my money on cars and instead invest it in property. He offered to help me get the necessary funds for a down payment on a house by scheduling additional overtime hours and selling the GT for considerably more than I had paid for it. It was really thanks to Victor and his guidance that my wife Cathy and I were able to purchase our first home in 1972.

However, prior to owning that home, like most newlyweds, we rented and sometime in 1968, we moved into a rented house on Stanley Street in Ormskirk, which was where Cathy became friends with a young lady that worked at the corner general store. By sheer coincidence it turned out that she was the wife of Dave McClure, a former 'Abstracts' member. This chance association ultimately resulted in a life-long friendship between us.

Dave had extended the garage at his house such that it would easily accommodate two cars and he had also installed an inspection pit to facilitate repair work, so immediately after I finished my day's work at the Volkswagen dealership, I would drive to Dave's house and we would work on whatever 'customer' car needed attention until heading to the nearby local pub at 10:15 pm to down a pint or two before the (then) 10:30 pm closing time.

One memorable occurrence was the time we repainted Dave's own Ford Cortina in that garage. I remember that the garage had only one very small window so Dave had installed one of those translucent fiberglass corrugated roofs to help with visibility during daylight hours. However, it was night time when I set about painting the car and it was also early on in the year and still very cold. Dave had one of those 'jet engine' paraffin space heaters so we fired it up and warmed up both the car and the garage prior to starting the paint job. Unfortunately, due to the lack of the insulating properties of the roof, the garage cooled down very quickly, to the point that I was concerned that it was too cold to allow the paint to flow properly. Consequently, we made the decision to fire up the heater again and carry on. The paint used in automobile refinishing at that time was nitrocellulose lacquer and as I proceeded to spray the car, the air inside the garage became almost foggy with lacquer fumes, all of a sudden there was a minor explosion (that rattled said roof) accompanied by a flash and the air cleared instantly.... the space heater had ignited the lacquer fumes. Dave and I stood quietly looking at each other and then he started to laugh, so I said:

"What's so funny, we almost got killed".

He said "Your hair and eyebrows are all torched"

I said "so are yours".

Every inch of our clothing was covered in sticky white fuzz as a result of the spontaneous airborne ignition so we decided to call it a night and went down to the pub for a few pints. Everyone in the bar kept sneaking sideways glances at us, I am sure we both reeked of lacquer thinner and burnt hair.

In 1978 Cathy, Mandy and myself were on holiday in Benidorm, Spain and we toured a guitar factory that was manufacturing inexpensive 'Spanish Acoustic' style guitars and on a whim I purchased one. Although ten years or so had gone by since leaving the 'Notions' and not owning a guitar, this purchase began to renew my interest in playing once again.

Also in 1978, I was working as a 'finish spray painter' at the British Leyland plant at Halewood in Speke where the Triumph Dolomite, Stag, TR6 and its replacement the TR7 were being assembled. Unfortunately, the TR7 was a huge flop and coupled with employee unrest with pay and working conditions, British Leyland made the decision to 'lay off' or make 'redundant' the majority of the employees. I decided to take a portion of my redundancy pay and visit Dave who had emigrated to the USA earlier that year.

When we returned from that holiday, I worked a number of part-time jobs at various garages doing paint and body repairs. However, I eventually ended up working full-time as a stainless steel polisher, a job I worked at until 2004 when I was diagnosed with a hereditary heart condition and was declared medically unfit to work at any sort of manual job.

In 1979, along with Cathy and our then 12-year-old daughter Mandy, we visited Dave again and, as he had left his 12-string Harmony acoustic guitar in the UK when he emigrated to the USA, he asked me to bring it along. I checked-in the guitar (in its hard case) along with our luggage and when I retrieved it from the luggage carousel in the USA I was devastated to find that it had been badly damaged. It had apparently fallen off a baggage truck and then been run over!

In August 1990 while visiting the USA again, Dave's wife, Lynn, through her business associates, had located a pristine used 1966 Fender Jaguar for sale and, as Dave's interest in guitars had waned, I decided to purchase it and my reintroduction to playing the guitar had come full circle. It was around that time I also realised that by buying 'high end' guitars in the USA and bringing them back to the UK to re-sell, I could almost pay for my trips, as the UK selling price was almost double the US purchase price.

So in August 1991, on yet another visit to the USA, I purchased a couple of guitars to re-sell plus a white 1983 'Dan Smith' era Stratocaster, which became part of my personal collection. In September 1992 it was back to the USA yet again, this time I purchased four guitars, two Fender Stratocasters, a Gibson Les Paul and a Gibson Flying V. During the 90's my trips to the USA became more frequent but, unfortunately, the guitar-purchasing opportunities began to decline. However, I always seemed to manage to find something to re-sell or add to my collection. My friendship with Dave and Lynn had grown over the years and it was not unusual for me to visit them two (or more!) times in a single year.

In 1993 I expanded my purchasing opportunities to include a car, a 1984 Corvette, which I shipped back from the USA to the UK.

In 2005 a particularly humorous 'purchasing opportunity' occurred. Dave spotted a guy trying to sell a 1989 Fender Jazz Bass to a salesman at one of the local music stores, apparently with no success. Dave followed the guy out of the store and got the necessary details so that we could email my good friend and bass player Steve Faulkner in the UK to see if he was interested in buying it. Dave explained the situation to the guy and asked if he would hold it for twenty-four hours pending Steve's response, to which he agreed. He then said "You can call me at the San Antonio International airport. I work there as a security guard, so I can't take personal calls but the main switchboard will patch you through, just ask for Elvis". Dave was sure he was the butt of a huge joke and that when he called the airport he would be met with the standard "I'm sorry sir, but Elvis has left the building". However, everything worked out OK and Steve now owns a bass that he can honestly claim was at one time owned by Elvis.

In 2010 while shopping at the local Tesco's Supermarket I had a chance meeting with the 'Notions' drummer Dave Armstrong. It turned out that he was still in contact with Dave Delaney and provided me with Dave's contact information, so I was able to renew my association with him after a gap of forty-five years! Through a series of personal friends and associates, Dave Armstrong was also able to establish the whereabouts of Joe Short and both Dave Armstrong and I were able to reconnect with him. This ultimately resulted in a meeting of all four of the original 1963-64 'Notions' line up on October 29, 2011 at the Pheasant Pub in Hightown, near Liverpool. Subsequently, Dave Delaney was also able to re-establish contact with Dave McCarthy who now lives in Pensacola, Florida.

Since that October 2011 meeting we have had a few 'jam sessions' that, at different times, included myself, Dave Armstrong and Joe Short, and I would like to think that maybe, at some point in the future, the 'Notions' may be reunited as a group and play together once again.

FOOTNOTE by Dave & Lynn McClure

As a result of his medical condition Keith sadly passed away on June 27, 2016 and never got his wish for a 'musical' reunion of the Notions or to see this completed book. However, during his frequent trips to visit with us, he did see the book grow from a concept into an almost finished draft. We will miss his visits as he was always a generous, amusing and entertaining guest who demanded nothing in return but our companionship.

DAVE ARMSTRONG

After the Notions disbanded in 1967, I carried on playing the drums with various bands and artistes for many years as a professional musician. One of these bands, 'Candy', featured the late Vic Grace on lead guitar and bass player Gordon Loughlin. I also played with Taste of Honey (formerly the Easybeats),* which was a Beach Boys cover band fronted by Frank Townsend.

After playing in bands for a few years I decided to go solo and became an independent, stand-in drummer working in many of the clubs around Liverpool and at other locations in the North West, such as Manchester and Blackpool. At these venues I often found myself supporting resident keyboard players who provided the backing music for visiting artistes. One artiste that I particularly remember was a relatively unknown singer by the name of Russel Watson, who went on to become an internationally famous star in the world of classical music and opera.

Several years later I joined my final band, the Takers (formerly Liverpool's well-known 'Undertakers'),* a blues and soul outfit that played gigs all around the country.

Eventually I decided to take up a 'proper' job as a Call Centre Customer Service Advisor and successfully studied for City and Guilds and Health and Safety qualifications.

Now, at the grand old age of seventy, I have finally decided to call it a day. I still play occasionally at Merseycats, but mainly I concentrate on family life with my wife, Lynn, whom I married in 1971, four years after the Notions finished. We met in the Cavern in the mid-sixties when she was just seventeen and have been together ever since. We still live in Liverpool.

The 'Sixties' were the best time of my life and, unfortunately, nothing like it will ever happen again. It was a fabulous experience and I am glad I was there and that I was involved in one of the greatest musical experiences of the century.

* The stories of these two groups can be found in the book 'Beat Waves 'Cross the Mersey by Manfred Kuhlmann ISBN 9781588502018.

JOE SHORT

When I left the Notions I went to study for the Catholic priesthood at Campion House, Osterley, near London. I was there for two years and then I went to a Franciscan friary in North Wales. After about nine months I came back home after my health deteriorated.

Following a recuperative period I continued my studies at the Upholland seminary near Wigan; however, in 1969, after the first term I came to the conclusion that I should return to the secular world.

I took up the bass guitar again and played in a number of groups in the Merseyside area. I played in different types of bands including rock, country and western and even jazz outfits! After a trip across to Germany, as a member of a session band, I decided finally to sell my guitar and bass amp and give up playing altogether. Shortly afterwards I joined the Civil Service as a Tax Officer.

I left the Civil Service in 1970 and joined Olivetti as a sales representative in the Liverpool branch, spending the rest of my career selling business hardware and software systems.

At the start of 1990 I spent six years studying with the Open University and obtained a Bachelor of Science degree. I am now retired but continue to study - a habit created during my time spent with the Open University.

KEVIN SHORT (as related by Joe)

After the Notions ceased performing, Kevin continued playing in a solo capacity at various venues around the North West. After a couple of years he decided to leave his playing days behind and he left the UK for India. He spent a couple of years there before returning to the UK.

He settled in Derby and started work again in the printing industry as a print job estimator. He had started his career in the printing industry as a 'black and white' artist. This was a highly skilful job which required great precision in creating lettering and other design work. However, the arrival of the personal computer and desktop publishing software eventually made these skills redundant, hence his decision to work as an estimator instead.

Kevin was a very talented guitarist, singer and artist. When he was in his teens he had a passion for painting pictures of ships — very appropriate considering he lived on Merseyside.

In his very early fifties, Kevin suffered a minor heart attack; however, he kept this information to himself. We were therefore surprised and deeply saddened when he died suddenly at the age of fifty-two from a massive heart attack.

DAVE DELANEY

In the summer of 1967, when the Notions had ceased performing completely, it felt very strange for me to be inactive after the years of playing and performing so many gigs. I missed the regular contact with my band-mates and the 'buzz' of playing music live, but I had made my decision and I was determined to knuckle down and make a success of my new career. I knew I would have to give it my full attention from the outset, science-based studies being somewhat more time and energy consuming than most other subjects. Even so, I realised that it was not going to be a simple task and that there would be no guarantee of success, certainly not without a lot of hard work. It was definitely not an easy option but, barring unexpected difficulties, it offered a more deterministic career path in comparison to that of a full-time musician.

Subsequently, after four years work, I completed the engineering degree course at Liverpool Polytechnic, which then opened up several new options as to what to do next. As I was by no means desperate to dive straight into a full-time job in industry, I decided to continue by studying for a Master's degree at the University of Bradford, which eventually led to undertaking a research project for a Ph.D in the field of Automation Engineering.

A decade earlier, when Keith Balcomb and I were in our very early teens and before our interest in music overtook everything else, we used to make and fly model aeroplanes together. In fact, even before then, I had thought about becoming a pilot and so it was a happy coincidence that in 1971, when I was a postgraduate student at the university, I was offered the chance of learning to fly with the Royal Air Force, whilst still pursuing my research project. There was no way that I was going to let such an opportunity pass, so despite having to suffer an appallingly short haircut at a time when everyone I knew had flowing locks, I signed up for two years as a part-time student pilot with the RAF Volunteer Reserve.

It was a good decision — I had a great time, made many friends and enjoyed free, top-class flying tuition. Although my training period was not without its hairy moments (no pun intended), particularly when all alone in the sky with not everything going quite according to plan, I did think seriously about joining the RAF at the end of the stint. Unfortunately, that meant I would have to abandon my Ph.D project, which I really wanted to finish and so, when the two years were up and having also concluded that I would probably live longer by keeping my feet on the ground, I decided to stick with my chosen career path.

Achieving these academic qualifications took me through to 1975 and I then continued as an employee of the university as a Research Fellow for a few more years. During this period, in 1973, I got married and with my wife, Sue, moved into a small, picturesque village near Keighley in the West Riding of Yorkshire. We led a very pleasant existence in that area for a total of eight years, surrounded by the lovely dales and moorlands of the local countryside with its historic connections to the famous Bronte sisters of Haworth.

In April 1978, we moved southwards from Yorkshire to a village near Uttoxeter in North Staffordshire, as I had decided to leave the university to take up a post at the British Coal Research Centre near Burton-on-Trent. I started there as a Software Development Engineer, joining a world-leading project designed to bring much-needed automation and greater safety into the coal mining process. It was cutting-edge work (again, no pun intended) involving advanced machine control techniques and it became a significant success story within the coal industry. Gradually I worked my way up to become a Senior Technical Manager, with responsibility for a number of major projects. I stayed with British Coal for fifteen years, until the industry was decimated and then finally privatised by the government of the day.

In 1993 I left British Coal and began working in Derby for British Rail (as it was at the time) on the development and support of computerised signalling systems. Well, they say that lightning never strikes twice but, a year later, British Rail was also privatised and I was then transferred to the company which took on the same specialised area of work for the new owner of the UK's rail network, Railtrack (now Network Rail).

That same year, 1994, my father, Frank Delaney, the Notions' manager, passed away after a brief illness. When the group disbanded in 1967 he had set up an entertainments agency in partnership with his friend Ted Lambe, who had been the secretary of the NALGO club in West Derby and who had booked the Notions to play there many times. They named the agency 'Abendsterne Promotions', meaning 'Evening Star' in German, and established an office above a row of shops in Hanover Street, opposite Cranes music store and theatre. Their business was very successful and for several years it provided work for many Liverpool groups at venues all over Merseyside and the North West. However, my father closed down the agency after Ted died and he then retired completely from the music scene.

During the next thirteen years I moved gradually up the ladder and eventually became a vice-president of the signalling business within the railway company.

At the tender age of sixty, in 2006, I retired from 'active service', having enjoyed my various jobs over the years and especially the comradeship of many friends and colleagues. However, after a couple of years break, I was persuaded by a recruitment outfit to slip back into 'harness' and since then I have worked on a variety of limited duration, part-time contracts as a Consultant Engineer and Project Manager, which has involved periods of working in London, Birmingham, Liverpool and Derby.

When I look back now at the key decision points in my life, I find myself wondering what might have happened if I had chosen to take the alternative path. Maybe I could have become a famous and fabulously wealthy artiste in the world of musical entertainment (highly unlikely) or, much more likely, a jobbing musician trying hard to make a living. Perhaps I could have been a professional airline pilot flying jumbo jets around the globe (possible, I imagine, with luck) or maybe a military flying legend (more likely a dead one). At each of those moments I probably chose the option for which I could visualise more readily what the future might hold — I think that was more my style, not being a great risk-taker by nature. Nonetheless, I have done what I decided to do each time and consider that I have fared reasonably well in the grand scheme of things. I am very fortunate to have had a happy and enjoyable life, thus far, with the added bonus of my wife and I being blessed with two daughters, born in 1979 and 1981 respectively, and more recently, a granddaughter.

All in all, despite leaving behind the wonderful musical adventure I experienced as one of the Notions in that unforgettable sixties era, I have no great reason to feel any regret about the choices I made subsequently. Of course, deep, deep down, the lingering thought 'What if .....?' will always be there. But, in a similar way, that same unanswerable question could probably apply to most of us!

On a final note (pun intended!), it was back in 1996, whilst I was working for the railway company, that I was persuaded by a guitar-playing colleague to dig out my old 'Strat' from under the bed, where it had lain neglected for almost thirty years, blow off the dust and start playing again. Surprisingly, it took very little effort to jog the musical memory, get back in the groove and join a local band.

I'm still playing in the band! .... Full circle or what??

FOOTNOTE by Dave Delaney

In March 2017 I received a 'phone call from a friend to say that a photograph of the Notions performing at the Cavern had appeared on screen during a BBC television show called 'The House that £100K Built'. I watched the programme on BBC iPlayer the next day and discovered that it was all about a couple who were building their own house in Kent.

About five minutes into the programme some background information about the husband was given, in which it was mentioned that he had been the roadie for a group called the Notions in Liverpool during the 1960's, whereupon the photo of the Notions playing at the Cavern flashed up on the screen (wow, fame at last!). This guy could only be 'Big Ian' — we only ever had one roadie. There was no real doubt about his identity as he was easily recognisable, but for some reason he was called 'Derek' in the programme. Then I remembered that one of his initials was 'D', so he was simply using his other name. I rang Dave Armstrong to let him know about the programme and after watching it he confirmed that it was definitely Ian (or Derek).

We were both keen to get in touch with Ian if we could, so I 'phoned the film production company and gave them my contact details to be passed on to him. They quickly obliged and a day or so later I received an email from Ian, who happened to be on holiday in Australia at the time. Since making that first communication, Dave A and I have met up with Ian and spent several happy hours swapping life stories and reminiscing about the 'good old days' over a meal and a pint.

What an incredible fluke to come across an old mate after fifty years through a TV programme about building a house - truly amazing! Having re-connected after all this time, 'Big Ian' and the Notions will definitely not be losing touch with each other again.

'LET IT ROCK!!!'

The continuation of my musical adventures and misadventures
after my time with the 'Notions'

By

Dave McCarthy

'LET IT ROCK!!!' – By Dave McCarthy.
The continuation of my musical adventures and misadventures after the Notions

As the era of the 'Liverpool Sound' came to an end the predominance of the disbanded group members were faced with no alternative other than to seek out mundane daily employment. Unfortunately, we were the children of a generation that had suffered the hardships of a World War and Liverpool, being a port, was particularly hard hit by the bombing and our parents never new for sure if their home, place of employment, friends or neighbors would be around tomorrow. This insecurity caused them to instill in their children the need to learn a 'trade' or get a 'good job' and a career in music was certainly not high on that list. However, for some of us the musical apprenticeship we served during the 1960's would mold our future - and so it was with me.

As the Notions played such a huge part in preparing me for what subsequently turned out to be a twenty-six-year musical roller-coaster ride, I have recounted my full post-Notions story here for the sake of completeness, as without the experience I gained during my time with the group it would never have happened.

The story begins a week after my last Notions' gig at the Mardi Gras on 26th May 1966.

My first band after the 'Notions' was the London based the 'League of Gentlemen' a house band for the Roy Tempest Organization, an agency who specialized in importing middle-strata American talent for British tours. In those days, the British Musicians Union would not permit foreign artistes to bring their own regular musical accompaniment into the country, so the agency responsible for the tour had to provide ready-made back up bands. The 'League of Gentlemen' included a top-of-the-line sax player, a native of Toronto called Joel Shapiro who had worked as a regular with the Dick Clark Road Shows in the States and appeared with Little Richard, Check Berry, Jerry Lee Lewis and just about everyone who was anyone in the rock 'n roll bizz. He came over to join the Spencer Davis group with Stevie Winwood but it didn't work out.

Other bands in the Roy Tempest stable included the 'Senate' a seven piece band, including brass and keyboards. Hailing from Glasgow, they were the Tempest organization's top band, and used to back up the Drifters, Patti La Belle, and some of the better known artistes. However, we were assigned first choice to a tour with Lee (Working in a Coalmine) Dorsey which was a lot of fun.

The other band in the agency we used to hang about with a lot was called 'Bluesology' for whom the then-unknown Elton John was the keyboard player. I always felt sorry for 'Bluesology' because Roy Tempest always gave them dodgy gigs, like backing up the 'Inkspots' who were great lads, but were all in their seventies even at that time. The band also had to go all the way up to Scotland touring with the late Billy (Summertime) Stuart, who weighed about twenty two stone,* crammed into their van. Billy Stuart also suffered from a bladder disorder which necessitated him having to stop for a piss every twenty minutes. Apparently it took them about four weeks to get to Carlisle!

The Tempest Organization had a large flat** on Chelsea Bridge Road which was used to accommodate all of his imported artistes. We also used to crash there regularly whenever we were in town. I remember walking in there one night, and Elton John greeted me, fore-finger to lips, with a theatrical "Sssshhhh."

*22 Stone = 308 pounds - **apartment

Apparently Billy Stuart, who, (with his arrival in London having been delayed due to a court appearance back in the States charged with shooting his road-manager) had thrown a huge moody upon finding the kitchen sink in the flat filled with everyone's dirty dishes. His reaction was to chuck them from the third floor window sending them all crashing down onto the pavement below, after which he had immediately fallen asleep on top of his diminutive Filipino girlfriend, the tips of whose tiny fingers and feet were only just visible, protruding from either side of the colossal mass of brown blubber sprawled across the bed. Understandably, Elton didn't want to risk waking him up for any kind of a repeat performance.

The last time I ever saw the lads from 'Bluesology', they were gathered solemnly - together with the afore-mentioned 'Inkspots' - around the engine of their broken down van on London's North Circular Road. We tried to help but the engine had already died of severe internal injuries. I bumped into Elton John in the Marquee in Wardour Street a few months later and by then he had started a new gig backing up Long John Baldry. His boyfriend during the 'Bluesology' era was a lad called Rod Harrod, a journalist with The New Musical Express, who was a fan of our band and always gave us good reviews.

Our last job with The Roy Tempest group was backing up one-hit wonder Roy C (Shotgun Wedding). The three week disaster of a tour culminated in a dressing room brawl at Toft's Club in Folkstone between Roy, who, like Lee Dorsey, was a former boxer, and the band, during which Joel Shapiro, the main focus of Roy C's wrath, had his front tooth knocked out, and as a result was unable to play the saxophone for a few days afterwards.

As soon as Joel had his grill repaired we departed for Germany for nine months, playing various residencies in Frankfurt, Cologne, and Hamburg. The 'League of Gentlemen' drifted apart after returning to the U.K. from Germany, and although some consideration was given to me rejoining the 'Notions' after a nine month absence, the sentiment wasn't unanimous, as I understand my childhood friend; the late Kevin Short was not in favour of my reinstatement.

In any case, the previous twelve months in my first professional job had been so hectic that I was not in a hurry to look for another band, so for a change of pace, I signed to a management deal at Allison's Theatre Club in Litherland and did the working men's and theatre club circuit as a solo-vocal traveling mainly in Yorkshire and the North East of England. Have Dickey bow, will travel!

Due to the vast disparity in the quality of musical accompaniment, the solo vocal idea was becoming unsustainable, so I returned to the guitar, and continued as a guitar-vocalist, working every sort of venue from cabaret clubs like the Batley Variety Club, the Stockton Fiesta, and the Stringfellow circuit and local pubs and working men's clubs closer to my Liverpool home....I would play anywhere, and although I had no problem handling the big stage gigs, I always preferred the atmosphere in the pubs where you didn't have to wear a stage suit and ponce about like Englebert Humperdinck on crack.

During my time with the 'Notions', I had a girlfriend whom I had met at the Cavern, (whose name, to my shame, I no longer even remember). She was a resident of the quiet, posh little village of Gayton, Wirral, Cheshire, just down the road from Heswall. Upon one of our romantic teen-age hand-in hand walks around the quaint Gayton country lanes, she pointed out to me a rambling old ivy covered house aesthetically entitled 'Rembrandt'. It turns out that this was the house purchased by Paul McCartney for his dad, Jim - which was a best-kept secret at the time, not widely known outside of the immediate area. After returning home to Liverpool from the 'League of Gentlemen' adventures and long after my association with the Gayton lass had ended, I had accumulated loads of songs I had written before, during, and after the 'Notions' period. Well I was a cheeky little bastard in those days, and predicated on the principle nothing ventured, nothing gained, I got off the bus from Birkenhead in Gayton one fine afternoon with a five-tune acetate in my hand, gathered my courage, scrunched up the gravel drive to 'Rembrandt' and knocked on the door. After a few seconds that seemed like an eternity, the door opened, and I had my first face-to face meeting with Jim McCartney....the exchange proceeded as follows:

Jim Mac. "What can I do for you son?"

Dave Mac. "Is Paul in?"

Jim Mac. "Who shall I say wants him?"

"My name is Dave McCarthy and I've written some songs."

Jim Mac. "Well you better come in then....Paul, there's a lad here called Dave McCarthy wants to see you, he says he's written some songs."

Looking back on it, it's hard to believe that it was that easy, but a few moments later the Beatles legend appeared, and after greeting me with a disarming "Alright mate", ushered me into the living room, and introduced me to the two other occupants of the room, his step-mother, and Jim's second wife Angie, and her daughter Ruth, who was then a precociously charming young lady of about thirteen years of age. Cups of tea all round accompanied by a plate of McVities Digestives biscuits (cookies) appeared shortly thereafter, courtesy of Angie Mac, and we all adjourned to the small room between the living room and kitchen containing a baby grand piano. Jim McCartney was first up, and his knarled old arthritic hands notwithstanding, proceeded to expertly plonk out a wonderful medley of old tunes from his roaring twenties dance band days. Paul sat down next to him, and seamlessly paid tribute to his paternal musical heritage with a twenties influenced, at the time unreleased original song, entitled 'Honey Pie'. I think the finished version eventually appeared on 'The White Album'. The song was so new, that Macca needed to refer to the pencil-written lyrics set in front of him as he played it. Unbelievably, I can claim some collaboration on the song. Because in the bridge, Paul had written; **'Will the wind that sent her boat across the sea, kindly send her sailing home to me'**. I suggested he replace the word 'Sent' with the word 'Blew' i.e. 'Will the wind that *blew* her boat across the sea....' Paul produced his pencil, crossed out the word 'sent', and duly obliged.

After that, another round of tea and bickies (cookies) appeared, and we started to discuss the recording of Hey Jude, and a few of the people on the session who we knew in common, such as the Undertakers lead vocal, Jackie Lomax, and Badfinger's Joey Molland, whom I knew from the old Birkenhead band the 'Pathfinders'. I won't forget the next moment, as Macca spontaneously began to play 'Hey Jude', and I sang the harmony with him, and even if I say so myself, it was a pretty tight vocal match. But then again, I always loved singing harmony, as much and, on that particular occasion, even more than lead vocals. I will always remember that moment as a rare and magical privilege, jamming vocals on 'Hey Jude' with the author himself.

For the rest of the afternoon Paul McCartney was then kind enough to listen to and critique my demo. He told me encouragingly that my songs were...'As good as our first hundred...' and offered me some excellent advice on song-writing. His approach was, (and this is the example he used):

"You might like the song, 'Please Mr. Postman' so you decide to write something similar using that song as a base, and make your first line, something like, let's say....I'm sorry Mr. Milkman. Well before you know it, you might have your second line *'I'm sorry Mr. Milkman that I let you down....I'll make it up to you next time you're in town.'* Drop the "Milkman" reference, and replace it with; *I'm sorry baby that I let you down...I'll get to see you next time I'm in town,'* and suddenly you have an entirely different song. You can even use the identical melody and the same four-bar chord sequence, in common with dozens of songs written by, Carole King, Smokey Robinson, Doc Pomus, Mort Shuman, and many more from that era which actually do. The song will still sound different. But you have to start somewhere, and allow the spin off to emerge. All you need now is to come up with a good middle-eight and a strong hook". Good advice indeed, which I have used ever since to generate the necessary momentum to overcome any creative inertia and get the little intellectual hamster pushing the wheel around once again.

The afternoon came to an end about three hours later, as Paul had to return to London that day. To save me catching the old green Crossville double-decker bus from Heswall to the Woodside ferry in Birkenhead, he kindly offered to transport me through the Mersey Tunnel and drop me off in Liverpool on his way out to the M6. His old sheepdog Martha eagerly jumped into the back seat of the smart little black Mini-Cooper parked in the driveway, but for some reason, she would not lie down until Macca had thrown his jacket in there with her....I had wondered why the garment was encrusted with dog hair. I jumped into the passenger seat, and we waved at Jim, Angie, and Ruth standing in the doorway of 'Rembrandt'. Paul turned the key in the ignition, and NOTHING! - not even a click, the battery was completely flat. A few minutes later, sweating my arse off while pushing a sturdy British-built Mini-Cooper containing rock-star and dog up and down the winding country curves of Well Lane, Gayton, I had the opportunity to reflect on the reality, that while it is far from a perfect world, it's still possible to be happy. In fact, the almost-perfect day for this aspiring young musician got significantly better as the car engine finally burst into life, and a little way down the road, Paul McCartney advised me that he was prepared to recommend that I become signed to Apple as a writer. He explained that he was not prepared to offer me a deal as an artiste at that point, since with James Taylor, Jackie Lomax, Mary Hopkins, Harry Nilson, and Badfinger in the pipeline, there was just too much going on for a company in it's first year of inception. Nonetheless, he promised to set up a meeting at Apple offices in Saville Row with the new head of his publishing department, an American recording executive named Dennis O'Dell, which he subsequently did. Thus I became the first, and I think only writer, ever signed to Apple.

Paul had this vision of cubicles full of writers, all collaborating, and exchanging ideas like the song-factories with a stable of house writers, reminiscent of the early New York tin-pan-alley labels of the fifties that spawned Carole King, Jerry Goffin and the rest of those legendary writers. Unfortunately, due to the suicidal chaos and corruption that eventually engulfed Apple Records, like all the other dreams, this vision never came to fruition. Eventually, things got so out of control that the entire organization finally imploded. Regrettably, except for a few notables like James Taylor, and Badfinger, Apple's impact on the industry was sadly limited, and ultimately suffered a spectacularly-painful and premature demise. In other words, nothing ever came of my writers' contract, but it was a great way to bomb out. I subsequently visited Jim, Angie and Ruth several times, in Heswall, then London, and later following their relocation to Kings Lynn Norfolk after Jim sadly passed away in 1978. Angie and Ruth now live in L.A. and we still keep in touch.

Eventually I became a bit fed up with traveling, and in the spring of 1969 I took a residency with a fourteen-piece house orchestra - the 'Alan Ross Band' - at the newly-opened Top Rank Ballroom in St John's precinct in Liverpool. After that, I did the same front vocalist job with the house band at the Shakespeare Theatre Club, together with Brian Griffiths (ex-member of the 'Big Three'), and then finally back for a second stint at the Top Rank with the new band that had taken up residency there. In that band I became reacquainted with John Wiggins the keyboard player from the 'Bobby Patrick Big Six' who I knew from Hamburg. He had married Sylvia Saunders the drummer from the 'Liver Birds' and was living in Liverpool at the time.

These residencies cover the period from 1969 until 1972, at which point I left for a summer season at Butlins Holiday Camp in Clacton-Upon-Sea in Essex, which is marginally posher than Southend, with not quite so many West Ham United fans and jellied eels.

Upon returning to Liverpool, I went back to the pub and club circuit as a solo guitar vocal in Liverpool, South Wales, and the North East. Around that period, I also did a stint as a compere at the Wooky Hollow Theatre Club, where I had the pleasure of working with some of my favourite bands, as diverse as - the 'Chi Lites' and the 'Grumbleweeds', with whom I had first become friends while playing at the Top Ten Club in Hamburg. Around that time I also did a few weeks in Naples Italy, doing service clubs for the N.A.T.O. Armed Forces. I continued to earn a living as a solo guitar vocalist, working locally in Liverpool, and throughout England, Scotland and Wales until 1975, at which point I joined my first band in almost ten years. The band was from Sweden, but the two band leaders were Czechoslovakian refugees who emigrated to Sweden as kids to escape the Russian invasion.

They had a current hit on the Swedish charts but had parted company with the rest of their band members due to personal disagreements, and had arrived in London on a mission to urgently recruit new musicians to tour behind their hit record. After two weeks frantic rehearsal with two other successful candidates; a Scottish drummer from Glasgow, and an androgynous keyboard player from Hampton Court, sleeping in the midst of our equipment at a friends flat just off Kilburn High Street; we drove to Stockholm ready to hit the road. Unfortunately the Swedish authorities, now famous for their acceptance of half a million Syrian immigrants, were at the time a bit stingy with work permits, a fact that had escaped the attention of the Czech boys, and as a result we Brits were unable to work officially in Sweden.

Stranded in Sweden without much work except a few under-the-radar gigs with the band backing up strippers in the red-light district, I busked on the streets of Gamla Stan the Stockholm old town, and the Stockholm underground the Tunnelbana (usually referred to as the Tunnel Banana) until it became too cold, then it was into the Czech National club, whose occupants, due to my association with the other two Slovakian lads, had grown to treat me like one of their own, for some ridiculously inexpensive (Thank God) eastern European scran (Liverpool slang for food) and a few warm Pilsners.

Upon my eventual return to England, I sought comfort (and income) once again on the Liverpool/Newcastle/Middlesborough/Sunderland/Cardiff, pub, club and cabaret circuit until March of 1976, at which point, at the ripe old age of twenty-nine, I made a big change in my life. I boarded a plane to Canada, having assigned myself three years to complete a voyage across the North American continent.

At first I shared accommodation with my old mate, Brian Griffiths from the Big Three, who had relocated to Canada the previous year. We played gigs in the Toronto and Southern Ontario area with a band oddly entitled 'Quadrac' formed by Griff's brother Billy, together with a couple of local Canadian lads.

A year later in 1977, I moved out to Calgary Alberta, and immediately stumbled upon a British booking agent lady, who sent me out onto the snowy Canadian road, playing pubs and clubs across three Western Canadian provinces, from Skookumchuck, British Columbia, to Moose Jaw and Swift Current Saskatchewan. Did you know that in Swift Current Saskatchewan, there is a Chinese restaurant called 'Willie Wong's' that regularly features live music? Not many people know that. Played there!!! (Funny...I just remembered...I was doing a job at Willie Wong's when I heard that Elvis had died....)

Anyway, I think it was around January 1978, I was engaged to appear at the Assiniboia Hotel in Medicine Hat Alberta. Medicine Hat is primarily an oil town that sits on the edge of Suffield Canadian army base, which is the largest British Army tank training ground in the world. I was playing in the predictably cheesy 'Grotto Lounge'. I had a dose of the flu and felt like shit, and probably sounded like it, but on my first break I took the opportunity to check out the band playing in the bar, located on the opposite side of the huge old Victorian red-brick hotel.

The place was chaotic, chokka (Liverpool slang for 'full to busting') to the bulging walls with insanely rowdy British squaddies, all pissed as proverbial farts. As I struggled my way across the expansive room towards the bar, the band took the stage, kicked into gear, and immediately stopped me in my tracks. They were loudly and clearly the best live band I had heard in ten years. There was a good reason for that. I later discovered that the drummer, Rick Pobst, had backed up Charlie Pride. The lead guitarist, Dennis White from Mobile, Alabama, had originally played with Southern Rock icons 'Wet Willie', while the lead-vocal/second guitar/keyboard, Ronnie Poss, had played in Porter Waggoner's band on the Grand Old Opry' Radio Show at the ripe old age of thirteen.

Musicians from the South-Eastern United States of America are entirely fluent in three musical languages; Rock, Blues, and Country. Shaded and coloured by their peripheral dialects Bluegrass and Gospel, Southern musicians are able to either express these languages individually and discreetly, or to flexibly combine them into the fusion of a uniquely modern melodic dialect that we conveniently categorize as 'Southern Rock'. It was a defining moment in my musical career, as I discovered the source of the sound I had originally crossed the Atlantic to discover.

It turned out that the feeling was mutual. Unbeknownst to me, on their band breaks, the members of 'Sundance' had been surreptitiously checking out my sets in the Grotto, and after having been invited to have a drink with them in their hotel room, they revealed that their bass player/vocalist was leaving the band due to family reasons. They offered me the job and of course, I accepted. The plan was for me to finish out the remaining month of their Canadian tour, making the best of the on-the-job-rehearsal time to get tight with their program on bass guitar and vocals. The band would then take a month off, followed by a three month residency in Sitka, Alaska.

The first part of the schedule proceeded according to plan as I cancelled my remaining solo bookings with my long-suffering Calgary agent Irene Marjoram, (I loved her) and hit the road with the fifth, and probably the final band of my musical career. At the end of the Canadian stint, the other lads had returned to Atlanta for a long-anticipated reunion with their families, while myself and Ronnie Poss, the other guitar vocalist, planned a month vacation in Las Vegas. We would then proceed to hook up with the band in Los Angeles en route to Seattle to catch the ferry to Alaska for our next tour of duty.

We subsequently proceeded to blaze a chaotic trail from the final job on the schedule in Edmonton Alberta, down through Idaho, stopping only for beer in Salt Lake City (or was it for salt in Beer Lake City?) Is this a full bottle in front of me or a full-frontal lobotomy? Let's just say that there were points during the excursion that were distinctly indistinct. We arrived in Vegas - the old sleazy Vegas - not the modern theme park model, spending money like drunken sailors, or in this instance, musicians, with fear and loathing, like Hunter Davis, loving life to the proverbial max in Las Vegas....If only we had known....

If you have ever pondered the eternal mystery of what we ever did before the advent of cell 'phones and the Internet, I'll tell you exactly what we did. We missed vital communications regarding serious family illnesses, resulting in the cancellation of Alaskan tours for Southern Rock bands, because there is no way to notify nomadic band members, wandering in a state of profound stupefaction around the country, staying in random hotels, with no forwarding addresses, of the unexpected and late cancellation of musical engagements! Yes you guessed it. No Alaskan tour, and worse still, no money left following our only partially-memorable holiday, we arrived almost penniless for a non-existent rendezvous in Los Angeles, with no fixed abode except for my faithful old 1969 Ford LTD which, in common with its understandably stunned occupants, was rapidly running out of gas. Rewind to the earlier narrative of the Swedish band debacle beginning with the rehearsals in London.

The Czechoslovakian lads who originally formed the band had a couple of American girlfriends studying at the London School of Economics in whose apartment we stayed for a couple of weeks while rehearsing for the ill-fated Scandinavian tour. Fortunately, they had since returned to the U.S.A and even more fortunately, were residents and natives of Los Angeles. As luck would have it, the girls had both become good friends and had later visited me in Liverpool, after which, we had stayed pretty much in touch. They were unbelievably understanding and helpful with regard to our plight, and managed to arrange accommodation for us with a brother of one of the girls, the manager of an apartment complex off Venice Boulevard, who kindly allowed us to doss free of charge in a vacant apartment scheduled for renovation.

That was the most urgent problem solved, but we still had to find some work which, as a musician in Los Angeles, can be a daunting proposition. Based on the universally accepted theory that you can't be in the race unless you're in the stadium, Los Angeles is a holding area for an enormous volume of front-line talent of every conceivable variety. As a result, there are very few paying gigs for unknowns. Clubs don't need to hire talent when they can hold showcases to provide aspiring artistes with the only opportunity to be seen by agents and recording execs. In L.A. you have to play for free, or you don't play at all.

Except for my old Ovation electric/acoustic guitar, Ronny and I had no electrical equipment, which had all been packed up and returned to Atlanta with the other lads, and nowhere to earn any real money even if the equipment had been available. The first scheme to raise money and raise our profile was to audition for a N.B.C. nationally networked T.V. show called 'The Gong Show'. You can still find episodes of this bizarrely abusive program which, based upon the public execution mentality, would feature original talent whose criteria for qualification had to be severe delusions with regard to their ability.

The show which aired weekly on Network T.V. would feature five truly awful acts who sincerely thought they were great, appearing before a live studio audience. Each of the respective contestants would have their performance prematurely interrupted by whichever member of a trio of celebrity judges was the first to become sufficiently appalled by the performance to leave their seat and bash loudly on a huge oriental gong located next to the panel, to the raucous delight of the rowdy studio audience. The only saving grace from our standpoint was that the winner was always a really good act, which was the only way the show could maintain any pretence of credibility. Our strategy was to be that token act and receive the $1000 prize awarded weekly.

Our first audition performed before a video camera in a small room with only one technician in attendance. We must have done okay, because it turns out that the show had called our friends whose number we had given as a point of contact even before we got home, and encouragingly, we were invited to appear before the Gong Show's producers at a suite on the ninth floor of the Crocker Bank building, located immediately opposite to the iconic Mann's Chinese theater on Hollywood Boulevard the very next day. We performed an original song entitled 'I Can Dream' written by my partner Ronny Poss, who is an exceptionally talented composer, musician, and vocalist, and were subsequently scheduled the next week to attend the taping of the show to be aired at the end of the same month, May 1978.

After our successful audition, while sitting outside the Crocker Bank building, I remarked to Ron, that here we were, sitting on the richest street in the richest state of the richest country in the world, both so broke, that you couldn't have found a coin on either of us if you had subjected the pair of us to a thorough search with metal detector!

An entire month of Gong Show episodes were scheduled to be taped on a single day once per month at N.B.C. studios in beautiful down-town Burbank California. Acts selected to take part, upwards of around 100 people in total, mainly highly eccentric individuals, were assembled in a huge hanger of a room at the T.V. studios. One by one the aspiring contestants would be summoned to go into the studio, first to rehearse with the house band, without any audience present in preparation for the show being aired before a live audience to be recorded later on. As you can imagine, this is a time-consuming process, and we were trapped in room for twelve hours with an assembly of bizarrely attired and often extremely 'interesting' individuals. On our show, there was a really beautiful young lady whose specialty was to bark like a dog (I couldn't quite make up my mind about that one) and a guy who would walk on stage, immediately fall to his knees, cram his fingers down his throat and attempt to make himself vomit! The game show designer and host of the show, eccentric T.V. impresario Chuck Barris, was to rush onto the stage interrupting the emetic procedure and dragging the contestant theatrically away by the collar immediately prior to the gastric ejaculation. Well as they say, timing is everything, and on both occasions the finale of the performance turned out to be 'a darned close-run thing', as the Duke of Wellington would say.

We spent most of the afternoon in the safe and pleasant company of two Israeli go-go dancers, fascinating and gorgeous young women who had recently completed military deployment on the Golan heights separating Israel from Syria during the ongoing Middle-East confrontation. War stories from go-go girls engaged in armed combat was an entirely new experience for me.

Another member of the company was a percussionist from New Orleans, a black lad with a variety of portable percussion instruments, who could really get a groove going; a great talent whom the producers deliberately made look ridiculous - the object of the entire exercise of course - by taping his live segment with a Louisiana style umbrella strapped around his forehead, while shaking a giant dried bean-pod. Stereotype safely reinforced....Job done!!!

So far all was going according to plan, until untypically for the usual format of the show, we found ourselves in direct competition with a really talented and tight boy and girl guitar and harmony duo with the same idea as ourselves of providing the 'respectable' option to produce the winner. This was going to be an unlucky break for one of us, and we both realized the fact.

Our panel was comprised of impressionist and comedian the late Fred Travolina: ventriloquist, 'Waylon and Madame' and Michele Lee the glamorous star of the long-running American seventies soap-opera, 'Knotts Landing'. We went on immediately after the dog-barking lady, and immediately prior to the vomiting man. No gong was bashed during our two and a half minute slot, and the score cards were held aloft to reveal three tens, maximum points. As he produced his 'ten' card, Fred Travolina, noting that we had been introduced as hailing from Atlanta Georgia, looked straight at me and said in his best Jimmy Carter impression: "Anyone who sings, 'I can't touch you but I can dream,' must have dee-sire in his heart."

We looked on with considerable anxiety as the other duo put on a predictably excellent performance. "Now we'll see who has the magic", I whispered to Ronny. The score cards were produced for our rival duo....two tens and a nine....we won, and were duly presented with an enormous cardboard check at the finale of the show to the accompaniment of loud acclaim, as a dwarf ran around amongst the cast members industriously showering all with confetti - a circus indeed. The anti-climax came as we realized that instead of receiving a real $1000 check at the end of the show as we had hoped and counted on, we were obliged to fill in some paperwork for the I.R.S. and informed that the check would arrive within thirty days. We left the studio dismayed but not disheartened. We still had to find a way to pay the bills.

In those days some enterprising mind in Common with the Gong Show, had devised an ingenious way to utilize the Los Angeles talent surplus. This particular example involved a restaurant called 'The Great American Food and Beverage Company' with two outlets. One of the venues was located at the top of Sunset Boulevard; the other was on Wilshire Boulevard at Westwood Village. The premise was that all the waiters, waitresses, bartenders and bus-boys employed there had to sing, dance, and/or play some kind of musical instrument. Everything was done acoustically with no microphones or electrics whatsoever. As luck would have it, they were holding auditions at the Sunset Boulevard branch, and of course minimum wage and tips was far better than the alternative which was bugger all! The Sunset Branch is adjacent to the U.C.L.A. campus and full of rowdy, noisy, obnoxiously-drunk 'Bruins'. The restaurant did not hire duos, so Ronny and I auditioned separately taking turns with the solitary guitar. He went up first, and in spite of standing on a chair to better project his outstanding vocal rendition of 'Midnight Rider', I couldn't hear a bloody thing even though I was only twenty feet away!!

I subsequently stepped up for my bit. Steve Miller's 'Keep On Rockin' Me Baby', using an occupied table to stand on this time in order to gain a bit more altitude and attitude. When it comes to being obnoxious my philosophy is; 'If you can't beat 'em, join 'em'. Anyway, later after the ordeal had finished and while in the process of evading randomly aimed beer projectiles on the way out of the restaurant, we were official notified that we had both passed the audition!!

Unfortunately, the experience turned out to be the proverbial bridge too far that broke the Camel's back for Ronny who decided to flee the stable with a stitch in time before the door was bolted. Fortunately, for the horse, the water was only skin deep.

To put it another way, my partner decided The Great American Food and Beverage Company was not the job for him, and advised me that he never intended to set foot inside "that fuckin' shit-hole" ever again, or as long as he had "a hole in his ass" or whichever option was longer.

He subsequently concluded the series of mixed metaphors with a trip back home on the midnight train (or, in this case, bus,) to Georgia a few days later. We both agreed sadly that it had been a great ride until the wheels fell off, wished each other the best of British, and agreed to stay in touch, which have done right up until this day, (In fact I called him only last week).

Ironically, he need not have worried. I was not assigned to work in the Sunset Boulevard branch adjacent to the U.C.L.A. campus where we had auditioned. Instead I was to work at the Westwood Village outlet on Wilshire Boulevard. I began my career as a bus-boy, clearing off and setting up table for the waiters. 'The Great American Food and Beverage Company' turned out to be an interesting job for several reasons. As I mentioned, everyone who worked there, had to sing and/or play a musical instrument. There was no sound system, so everything was done acoustically.

Whenever any staff member had any spare moment, they were expected to grab their instrument from the rack conveniently located on the side wall of the room, and launch into an impromptu minstrel style performance of whatever song came into their head. This format produced some wonderfully spontaneous moments, as whoever happened to be performing would be progressively joined by, for example; a violin, a string bass, various guitars, a portable keyboard, and sundry harmonic vocal supplementation. And of course, sometimes you would just end up doing a solo performance. Depending on the type and number of staff musicians available at any given moment, sometimes, you would be the lead, sometimes a member of a musical ensemble, a duo, or just a solo. Moreover, the identical song would potentially undergo a radical transformation in arrangement, key, tempo rhythm, and atmosphere, depending on how many musicians, and which of us actually performed the number. Looking back on it, I really regret not having recorded any of those sessions.

Not only did this venue turn out to be far more civilized environment, but the restaurant was located in a small quiet traffic-free shopping area, just off Wilshire Boulevard, immediately opposite to the Westwood 1, and 2 Cinemas. These cinemas were notable for screening informal movie premieres, where actors appearing in a production would have the opportunity to see the complete movie in which they appeared in continuous form for the first time.

During my time there, I had the pleasure of entertaining (hopefully) and attending to tables occupied by notables and local residents such as; Diana Ross, Jack Nicholson, Englebert Humperdinck, and the actor who appeared with Jack Nicholson in 'One Flew Over the Cuckoo's Nest'. It was the young vulnerable lad who eventually committed suicide if you remember. I can recall neither the name, of the actor, nor the character he portrayed in the movie, but I think you will know who I mean.

Also at that time I had the opportunity to renew an old Liverpool acquaintance, a lad called Bob Adcock, whom you may recall, eventually became the first manager of super group 'Cream', featuring the divine Eric Clapton, but who at the time served as road manager for the 'Roadrunners' featuring 'Henry' Hart. Bob lived in Litherland in those days, and he would come bashing on my door in Waterloo at about ten in the morning, waking me up to go and either break down, or set up the 'Roadrunners' equipment for their long running residency at Hope Hall. After that we would retire to 'Ye Olde Cracke' or the Philharmonic and get pissed for the remainder of the afternoon. Meeting him again was another memorable 'small-world' moment in Westwood Village.

As an illustration of the kind of town L.A. is; I was breaking down the outside patio in preparation for closing late one chilly relatively quiet evening in mid-week. The area outside the patio was virtually deserted, except for a lady attempting to use the pay-'phone located opposite the patio on the wall outside the cinema. She walked across and asked me if I could change a dollar for the 'phone (this era of course long preceded the onslaught of electronic devices.) I dug into my stash of tips and duly obliged, and as I spoke to her, she enquired if I was by any chance from Liverpool. The question from a middle aged black lady in deepest Los Angeles took me by surprise, but I complimented her on her musical ear, and asked her how she had been so perceptive. It turns out that she had toured with Joe Cocker for ten years, ever since he broke through with 'A little help from my Friends' back in the sixties, but that she had recently been working mainly as a session singer so she could spend more time with her family in L.A. The list of sessions she had been on and the notable artistes she had worked with during her career, was astounding. The people you bump into in this business (and how easily you forget some of their names) is truly amazing eh?

One of the hostesses responsible for the customers seating arrangements at the restaurant was a young lady with whom I frequently went out for a couple of drinks to watch a band after work. She was an aspiring actress who had been classically trained on guitar, and who showed me the correct fingering for 'Blackbird' (Watch it!!!) Her name was Patti Davis. It took a couple of months for another staff member, who assumed I must have known all along, to tell me to my astonishment, that she was the daughter of the current California Governor, Ronald Reagan. Bloody high profile for a music teacher I would say. I then discovered that she had recently terminated a long-term relationship with Eagles guitarist, Bernie Leadon (WHO DID YOU SAY SONNIE???? BERT WEEDON....). Never thought I could follow a guitarist like him with an act like mine!

Around this time, I also coincidentally bumped into Terry Sylvester. It wasn't at the restaurant, but at someone's pool party at the same apartment complex where I happened to be visiting a friend of mine. It's worth mentioning in the context of The 'Notions' history, that I almost left the group a year prior to joining the 'League of Gentlemen'. This came about when Terry left the 'Escorts' to replace Graham Nash in the 'Hollies', Mike Gregory and John Kinrade approached me to join the 'Escorts' as his replacement, and I agreed in principle to do so. The only problem was that Pete Clark wanted Frank Townsend from the 'Easybeats' to replace Terry. Mike and John were unable to persuade him otherwise, and wisely went along rather than risk losing Pete, who was far more valuable to the identity of the 'Escorts' than myself. Frank never really fitted in, and within a few months Mike Gregory had moved on to become a member of the 'Swinging Blue Jeans' and later 'Big John's Rock 'n Roll Circus'. I bumped into him while playing in Garmisch-Partenkirchen in Germany and spent an evening sharing some hilarious reminiscences over a few Weissbiers.

The restaurant manager, Jimmy, a young Vietnam veteran, became a friend, and I was getting plenty of hours and having a great time enthusiastically giving it the proverbial welly (Liverpool slang for 'kickin' ass') around Hollywood. But as they say, all good things must come to an end, and accordingly, my six-month tenure at GAFB was soon to culminate in an explosive conclusion.

I arrived at work around 4 pm one afternoon ready to begin my shift, to find the place in a bit of a panic. The bartender that was scheduled to work that evening had been delayed, and the place was beginning to get busy.

My mate, Jimmy (the manager) asked me to fill in behind the bar. He had been grooming me for the job anyway, teaching me how to concoct all the mixed drinks, and although you don't get much opportunity to hit the floor and join in with the musical adventures, the bar-tenders made fabulous money in tips.

Well I had been behind the bar for about twenty minutes, and in comes the bartender, breathless and flustered, and starts rushing round getting his set-up in order. I remember the first thing he did, which I had neglected to do, was to place a large can of chocolate fudge about the size of a gallon tin of paint, into the industrial size pressure cooker located on a shelf behind the bar to heat up in preparation for the perennially-popular Hot Fudge Sundaes, a specialty of the house. I hurriedly got out of his way, and returned to my normal duties on the restaurant floor. Not long afterwards, there was a sickening percussive thud the kind that hits you in the gut and chest rather than the ear drums. I was carrying a large plastic basin of dirty glasses to the kitchen at the time, but I instinctively hit the floor headlong, still holding on to the glasses in the basin outstretched in front of me, in order to avoid the consequences of what I was certain could only have been the explosion from a planted bomb. After a few seconds had elapsed, in the absence of any further explosions, I cautiously rose to my knees, and peered peevishly into the main room, bracing myself for the sight of what I fully expected to be horrific casualties. Instead, if not for the fact that it was so utterly bizarre, the sight that met my eyes was almost hilarious. It was indeed a surreal scene. Every single person in the crowded room, frozen into stunned silence by the explosion and still motionlessly seated at their tables, had been covered to some extent with liberal lashings of hot fudge! Faces, heads and bodies, all splattered, daubed or speckled to some degree with dark cloying confectionary. Tens of thousands of dollars in designer Rodeo Drive clothing utterly and forever ruined. What a mess!

It turned out that the bartender while rushing to complete his preparations had completely forgotten to puncture the hot-fudge can before it was placed inside the sealed pressure cooker, and at the time I did not know enough to recognize the imminent danger.

Well after we had managed to calm everyone down, and release them free of charge of course, for anything that they had eaten prior to the traumatic event, the restaurant was closed and the clean-up began. Somewhere along the way in the clean-up process, a tray of whipped cream canisters found its way out of the cold storage closet, and although not many people outside of L.A. know this, whipped cream is, or at least was, pressurized in dispensing spray cans together with Nitrous Oxide, also known by the colloquial sobriquet, 'Laughing Gas' as the propelling agent. Usually, a pocket of this gaseous substance permeates to the top of the canister and sits atop the whipped cream. When the dispensing button is pressed, not enough to activate the whipped cream, but just enough to release the gas, it is possible to inhale this little pocket of Nitrous Oxide vapour, and immediately become highly chemically amused.

Not satisfied with this relaxing pursuit, some of the 'cleaning' staff began to assault one another with the rest of the contents of the whipped cream containers, and predictably, widespread mayhem, anarchy and hilarity immediately ensued. Ten or eleven trays, or approximately one hundred and twenty whipped cream cans later, the restaurant was several orders of magnitude less inhabitable than it had been immediately after the initial hot fudge explosion, while the highly gassed cleaning crew, including yours truly, were now compelled to remain until around 7 am the following morning expunging all traces of the Great American Hot Fudge Disaster and the accompanying Whipped-cream festival, it had certainly been a gas! (Weak pun intentional). Ah yes…those were the days.

Predictably, within the litigious society represented by Western culture in general, and the United States of America in particular, it didn't take long before the legions of lawyers began to emerge from the surrounding woodwork and harass the company. Shortly thereafter myself and the bartender on the night in question were summoned before management to recount our version of the events on that fateful evening. In spite of the fact that I had not been directly responsible for the mishap and due to the fact that the actual culprit was an experienced, long serving, and indeed brilliant bartender, I was told apologetically by the manager, that I would have to be the human sacrifice and take the fall for the incident. I understood that there was not much my mate Jimmy the restaurant manager could do in the face of this corporate decision from the general manager of the entire franchise. So with considerable regret, I said goodbye to the 'Great American Food and Beverage Company' that had been so fortuitously good to me during a difficult period, and shortly thereafter, bade farewell to Los Angeles altogether.

I had not been idle in attempting to advance my career during my nine months in Los Angeles. I had made the rounds with my material, and Ronny's brilliant stuff, and succeeded in doing a few showcases and gaining access to a couple of record label execs. But it's hard, jumping through the same hoops as I had wearied jumping through during my times in London. The problem in L.A. is that everyone knows someone in the business. One day, while relaxing by the pool in my friend's apartment, I started a random conversation with the pool maintenance man, who had noticed my accent, and observed that I was British. Guilty as charged, I politely submitted to the usual interrogation. The pool man subsequently informed me that his brother in law was also a Brit.

"He's in a band as well, and he's a real asshole." He took pleasure in informing me.

After further discussion, it turns out that the British musical asshole married to the pool man's beloved sister, was none other than Mick Relfs from 'Bad Company'! Just another day at the office - that's L.A for ya'.

I have been sufficiently blessed to have available to me, a choice between extremely interesting careers. I was a reasonably decent footballer as a kid, and at the time the 'Notions' came along, I had been involved for over two years as a trainee with the youth development system at Liverpool F.C. As the 'Notions' began to gain momentum, there were increasingly more mid-week gigs, and after playing Monday nights at the Jacaranda until 1 am on Tuesday morning, and then again sometimes on Tuesday, Wednesday, and Thursday nights, I was not always available to attend the scheduled team training with Liverpool F.C. which were conducted every Tuesday and Thursday evening at the club training facility located at Melwood Drive in West Derby. Liverpool tolerated this almost-unprecedented inconsistency for close to a year before finally informing me, that there would be no more opportunities to redeem myself. The club had allowed me sufficient rope and I had obligingly hanged myself with it. Of course, I was absolutely heart broken, and to this day, I often reflect upon the wisdom of my choice, and wonder….'What if?' Nonetheless, the lesson I had learned during three marvelous years from the legendary coaches at that world class football environment enabled me to qualify for the top coaching licenses in England and the U.S.A., and pursue the rewarding professional career I have today. Furthermore, looking back I would not trade anything for the rich experiences acquired during twenty five years as a working musician. So, at the end of the day, hindsight is 20/20 - if you want a guarantee you have to buy a washing machine, and….Yes I will have no regrets….Yes! We Have No Bananas….God Bless Edith Piaf.

I left Los Angeles in late Fall of 1978. The $1,000 prize from The Gong Show check had evaporated on arrival about six weeks after the show, since we owed more than the gross amount to our friends and supporters for basic living expenses incurred prior to the commencement of my minstrel bus-boy job. We also were supposed to receive a trophy in the form of a miniature ornamental gong, to sit on the mantelpiece as a memento of the occasion. However, that particular trophy was apparently ripped off from the doorstep of our original empty apartment on Venice Boulevard the day it was delivered, so all that now remains of the Gong Show experience are the memories.

I directed the prow of my faithful old 1969 Ford LTD, Eastward onto Interstate 10, which in Los Angeles begins – or ends – depending on which way you happen to be pointing – as the Santa Monica Freeway. Funnily enough, the same highway which finds its destination in Jacksonville Florida, will also take you straight to Pensacola in about four days. But although I had no way to know it at the time, it would take me about ten more years to get there.

The plan was to follow Chuck Berry's directions in reverse - the directions outlined in the famous song-lyrics along the old Route 66, through Kingman, Barstow, and San Bernardino, with the musical pilgrimage pausing briefly to afford the opportunity to stand on a corner in Winslow, Arizona. Any corner will do of course, but the most popular one is adjacent to the main post office.

My eventual destination was Atlanta, Georgia, to visit my partner Ronny, and my old 'Sundance' buddies, to investigate the fragile possibility of reigniting the group. Ron was staying in Athens, Georgia, working in the family automobile body shop owned by his dad and brother. My cross-country drive from Los Angeles to Atlanta, eventually parted company with Route 66, and proceeded through Amarillo Texas, with a brief diversion to have a quick butchers (Liverpool slang for 'look see')* at Muscogee Oklahoma U.S.A. and Chattanooga, Tennessee.

However, although the musical pilgrimage had been relaxing and interesting, it turned out to be an end in itself rather than a stepping stone to revitalize the best band I have played in during my musical career. Regrettably, in the year intervening from the disintegration of the group following the Canadian tour, the other lads had all moved on to become involved in other projects.

Nonetheless, I stayed for a month visiting my old partner Ronny Poss, and his family. Ron's father Alan Poss, the owner of the family body-shop repair business, and father of seven, was an imposing figure. In his late fifties, standing around six-foot three, he was an ex-prize-fighter who had fought bare-knuckled in his youth, and as a result, had acquired more scars than a butchers block. I was more than relieved to discover that he had actually taken a liking to me.

He had later become ordained as a Baptist preacher, and traveled throughout the Southern United States preaching at revival gatherings with his wife and three sons comprising a family gospel musical troupe. Ronny was already proficient on guitar, pedal-steel, harmonica, vocals and key-boards at the age of nine. What a background! At the end of the day this was the cultural heritage – the prize-fighter/preacher/body-repairman/musician – fluent in Gospel, Country and Rock n Roll music - the traditional iconic American musical image with which we scruffy primitive musicians from Liverpool had become so enamoured at the outset of our own musical movement.

British people are born explorers. There is a saying to the effect that a Briton is never at home until he's abroad. We have an innate compulsion to stray from the road most-traveled, becoming absorbed into unfamiliar cultures in order to better understand them. And since discovering the original source of the traditional American music that had furnished the artistic inspiration for lads like us, had been the motivation for my voyage of discovery in the first place, I felt I had arrived full-circle at this point. During my involvement with front-line Southern musicians – of both black and white heritage - with roots in North Georgia, and South Alabama - and during that visit with Ron's family in the rural South, I finally felt that I had reached the headwaters of the musical culture, thus realizing the primary objective of my own 'Leaving of Liverpool' three years earlier.

The visit to Dixieland was another natural turning point on the journey. With nowhere to start the next phase of my musical career, and with the funds saved from my minstrel bus-boy job in Los Angeles rapidly dwindling, I called my old trusted agent, Irene Marjoram, in Calgary, and asked her if she had any jobs she could send my way. I made the 'phone call on a Friday afternoon from Athens, Georgia. She informed me she had a late cancellation, and if I could get to Swift Current Saskatchewan, 2,200 miles away by Sunday afternoon, I could do a month at 'Willie Wong's' where I had played several times previously, and had made quite a few friends among the locals in the town. No problem!

Fifty-two hours of literally non-stop driving later, I chugged into Swift Current (known to the locals colloquially as 'Speedy Creek') with eyes like hat pegs and a busted muffler. The front end of the exhaust pipe had detached itself from the engine manifold somewhere around Nashville. Of course I heard it go, but I did not realize that I was pushing the front end of the broken pipe along the highway underneath the car, until it got dark, and in my rear view mirror I was alarmed to observe a profuse shower of sparks spraying from beneath the rear end of the car next to the petrol tank! The vehicle must have looked like one of those space-ships spewing molten particles and smoke that Flash Gordon used to fly on Saturday morning matinees at the

Waterloo Odeon, or whichever cinematic venue lads of our age would typically spend Saturday mornings watching cartoons before the current onslaught of electronic devices.

By this time I was approaching the city of Paducah, Kentucky. Since at 9 pm on Friday evening, there was no chance of finding a repair shop open, I was obliged to allow the engine to cool, before crawling beneath the vehicle with a flashlight, in order to re-attach what remained of the molten exhaust pipe to the engine manifold by means of interlocking wire coat hangers scrounged from my luggage. Turning up the radio to conceal the appalling noise in the car from the busted muffler, covered in oil and grime, I continued on my journey. All went well until around 3 am, at which point while passing through a tiny town somewhere in the middle of the Kansas wilderness, I blew a tire.

It's worth mentioning at this point that after driving down to Los Angeles directly from a Canadian winter the previous year, I had spent an entire year driving around sunny Southern California and across the scorching deserts of Arizona and New Mexico to Atlanta with a set of studded snow tires on my car! Attention to mechanical details was never one of my strong points. To make things worse, the spare tire was the wrong size, so to add to the deafening racket from the muffler which I had endured for the past nine hours between Nashville and Kansas, the car was now also hopping along the road on a miss-sized rear tire, limping and bobbing up and down like a three-legged dog, to the accompaniment of a loudly disconcerting rhythmic 'bump-bump-bump' sound.

It was getting light by the time I stopped in St Louis Missouri to find a tire service to fix the tire. However, taking into account the fuel required to complete the rest of my trip, I could not afford to repair the broken exhaust. After pausing for fifteen minute naps in Omaha, Nebraska, and Sioux Falls South Dakota, I finally crossed the Canadian border into Manitoba, at Fargo North Dakota on a dark and windswept prairie night at a lonely border outpost, forty-two straight driving hours after leaving Athens, Georgia - only ten more hours to Speedy Creek.

I have only done one other trip to match the Georgia to Saskatchewan expedition; that was performed without safety belts (literally) non-stop in a Ford Transit van from London to Stockholm with the Czecho-Swedish band. That was a mere twenty four hours driving, up through Germany to Hamburg and Copenhagen, not including an all-night piss-up on the Danish ferry.

I finally chugged into Swift Current Saskatchewan fifty-two hours and 2100 miles after leaving Athens Georgia, to find light snow already on the ground. I had been in town not more than ten minutes, when the lights of the Royal Canadian Mounted Police car flashed in my rear-view mirror. The Mountie dismounted just long enough to issue me a citation for the broken exhaust. After driving half way across the continent with a busted muffler without a murmur from anyone, ten minutes in Saskatchewan and I'm busted. Welcome back to Canada! (at least he couldn't complain about the studded snow tires).

The original month residency at 'Willie Wong's' turned into two months, then three months, and eventually, a five month house gig. Twenty weeks that mercifully kept me off the Canadian road throughout the winter of 1978. I had and still have many friends in that little farming town, located about 200 miles south of Saskatoon, and many happy memories of my numerous visits there.

The snow was beginning to melt in March of 1979 heralding the end of my two week engagement at the Williams Lake Hotel, located in the town of the same name, deep in the mountainous interior of British Columbia. It also was my last job in Canada. After the unforgettable three years I had originally allocated to travel across the North American continent, I had finally run out of space, completed the huge circle, and it was time to go home. I wasn't working to the clock. Strangely enough, it was just the way it happened - unusually for me - right on time.

There are certain patterns and connecting points in the life of an individual that become recognizable only retrospectively.

When I left Canada and the U.S.A. in the Spring of 1979, the biggest wrench came from having to leave my old faithful 1969 Ford LTD, that had never let me down, through thousands of miles of sometimes dangerous and usually appalling weather conditions, traveling between jobs through the mountainous interior snow and ice covered highways of the Western Canadian Rockies, the congested freeways of Southern California, and across the vast prairies and burning deserts of the South Western American Continent. I have liked and appreciated many of the cars I have owned, but I have actually fallen in love with only one, and this was it. Air conditioned, with power windows, power adjustable seats, power steering, power every bloody thing. The LTD was a veritable tower of power, all new to me and I absolutely loved it.

The amazingly coincidental connection with a former life had been the purchase of this beloved vehicle upon my arrival in Calgary, from none other than Joel Shapiro, whom the reader will recall as the sax-player from the 'League of Gentlemen', who had actively recruited me from the Notions, and whom, since I had last seen him in London almost twelve years earlier, had moved back to his native land, and restarted his career as a chiropractor in Calgary.

I stayed with Joel at his home upon my arrival in Calgary in 1978, but more significantly, how this coincidental and unlikely reunion occurred after totally losing touch with him for more than eleven years represents a great small-world moment, and a prestigious addition to the catalogue of adventures recounted by a rock and roll musician.

Joel, as I have already mentioned, had originally been a back up musician for the legendary 'Dick Clark Road Shows'. He told us many entertaining war stories from those days, but never failed to mention one of his favorite artistes with whom he had regularly worked, was the legendary Bobby Vee.

Fast forward to when I first moved to Canada and was staying with Brian Griffiths in Kitchener, Ontario, near Toronto, there was a local road venue called the Coronet Hotel, with a big concert room that would regularly feature well-known artistes. Around the time I was planning to relocate to Calgary, Bobby Vee was appearing at the Coronet, and of course, as a huge fan ever since my early teens, I was not going to miss the event. Furthermore, although my experiences in London and Los Angeles had taught me that I was not a hyper ambitious type 'A' upwardly-mobile kind of artiste, my instinct for an opportunity that had prompted me to knock on Jim McCartney's door in Heswall, had not entirely deserted me. So armed with a few original songs, I strategically dropped Joel Shapiro's name to Bobby Vee's main roadie, told him I had worked with Joel in London, and requested a chat with Bobby after the show.

Later that evening in Bobby Vee's suite at the Coronet hotel, we discussed our mutual experiences with Joel Shapiro, swapped a few road stories, and jammed on a few songs while sharing Bobby Vee's acoustic guitar. I told him that I liked Neil Sedaka's recent ballad rearrangement of 'Don't Take Your Love (Away from Me)' and demonstrated a similarly laid back arrangement I had worked up of Bobby's own mega-hit, 'Take Good Care of My Baby' one of my all time favourite songs, and the same arrangement that I had been performing for years in the Liverpool pubs as a regular item in my own solo guitar vocal song list.

So it came about in the thrill of my musical career, second only to singing 'Hey Jude' with Macca, that Bobby Vee himself jumped in on back up harmony as I took the lead vocal on my arrangement of his own song 'Take Good Care of My Baby' Come on mate...You can't just make this stuff up!!!

Bobby Vee liked my original stuff, said he thought I was a good writer. He scribbled down his agent's number in Los Angeles, and invited me to send in some of my material. I still have that information written in Bobby Vee's own handwriting on a Coronet Hotel note pad. He was a real gentleman, and we hit it off in that brief moment of time when I had the opportunity to meet face to face with yet another of my musical heroes and influences. I was greatly saddened to learn of the passing of this iconic and influential pop artist several years later.

But the real psychic connection came when I casually mentioned to Bobby that I was relocating to Calgary the following month. You could have knocked me over with a feather when Bobby Vee delivered the bombshell information; "well you know that Joel lives in Calgary these days don't ya'!!!"

Anyway, that's how I ended up with my car.

A frozen rosy dawn was just breaking as I looked out of the cabin window of the Boeing 747 as the herds of shaggy sheep, in their long winter fleece, startled by the noise of the descending aircraft, scattered in panic over the rocky terrain of the Isle of Arran as we began our short-approach to Prestwick Airport in Glasgow.

When you walk into the local ale house in Liverpool after any kind of extended absence, the same lads are sitting in the same place at the same bar where you last saw them when you left. No one looks up as you walk in but, one of the regulars, still peering over his specs, eyes fixed un-waveringly on the Echo, might utter the greeting….

'"Orite Davey lad....where've you been?"

"Oh I emigrated to Canada, and travelled all over America, and this is my first time home in three years."

This information will probably be acknowledged with a cynical, "Oh aye?" followed by silence.

They don't believe a word of it mate - they think you've been in jail!

Liverpool had not changed much in the three years I had been away. I had never noticed this previously, but it rained every single day for the next two years! I stayed busy with the local pubs and clubs for about eighteen months, during which time I revisited my old career vocation, by taking the Football Association Preliminary Coaching Certificate on a course conducted at Everton Park Sports Centre on Netherfield Road.

Other candidates on the course included Chris (Kit) Fagan, whose father eventually became Liverpool manager after Bob Paisley retired, and who had been my old mentor at the club. Also on the course was ex-Liverpool forward, Tony Hately, who was at the time a youth coach at Everton. So it was all pretty familiar territory. Having passed the course, I immediately enrolled on the F.A. Full Badge course to be held at the historic Lilleshall Hall in the summer of 1980. In this way, just for want of something different to do really, I unknowingly took the first steps on what was eventually to become my new career.

Meanwhile one night while jamming with my old mate, the original keyboard player with Ted 'Kingsize' Taylor and the 'Dominoes', Keith 'Sam' Hardie, at St Patrick's club in Park Road, we were reminiscing about jobs we had done in Germany, and he mentioned a solo gig his brother had done at the U.S. Armed Forces Recreation Center, in Garmisch-Partenkirchen, Southern Germany, in the Bavarian Alps.

It sounded interesting, so I followed up and sent a demo to the U.S. Army Sergeant responsible for booking the entertainment at the facility. He got back to me within a few days, and offered me a residency at one of the recreation area hotels for the month of March, 1981.

Sitting at home a few weeks later, at the end of January the 'phone rang. Apparently, a vacancy had opened up for the month of February, and if I could get to South Germany in two days, the job was mine.

At the time I was driving round in a diesel engine Ford Transit van purchased from Old Swan Conservative Club. This was no secret, since the name of that worthy establishment had been emblazoned in three-foot high white lettering on both sides of the dark-green vehicle. I had been experiencing some electrical difficulties attributable to a faulty alternator, which I had planned to get fixed in preparation for my trip down to South Germany in four weeks. However, this latest development did not allow me time to have the vehicle repaired, so I packed up the 'Old Swan' and left Liverpool once again early on Saturday afternoon for the cross-country drive to Hull in time to catch the Saturday evening Zeebrugge Ferry. This would give me Sunday and Monday to drive across Belgium, and down through Germany towards Munich in time to arrive in Garmisch Partenkirchen for the start of the job on Monday night. Here we go again!! Yet another one of those last minute shit-or-bust efforts that have so often characterized my mottled musical career.

It was absolutely pissing down as I left Liverpool heading for the M62. I had lost the headlights by the time I reached the East Lancashire Road, and the windshield wipers packed in shortly thereafter. I was reduced to driving in a semi-reclining position with my head down towards the passenger seat, my foot jammed up against the top of the drivers-side window, while holding the steering wheel in my outstretched right arm, so I could get my face low enough to peer through the only clear space on the rain-spattered windshield – that little arc at the bottom where the seized-up wipers were somehow diverting the rain away from the tiny semi-circular space.

By the time I got to Shap Fell at the top of the Pennines, the rain had turned to sleet, totally obscuring the entire windshield except for the tiny peep hole which afforded my only view of the road. Of course at this point I was seriously regretting the decision to leave in the first place, but I was by now past the point of no return. With no electrics whatsoever, I knew that if I stopped or stalled, I would not be starting again, so there was no real choice except press on to Hull, or freeze to death on the snowy late-February Pennines. It was getting dark by the time I got to Hull, and of course, I had no lights. Gratefully, I made the Ferry with literally seconds to spare, and gunned the 'Old Swan' up the steep gang-plank on to the car deck. Don't stall now for God's sake!

After spending most of the night returning my joints to normal after being forced to assume and maintain such a bizarre body configuration all the way to Hull the previous afternoon, I made my way up to the deck as we entered Zeebrugge harbor on a perfect gem of a Sunday morning, given an even more spectacular dimension after the appalling weather blanketing England the day before.

The alternator was totally shot, so the deckhands could not even jump start the engine. So after waiting until all the other vehicles had cleared the vessel, they pushed the van to the edge of the gang plank, and let her roll. I popped the clutch and 'Old Swan' burst into life once more in a cloud of smoke, as I chugged off into sunny Belgium seated in a normal driving position, headed for Brussels. After a spectacular drive through the Ardennes, I crossed the German border at Osnabruck. (That's where Brian Griff's first wife, Lottie, whom he met in Hamburg, was from by the way….) It was here that I picked up a hitchhiker, a young English lad from Burnley, en-route to start a job in Munich.

We had to book into a hotel somewhere on the autobahn near Frankfurt when it got dark, because of course, I still had no lights. The hitchhiker came in useful the following morning, as after a liberal dose of 'Easy-Start' had been sprayed in to the carburetor, he was able to help me push 'Old Swan' down the fairly steep hill at the top of which I had presciently parked the previous evening in preparation for another high-speed clutch start the next day. The 'hitched hiker', thanked me as I dropped him off across the road from the Olympic Stadium in Munich, and I headed the Old Swan towards the E3 for the last fifty miles to Garmisch.

Garmisch Partenkirchen is a fairy-tale village, the site of the 1936 Winter Olympics, nestling between the giant peaks that form a picturesque Loisach valley in the Bavarian Alps. After the war, the American Armed Forces invaded Germany from the South through Italy, and in the process they captured all the scenery. They subsequently converted all the luxury hotels that the high-ranking Nazi's had built for themselves in breathtaking traditional German resort locations like Garmisch, and Berchtesgaden, where Hitler lived. These hotels were then made available as holiday destinations for servicemen and their families, who would be charged an accommodation fee directly commensurate with their military rank or pay-grade. I was to provide the entertainment at one of these vacation hotels, of which there were four in Garmisch, and three in nearby Brechtesgaden.

The following chapter of my life would require a book in itself, but suffice to stay that Garmisch became my home for the next eight years. It was here I met my second wife Marybeth Hanisko from Walingford, Connecticut, at the outset of a union that would endure for seventeen years, before finally culminating as we shall see, in Pensacola Florida, which has been my home ever since. I had previously been married to Irene Johnson from Liverpool, (now regrettably deceased.) But the ten-year marriage had finally fallen victim to the unrelenting continuity of showbiz separations.

Marybeth and I were married in Connecticut in October of 1982. She was a ski-instructor with the American ski school in Garmisch, who also taught tennis at the resort during the summer months. We began our honeymoon in Georgia, visiting my old mate and partner Ronny Poss and his family, and finished up with a month in Aspen Colorado before returning to Garmisch for the winter season. Apart from a couple of sabbaticals in the States at Fort Rucker Alabama, in 1984, and 1987, we remained in Germany, with Garmisch and Berchtesgaden as our primary base. With the apparent end of the 'cold-war' in the mid nineteen-eighties, the 350,000 active duty American troops permanently stationed in Europe since 1945 had dwindled to around 50,000. The funding for services at the Armed Forces Recreation Centers had been reduced accordingly, and as a result the recreation programs were becoming increasingly difficult to maintain. With these factors in mind, after eight wonderful years in Garmisch, we decided in March of 1989, that it was finally time to call it a day, and get back to 'the real world'. Our first stop was at Fort Rucker, the U.S. Army Aviation training center, located in rural South Alabama, staying with a couple of flight instructors, with whom we had established a lasting friendship during our time in Germany, and who we had previously spent time with during our visits in 1984 and 1987. The musical opportunities were limited in the area, so I booked a summer season in Panama City Florida, playing music on a gambling cruise ship. Gambling was illegal in Florida at that time, so the mafia had purchased an ancient ferry boat from a Swedish scrapyard, entitled it 'The Southern Elegance', installed a state-of the art casino manned by British Ladbrokes trained croupiers, which would twice daily sail the three miles into international waters outside of U.S. legal jurisdiction, stop engines, and commence operations. I would play the music in the lounge, on the way out and on the return voyage, so it was a pretty easy job, since I would be off duty while the casino was in session.

When the ship was at rest way off shore, idling in the moon-lit mill pond that the Gulf of Mexico sometimes presents as one of its many schizophrenic personas, pods of Dolphins would round up schools of Flying Fish, and stampede them towards the ship. Apparently, Flying Fish actually fly only when they are being chased, so the Dolphins would herd them together and put the pressure on about thirty yards away from the side of the boat. Their prey would come flying out of the water, and smash straight into the ship, knocking themselves senseless in the process, and while floating motionless on the surface, provide easy pickings for the hunters. I saw one Dolphin catch a stunned fish as it rebounded from the side of the boat, before sinking back, teeth firmly clamped around the helpless victim with a satisfied look on its face. I was close enough to hear the bones crunching between the animal's jaws as it sank below the surface.

On weekends we would do two cruises a day. The afternoon cruise was mainly for senior citizens and families, who would leave young children in the nursery while they visited the casino. On this particular afternoon, the Gulf was not in one of its better moods. After sailing through the pass from the relative calm of St Andrew Bay into the Gulf, we immediately turned sideways into a four foot swell. My musical equipment was catapulted across the lounge, as glassware behind the bar came crashing down from the shelves. Fortunately no one was injured. After cleaning up the mess and calming everyone down, some semblance of order was restored as the Captain straightened up the ship, the musician began to play, and we continued somewhat turbulently on our short voyage. However, by this time, not only had many of the passengers become sea-sick, but this so-far unpleasant trip was about to become even worse.

When it was time to go home after our usual three hour gambling hiatus, I discovered that there was no electrical power on the small stage. The bartender reported the same situation from his cash register, and, during summer in the Gulf of Mexico, even on a cloudy rain spattered day, it did not take long to notice that there was no air conditioning either. Just then the chief engineer, a Scouse (Liverpool slang for anybody that hails from Liverpool) lad called Barry Foulkes from Breeze Hill, Anfield, with whom I had become friends came charging into the bar, his overalls covered in shit....I mean real shit....with turds of varying dimensions clinging tenaciously to the fabric before giving up the gravitational fight and plopping messily to the luxurious carpet of the Southern Elegance lounge.

"Is there any power in here?" He yelled.

"No Barry....what's going on mate?"

He didn't bother to answer and charged off out of the lounge once again in an even more agitated state than before.

It turned out that the cause of the original lack of equilibrium on entering the Gulf was attributable to the fact that only three of the ship's five stabilizer ballast tanks were in working order, a dangerous maintenance oversight which had only become apparent during the first rough sea. Worse still, during the voyage a toilet had overflowed, allowing waste water to seep down between the decks and short out five electrical switches on the main board. The cause of the engineer's agitation and disgusting condition was that he had been wading chest deep through raw sewage to fight a fire behind the main electrical panel on the ship! Dead in the water in the middle of the Gulf of Mexico, decks awash in shite and spew, with a fire aboard a ship loaded with kids and senior citizens. What a disaster that could have been!

In retrospect, the only important facility on board that ship was the casino. Once again, the financial bottom line had superseded all concerns for safety, and without the heroic actions of our Scouse engineer, events could have taken a really catastrophic turn. Of course, just like my earlier experience in the 'Great American Food and Beverage Company', Barry was made the scapegoat, and was fired after taking the blame for the lack of maintenance.

The real story was of course that the mafia had purchased an ancient ferry boat from a Swedish scrap-yard, installed a state of the art casino, operated the ship in a systematically unsound condition, and started raking it in, just outside of any U.S. regulatory jurisdiction. Barry didn't care. He was a deep sea merchant mariner, and had only taken the job because he had been between big ships. We shared a few Scouse laughs on the ship and around the pubs of Panama City Florida during that summer. And although we have long since lost touch, I have some good memories of him....in spite of the fact that he was (and probably still is) a bleedin 'Evertonian' (A supporter of one of the two rival Liverpool soccer teams).

The summer came to an end, and I relocated about one hundred miles west, to base myself in the City of Pensacola, Florida. From this central location, I could easily access pubs, clubs and restaurants across the entire one hundred mile beach strip on what they appropriately call, 'The Emerald Coast', from Panama City, Florida, to Mobile Alabama, which I did for the next two years. Pensacola is a Navy town, the home base for the Blue Angels flight demonstration team, and predictably, the home of quite a few good pubs. As a realist, I had long ago come to terms with the fact that I was not going to become Elvis Presley. And although I did not consciously realize it at the time, the move to Pensacola was to be the beginning of the end of my long musical journey, as I was soon to be offered and accept a job that would return me to involvement in my previous career, as coach of the University of West Florida Men's Soccer Program.

There's a song that I learned in Liverpool while playing with the 'Notions' as one of our individually-selected repertoire numbers. The song was 'Let It Rock' by Chuck Berry, which features as its opening line the lyric; 'In the heat of the day down in Mobile Alabama....' Dave Delaney eventually talked me into letting Joey Short perform it instead, since he didn't have as broad a vocal repertoire as we did.

My first appearance on stage was in Liverpool with the 'Notions'.

My last public appearance as a working musician was at 'Paddy O'Toole's Irish Pub' on Airport Boulevard, Mobile Alabama.

One of the first songs I ever learned in Liverpool, and the last song I ever sang twenty-six years later in Mobile Alabama, began; 'In the heat of the day down in Mobile Alabama....'

From Liverpool to Mobile - symbolically and actually - that particular song at once came to represent both the beginning and end of my musical career, *and* my geographical journey.

From Liverpool to Mobile.

"LET IT ROCK!!!"

MORE 'MERSEY SOUND' BOOKS FROM
www.VelocePress.com

BEAT WAVES 'CROSS THE MERSEY
Manfred Kuhlmann

Originally published as 'The Sound With The Pound', this revised and updated edition includes an additional 142 illustrations and 112 pages. A comprehensive anthology of the 'Merseybeat' era, this book chronicles the complete stories of 164 Merseyside groups, plus an additional 100 line-ups and a list of 344 group names, for a total of 607 groups that were active in Liverpool and the surrounding area in the late 1950's to the end of the Sixties.

SOME OTHER GUYS
Manfred's follow up book

Featuring the complete stories of another 66 Merseyside groups of the 1960's. NONE of these stories are included in 'Beat Waves 'Cross The Mersey' they are all 'new'. Also includes an additional 104 line-ups ~ for a total of 174 groups! These are the 'Some Other Guys' who helped create the Merseysound

THE ABSTRACTS

Liverpool in the 60's was a wondrous place, it was alive with music and the sheer number of local musicians and the depth of the talent pool was mind numbing. Depending on your method of research, you will find that there were between 750 to 950 Liverpool based groups performing at any one time during the early to mid 1960's. So here's a story of one of the not-so-famous groups that's part of that total. While their story will always be overshadowed by those that made the 'big time,' it is an honest and down to earth tale and a fairly typical representation of the many hundreds of other groups that created the 'Mersey Sound' and the real Merseybeat era.

**For more information please visit our website
www.VelocePress.com - Arts & Entertainment**

BLUES AT THE CAVERN
Raymond David

Following in the wake of the Beatles and the remarkable surge of Merseyside groups, there came a memorable resurgence of arguably the greatest grass roots form of music, the 'Blues', not only on Merseyside but throughout the UK. This unique spell in the mid sixties saw the only performances by some of the legendary American bluesmen at the world-renowned original Cavern Club.

Liverpool born Raymond David's book, 'Blues at the Cavern', is a fascinating journey through these times and is a story that has never been told before. If you love the blues, you'll love this book.

In addition, he paints a vivid picture of what it was like to grow up in the suburbs during the post war years with his own humorous recollections that are well worth reading in their own right and give a nostalgic glimpse of that period in an austere Britain.

A mix of wit and pathos, the author tells it as it is, pulling no punches of life in a tough, uncompromising city where the ultimate priority is a sense of humor.

CD's FEATURING THE GROUPS FROM
BEAT WAVES 'CROSS THE MERSEY & SOME OTHER GUYS

Subsequent to the publication of "Beat Waves 'Cross The Mersey" and "Some Other Guys" Manfred produced a series of music CD's that compliment the stories of the groups that are included in those books. They include many previously unreleased recordings, some from the famous Liverpool clubs, all digitally re-mastered. A total of 106 songs on 5 separate CD's this is the ultimate nostalgic collection of 1960's 'Merseybeat' music.

If for any reason you experience difficulty in purchasing a copy of this book, please contact us by email at LMG@AutoBks.com and we will be happy to assist you. All of the publications and CD's shown above are also available for online purchase under the 'Arts & Entertainment' link located on the home page of our website at:
www.VelocePress.com

www.ingramcontent.com/pod-product-compliance
Lightning Source LLC
Chambersburg PA
CBHW081917170426
43200CB00014B/2752